EXPLORING THE URANTIA REVELATION

Exploring the Urantia Revelation

Bridging Science and Spirit with the Truth of Reality

JJ Johnson

Urantia scholar and former US diplomat

Skyhorse Publishing

Copyright © 2025 by JJ Johnson

All rights reserved. No part of this book may be reproduced in any manner without the express written consent of the publisher, except in the case of brief excerpts in critical reviews or articles. All inquiries should be addressed to Skyhorse Publishing, 307 West 36th Street, 11th Floor, New York, NY 10018.

Skyhorse Publishing books may be purchased in bulk at special discounts for sales promotion, corporate gifts, fund-raising, or educational purposes. Special editions can also be created to specifications. For details, contact the Special Sales Department, Skyhorse Publishing, 307 West 36th Street, 11th Floor, New York, NY 10018 or info@skyhorsepublishing.com.

Skyhorse® and Skyhorse Publishing® are registered trademarks of Skyhorse Publishing, Inc.®, a Delaware corporation.

Visit our website at www.skyhorsepublishing.com.

10 9 8 7 6 5 4 3 2 1

Library of Congress Cataloging-in-Publication Data is available on file.

Cover design by David Ter-Avanesyan
Cover art inspired by Bob Debold
Author's note image created by Bob Debold in Sora. Text by JJ Johnson

ISBN: 978-1-5107-8543-4
Ebook ISBN: 978-1-5107-8544-1

Printed in the United States of America

This book is personally dedicated to my two sons, Michael Andrew and David Matthew. The love they show for my grandchildren reflects the love our Heavenly Father has for each of us. Grandparents who witness this love in their children are truly and richly blessed.

This book is also dedicated with love and admiration to those forward-looking, universe-conscious citizens who dare to construct a religious philosophy of living based on the truths of reality revealed in The Urantia Book. *As cosmic ambassadors on behalf of the love of our spiritual Father, they are boldly going forth, sharing this love with all our spiritual brothers and sisters.*

The cosmic truth, universe beauty, and divine goodness revealed in The Urantia Book, *lived and shared by these forward-looking men and women of spiritual insight, bring joy to my heart. Godspeed, ambassadors. Godspeed!*

Author's Note

I will be using *Urantia Book* or "Ol' Blue" for *The Urantia Book* to avoid spelling the name out repeatedly. Other general usages also appear: FER for Fifth Epochal Revelation; the UB for *The Urantia Book*; and sometimes just the book.

Ol' Blue is a sentimental name I use after fifty years of carrying the *Urantia Book* around. I purchased my edition in 1975; it retains the iconic blue hardback printing from the original in 1955.

For the citation format when referencing to a specific paragraph in *The Urantia Book*, we use the single-page citation recommended by the Urantia Foundation (https://www .urantia.org/urantia-book/text-standardization-detail): 123:4.5 (1361.5) designates "paper 123, section 4, paragraph 5" (of the section), or "page 1361, paragraph 5" (of the page).

In addition, throughout the ensuing pages, we use terms that the reader may not be familiar with. Words like *absonite* or *Ultimate* may not be surrounded by enough context to discern what they mean. If that happens, I point the reader to The Urantia Book Fellowship's Glossary Page at https://urantia book.org/English-Glossary-for-The-Urantia-Book.

Please do reach out to me with any questions at JJ@MajestonPublishing.com.

Contents

Foreword by Paula Thompson	*xi*
Preface	*xv*
Introduction	*xvii*
Before I Begin My Story	*xix*
JJ's Story	*xxi*

Part I—Science in *The Urantia Book*:
The Impersonal Nature of God and the Cosmos — 1

Chapter 1: The Precambrian Supercontinent	7
Chapter 2: The Genes of Adam and Eve	19
Chapter 3: Göbekli Tepe	38
Chapter 4: A Baker's Dozen	66
Chapter 5: Recent Discoveries and the Yet to Be Discovered	86
Epilogue to Part I	109

Part II—Religion in *The Urantia Book*:
The Personal Nature of God—Our Heavenly Father — 131

Chapter 6: The Dalamation Teachings	139
Chapter 7: The Edenic Teachings—the History of Adam and Eve	149
Chapter 8: Melchizedek of Salem	162
Chapter 9: Jesus of Nazareth	168
Chapter 10: *Urantia Papers* and *The Urantia Book*, 1955	229
Epilogue to Part II	255

Part III   **259**

Chapter 11: The Good, the Bad, and the Sad   261
Chapter 12: Cocreation: Where the Divine
                Meets Human Imagination   286
Chapter 13: Seat at the Table   291
Chapter 14: Dishes Are Done: Call to Service/Call to Action   321
Chapter 15: The Search for Truth: A Journey Without End   340

Appendix 1: Suggested Debates, Conferences, Discussions   342
Appendix 2: The Urantia Community at Your Fingertips   345
Appendix 3: Photo Gallery   350

Acknowledgments   *357*
Index   *359*

Foreword
by Paula Thompson

I've known JJ Johnson for many years. His infectious good-will, his natural and keen interest in all kinds of people, and his deep and abiding faith have always profoundly impressed me.

This book is ultimately the story of his courageous spiritual journey. It's a hero's journey of discovery, one that we all must take. It helped me to think about and recount my own journey and the many significant milestones I've had along the way.

JJ's book reveals how *The Urantia Book* offers a truly unique perspective that integrates science, philosophy, and religion into a unified framework of reality. Through careful exposition and lived inquiry, JJ shows that these domains are not in conflict but are complementary avenues to truth. Science examines the physical universe; philosophy builds the bridge between matter and meaning; and religion provides the direct, personal experience of spiritual truth of reality.

In tracing these threads, JJ's work demonstrates how *The Urantia Book* asserts that true wisdom emerges only when scientific rigor, philosophical insight, and spiritual faith are brought into harmony. He highlights the revelatory brilliance of portraying God simultaneously as the universal First Cause in science, the loving and personal Father in religion, and the self-existent unity in philosophy—each view incomplete on its own, but profoundly coherent when seen through the lens of revelation.

By weaving together empirical discovery and spiritual revelation, JJ's book fosters a kind of cosmic consciousness, which nurtures both intellectual depth and soul-deep faith. He encourages readers to take up this integrated approach, to expand their understanding of the truth of reality, and to live with greater purpose, clarity, and inner alignment.

It is good to remember the declarations we've made to the great unseen and unknown in the universe—the truths we longed for even as children, the ideas we rejected as unsound, and the personal insights that launched us into new realms of understanding. Hope calls out to us still—a persistent sense that something greater is possible. And moving in perfect tandem with it is faith—not faith in what we already grasp, but a trust in what remains unseen. Like two interwoven currents, like sine and cosine riding the same axis of experience, hope and faith rise and fall together—distinct, yet inseparable. Together, they generate the energy that carries us forward—the urge to explore, to seek, to reach for the affirmations and answers waiting just beyond the visible spectrum of our lives.

JJ's book is a resonant chord in that great wave of human seeking—a testament to the innate quest that pulses in all of us. The answers he found in the supernal revelations of *The Urantia Book* are, to him, so astonishingly luminous that he feels compelled to share them. We might not align with every conclusion he reaches, but the value of his work transcends agreement. Like a tuning fork to the soul, it invites the reader to once again ask the questions that linger just beyond the reach of logic—and maybe even reason. In this harmonic field of exploration, JJ's unwavering faith and tireless hope act as guiding frequencies. Together, they echo the enduring promise: if we seek, we will find; if we ask, we will be answered; and when we knock—faith and hope in tandem—the door will, indeed, open.

In a world where the quest for knowledge often leads us to ponder the farthest reaches of the cosmos and the deepest recesses of our past, this wonderful book stands as a beacon of enlightenment. It invites the reader on a journey through time, space, and the very essence of human existence.

From the ancient mysteries of Göbekli Tepe to the profound teachings of *The Urantia Book* (which is clearly JJ's touchstone), *The Urantia Revelation* delves into the intricate tapestry of our own human history and spirituality. Each chapter is a testament to the enduring human spirit and our relentless pursuit of understanding.

In part 1, we explore the *impersonal* aspects of God and the science of our world and the cosmos. We begin with the formation of the Precambrian supercontinent and the genetic legacy of Adam and Eve. These chapters lay the groundwork for a deeper comprehension of our origins and the cosmic forces that have shaped us and our world.

Part 2 shifts focus to the personal nature of God, as progressively revealed through the ancient teachings of Dalamatia and Eden and ultimately through the life and teachings of Jesus of Nazareth. This section presents a rich tapestry of religious history and spiritual insight—threads that converge in a series of 196 revelatory documents known as the *Urantia Papers*. These papers, unified and published together as *The Urantia Book*, form a comprehensive narrative that spans cosmic origins to personal destiny, offering an integrated vision of divine purpose and human potential.

Finally, part 3 brings us to the present, where the interplay of the good, the bad, and the sad aspects of our lives is examined. This section challenges us to consider the divine within our *own* imagination and the everyday acts that define our *own* humanity.

As you embark on this journey, you may find inspiration, wisdom, and a renewed sense of wonder. I know I did. As someone who has had a similar journey that culminated in the discovery of revelatory information, I found that this book is not just a collection of chapters; it is a call to explore the depths of our own existence and the heights of our own potential.

Paula Thompson is a dedicated leader in the Urantia Book community, having spent over four decades studying and sharing its teachings. She served as director of The Urantia Book Fellowship from 2006 to 2021 and previously as executive director of the Jesusonian Foundation from 1993 to 2006. Paula's spiritual journey began with a strong connection to Jesus and a calling to serve others, which deepened after discovering *The Urantia Book* at age twenty. Her work has focused on global outreach, fostering faith relationships, and promoting spiritual growth through the book's teachings. She has also contributed significantly to TruthBook.com, furthering the dissemination of these teachings. Paula's legacy is marked by her loving service and leadership within the Urantia community.

Preface

Quench your thirst for the truth of reality from the well of wisdom known as *The Urantia Book*. *The Urantia Book* derives its authenticity from its beneficent impact on the lives of those individuals who trust its teachings to lead them on the path to the Truth of Reality. It is a transcendent literary masterpiece of epochal significance gifted to our strife-torn planet, which can and will stand up to honest analysis.

Introduction

Just what is *The Urantia Book*? There is a lot to this book, parts of which might be called spiritual guidance and other parts revisionist history. In fact, Urantia is the celestial name for Earth within God's administration for the entirety of creation. Yet, *The Urantia Book* does not offer a new religion—but an enlightened perspective to faith, certainly. The core of Urantia's spirituality is the singular relationship between a human being and God, itself a progressive endeavor over multiple lifetimes toward achieving purity and a greater intimacy with our Creator.

The Urantia Book is unique in several aspects in comparison with the preexisting faith systems on Earth, though there is some alignment with Christianity—just not what you'd expect. Judaism, Christianity and Islam, Hinduism, Buddhism, and the other religions shared among the eight billion souls alive today are evolutionary religions—they have evolved from what they were conceived to be, and although elements of story (myth) exist in their sacred texts, the greater part of all revolve around the laws of the faith.

Not so with *The Urantia Book*, which is a complete and consistent narrative revelation that traverses the nature of God and Paradise,[1] the structure of the universes both physically and administratively, and the hierarchy of life-forms that exist within creation. *The Urantia Book* recounts Urantia's (Earth's) history from its formation through the four epochs that culminate in an extensive biography of the life example and personal teachings of Jesus restated in modern phraseology. If any "religious text" could be considered a bestseller, the *Urantia Book* would be it.

Endnote

1. The Urantia Book Fellowship (website), s.v. "Paradise," accessed January 12, 2025, https://urantiabook.org/English-Glossary-for-The -Urantia-Book.

Before I Begin My Story

Do you long to understand the nature of creation and your purpose within it but don't know who or what to believe?

So many—and contradictory—religions compete; their sole similarity is their inflexible antiquity, their patinas as worn and dull as their inconsistent truths and their circular logic that fails to warm your soul. If you feel this way, *you are not alone.*

Many of us have lost or forgotten our connection to God and creation, just as most of us are unaware of our ancient history beyond the achievements in anthropology and archaeology, dry subjects couched in specialized language few understand. We have been taught to be skeptical about anything that's not written in the Bible or, for that matter, other scriptures sacred to millions of people across the globe. And then there are those of us who have neglected our spirituality. We spend so much time focused on what's going on outside of us that we forget to reflect on what is calling to us from the inside.

I've been lucky to have my eyes opened wide, although it took some doing to get there. I invite you to pause, reflect, and look up at the stars. Take this opportunity to examine your life and realize you are far more special than you ever imagined. Join me and learn of the greater truths about yourself and the universe through the faith journey I began decades ago.

JJ's Story

As far back as I can remember, I have always possessed an inner peace.

I was born on a farm on the outskirts of West Liberty in Morgan County, an undeveloped corner of Kentucky nestled in the foothills of the Appalachians. We didn't own a car or truck, so my Uncle Jess rode a horse into town to get to the doctor when I was born. My mother worked as a waitress, but her salary was not up to the challenge of raising four children, so for a few years my brother and I lived on my grandparents' farm. We helped as much as we could and learned self-respect and the value of honest labor.

"Mamaw" and "Papaw," I called my grandparents. They were as close to the land as they were to their faith and even built a small tabernacle on their property to host weekly sermons delivered by traveling preachers. Erected on the rise of a low hill above pastures of grazing cows, the small, dilapidated, whitewashed chapel was regularly filled by our farming neighbors who squeezed into tight rows of wooden chairs so they could worship together. Yet their worship terrified and agitated me, not because every preacher echoed the same fire-and-brimstone fear of God, but because my familiar neighbors were transformed into strangers who spoke in tongues and scattered my normal sense of peace. When a service concluded, the preacher often spent the night on a cot in the corner near the woodstove in my grandparents' home, leaving the following morning on the road to his next performance. Itinerant preachers were common in the late 1940s and early 1950s, and as far as my young self knew, that was the way of life. I never gave it a second thought when an unfamiliar preacher sat with aunts and uncles on the front porch in the afternoon, ate supper with us, made use of the cot by the stove, and then spent the next day in the tabernacle preparing that evening's sermon.

Then, one early evening, I could take no more. When the preacher began to wave his arms and raised his voice to a fevered pitch, I ran from the chapel and into the field next to my grandparents' house. I remember that I must have been five years old because, back then in this neck of the woods, kindergarten was unheard of, and I hadn't yet begun the first grade. Even then, I knew the risk I took by turning my back on God, so when I was a safe distance away, I halted, widened my short legs to balance myself, and braced for the bolt of lightning that would surely strike me dead for the sin of fleeing the *Halleluiahs* and *Amens*.

"I can't believe in God," I affirmed to myself into the fading light. "If this is what God is about, I don't care to have any part of Him!" Even so young, something in me could not accept that God was so intolerant and punitive and angry. I was ready to accept the consequences, but when nothing dropped from the sky, a comforting peacefulness followed. But as it was to me at the time Godless, it held a certain spiritual void that remained so for the next seventeen years of my life. These were my thirsty years, yet they led me to the experience that eventually refilled my ethereal emptiness.

My Spiritual "Birth Day"

Some of my friends call it my "spiritual transformation." During those intervening years, I remained curious about—what I would call thirsty for—truth, and I wondered why so many others didn't share that same curiosity. I didn't equate any spiritual aspect to my quest because I considered myself an agnostic for a lack of a better term. Nevertheless, I knew that if there was a God, He would recognize my sincerity and someday show me proof of His existence. I also knew it would have to be all about a loving experience, not the fire-and-brimstone kind of faith from which I fled as a child.

I was only twenty-two years old when I finished serving my four-year enlistment in the marines and settled in Chicago. Having spent more than half my time in the military in Vietnam, I was thankful to have emerged with my life and all four limbs. I was single and having a good time, despite my continuing search for some kind of spiritual truth.

While still waiting for my dream job, I ran across a business group that organized weekend retreats where one would learn strategies to achieve potential and become more successful. This was around the time Werner Erhard founded Erhard Seminars Training (EST), so self-actualization was the new big thing. Even though I didn't have much money, I decided to sign up for the business group's weekend retreat. It was at a small lodge, and you couldn't leave once the retreat started. You had to commit yourself to the entire weekend. The facilitator who ran the program was a young, well-dressed guy who introduced himself as Jack English, a very charismatic individual, and said he'd made $90,000 in the last three months or something like that, letting us know he was very successful and good at his profession. One of the main portions of the retreat was to bring attendees up in front of the others to break them down. He would call them a failure, tell them what they did wrong. Well, when he got me up there, the more he berated me, the more I resisted it. I just built a wall. I just didn't buy into that. For me, as long as I didn't give up, I wasn't a failure. I just stood there and let him do his thing.

And Then It Happened

At the end of the retreat, the group had a champagne cocktail party in the conference room. And everyone was standing around in groups of two or three talking about the weekend. I must admit, a lot of people, including myself, did get a lot out of the course. So, we were feeling ten feet tall and toasting each other, celebrating that we had "graduated," when I saw Jack English. Even though I didn't agree with everything, I wanted to thank him for giving such a good class because it certainly stimulated a lot of thought. So, when Jack got in front of our small group, I stepped forward and said, "Thank you, goddamn it." I shocked myself; I have no idea why I stated it that way. I never cursed using that phrase, even though I cursed every other four-letter word growing up on the streets of Chicago. And I never cursed in social settings like that. You can take the kid off the streets of Chicago, but you can't take the streets of Chicago out of the kid. When I said that to Jack, I shook his hand.

He looked me right in the eye and said, "Think about that."

I just wanted to catch his overflow. I'm a literal kind of guy, so I took a step back and did exactly that; I thought about it. And as I did, a presence manifested itself. A loving presence illuminated everything around me in a shimmering golden light and communicated to me—not in words, but in feelings that lie too deep for words. It was hard to describe, but the most accurate, most appropriate words I have thought up over the past fifty years to explain it is a *loving presence*. It illuminated the world around me—my reality—in an entirely new palette of spiritual depth and meaning.

The experience was so profound that I knew it wasn't my mind making this up; I knew in my being it was a real loving presence that somehow kept getting even more loving, which was a clear message from a loving heavenly Father. I consider that moment my spiritual "birth day," what some of my friends call my spiritual transformation.

When I think back on it, I'm reminded of Christian people who say they're born again when they experience a spiritual transformation. That's what happened to me. There is simply no comparison to the inner peace I experienced after my spiritual birth day compared to the peace before, when I was thankful to be that way but unable and unwilling to connect it to a spiritual nature. This is a peace that passes all understanding, and as long as we desire to remain receptive to the spirit of truth it cannot and will not leave us. From my spiritual birth day on, I could finally, for the first time in my life, recognize things of a spiritual nature and make decisions on it and determine their authenticity because of the spiritual insight I was now receptive to. The experience of this personal spiritual insight is real and can be recognized in our mind, but it's left up to our mortal free will to accept or reject this spiritual insight and act on it. I had been a doubting Thomas who sincerely believed I could not have living faith in order to believe in God. I never thought it would happen to me. But sure enough, it did. Even though my spiritual void was finally filled after seventeen years, my thirst for the truth of reality had not been quenched, so the search continued.

It was the most profound moment of my life, and like a window opened to the breeze, I felt the brush of spiritual awakening in those gentle currents. Suddenly, I knew myself capable of weighing and deciding my own spiritual nature, confident I possessed the required wisdom to find my path within any ephemeral topic I encountered. From then on, I would eagerly and honestly consider all I learned for its authenticity, universal beauty, and divine goodness and so discover my own cosmic truth. My spiritual void had been filled. My experience of personal spiritual insight was real, and my mind recognized it as such. My mortal free will accepted the truth of my experience of personal spiritual insight, and thus my spiritual search found new life. Furthermore, the event became the foundation of the experience of faith, which enabled me to discern spiritual truths and reject those which failed to connect with my heart. As I began to study and fill those gaps I found in my questions, I read obsessively. Yet none of the books I collected or of those experts I sought out sufficiently aligned with my expanding experience. My quest for a belief system that resonated within my heart saw me turn away from one path after another, discarding all that failed to harmonize with what I was certain had to be true.

My thirst for the truth of reality remained unquenched, despite my recent experience and a revitalized determination to seek greater wisdom. Still, compared to my Godless inner peace from my youth, I recognized the deepening wisdom gained with each small step and was grateful for its spiritual nature. This was a peace that defied understanding yet remained resilient and receptive to the spirit of truth, refusing to abandon me. All I could do was continue my path.

I began to study on my own in more earnest, but none of the books I read or the people I encountered sufficiently aligned with my experience. I would take six more years to find a belief system that resonated with me. However, not long after the retreat, I finally found a job. I won't say I stumbled onto it, because I constantly put the word out about wanting to work overseas, so people would often suggest I check out this company or that in addition to keeping my own eyes open. I'm a gypsy at heart and always curious how other folks lived across the pond.

The first job where I got my foot in the door was working at an early-warning system designed to deter any Soviet aggression. After a few weeks of training in Chicago at a remote site, they kick you out the door, issue you a parka, and instruct you not to eat the yellow snow. The Distant Early Warning Line, also known as the DEW Line, was a Cold War–era system of radar stations in the northern Arctic region of Canada, the north coast and Aleutian Islands of Alaska, the Faroe Islands, Greenland, and Iceland. As you might imagine, it didn't take me long to find a more salubrious climate to hang my hat.

With a top-secret clearance, crypto access, and current passport, after the brief DEW Line stint, I found myself on a beautiful tropical island located in the Pacific Ocean between Hawaii and Guam, an idyllic paradise known as Kwajalein. On Kwaj, as the contractors called it, those not native to the island fell into one of two social groups, though of course there was some overlap. There were those who drank alcohol and those who preferred to smoke cannabis. While I chose not to partake, I had much more in common with the dope smokers. They tended to be more creative and philosophical and often talked about spiritual matters, which appealed to me. Bear in mind that I'm still consciously searching for a spiritual written source in harmony with my personal revelation. I encouraged people to share their spiritual experiences, stories, and beliefs with me—anything they felt spiritually worthwhile—but a religion or belief system that felt right remained elusive. I admired and respected the born-again Christians above all, not for their beliefs but for their unequivocal enthusiasm. I have always been a gypsy at heart but have also always managed to leave on good terms with the relationships I left behind.

And so, a few months after I moved to Hawaii in 1974, I received a letter from a friend on Kwaj who had yet to complete his one-year contract. I tore it open to catch up on events since I left. Kwaj is a quiet, out-of-the-way kind of place, so I was caught up on all the news within a single paragraph. But the second one caught my attention. My interest in all things spiritual was well known, and though my friend, Bill Ibarra, was somewhat of a geek, I was puzzled as to why he mentioned *The Urantia Book* without any explanation. In fact, the title hooked me, even though I had not the slightest idea of its contents. Three words—blunt and without "secrets of" or "truth" or any such seductive vagaries—held my attention. "Book" implied reference or guide, but "Urantia"?—an exotic word unknown to me. I had to learn more. I felt compelled to discover what this book was, so I called my local bookstore.

It didn't have the book, but another of its branches did. I tell you, that was a very long day selling concert tickets in the Pearl Ridge Shopping Center, and I still remember running across the parking lot to my car. All I could think of as I crept along with the rush-hour traffic was *Why do I feel so compelled to own a copy of a book I had never heard of twenty-four hours earlier?* It was over two thousand pages and with a price tag almost as much as a week's rent back then—$25—yet I never flinched as the clerk ran my credit card through the store's card imprinter.

It was the biggest, heaviest hardcover book I had ever seen, let alone owned, but as I lugged it up the stairs to my apartment, I felt a knot of tension slide away, and the tightness in my chest from the moment I read the title slackened. I kicked off my shoes, dropped into my only chair, and opened the stiff cover. I paged through a table of contents worthy of its own volume and was genuinely surprised that a spiritual book would address so many disparate topics. I found the foreword and the meaning of *Urantia* on the same page. Urantia is another name for the planet Earth, and the intent of the book is to "present enlarged concepts and advanced truth."

The Urantia Book's introduction made clear its aim was to finally reconcile religion with science and philosophy by explaining the origin and meaning of life, mankind's place in the universe, the relationship between God and people, and the life of Jesus. Well, such an authoritative claim captured my attention. I was looking for truth wherever I could find it. Somehow it didn't even bother me that it was written as directly presented by celestial beings to a group of people in Chicago, who dutifully transcribed it sometime in the first half of the twentieth century and published it in 1955.

In truth, I was simultaneously cautious and intrigued. Based on my experiences with other books recommended by friends, I assumed there would be no reason to waste my time reading every page. Yet what compelled me to buy the book, costing a week's worth of groceries, in the first place? So, I opened the foreword. Right away, certain thought-provoking paragraphs rang true and kept me grounded, so I kept reading. When I got to paper 1, page 24, I had an epiphany. I was certain no human could have written this sentence by him- or herself:

"Those who know God have experienced the fact of his presence; such God-knowing mortals hold in their personal experience the only positive proof of the existence of the living God, which one human being can offer to another" 1:2.8 (24.6).

Now, for the first time I could point to a written source of a revelatory nature and unequivocally confirm that this passage is what I identify with, that my personal revelation was in harmony with an epochal revelation, *The Urantia Book*. I had found a source to quench my thirst for the Truth of Reality. Upon discovering *The Urantia Book*, I could consciously and truthfully give credit where credit was due—to the Spirit of Truth and my Indwelling Spirit.

I was reading it in black and white from a revelatory source. My personal religious experience confirmed it was true. More specifically, *The Urantia Book* confirmed my personal religious experience was real and valid. I was no longer alone.

Right away, I carried the hardcover wherever I went. No softcover printing of the book existed at the time. One day I was walking in downtown Waikiki when a bearded young man emerged up the stairs from a pizza parlor and onto the street. "Hey, man," he said to me. "I read that book in one afternoon on Maui."

Yeah, right! I thought to myself, but I was still impressed. As my constant companion, the book had the word *book* faded from the title because I carried the tome around every day, but, somehow, he had recognized it anyway.

That was just the first of scores of my encounters all over the world with truth seekers, tourists, and natives alike, who had read and studied *The Urantia Book*. When I left Hawaii, I had managed to locate and was participating in three Urantia study groups every week. These were the first experiences of what would become my life's passion—disseminating the truths of *The Urantia Book* in loving ministry to every corner of the globe.

In late 2001 I joined the Foreign Service as an information management specialist. During the ensuing eleven years, I served at over five assignments and major postings. After six months of orientation and training inside the DC area with other agencies, my first posting was US Embassy Islamabad in Pakistan or AmEmb ISL, as we referred to it. It was right in the wake of the 9/11 attacks, and we hit the ground running. I was on the third wave of evacuation during my first posting in ISL and hung my hat inside the Washington, DC, Beltway until events cooled down sufficiently to warrant my return. As you can imagine, because of the aftermath of 9/11, the medium-sized embassy was much busier than even large embassies like those in Moscow and Beijing. I served next at another small-to-medium-sized embassy, US Embassy Yangon (Rangoon), Burma, the region now known as Yangon, Myanmar. The Brits and Americans were still in the habit of calling it by its former name. A larger, updated embassy was being built when I left for my next assignment inside the Beltway. I next served on the executive secretariat's Special Communications team in Washington, DC, for two years. the work included thirty separate trips abroad with then U.S. secretary of state Condoleezza Rice. After those two years, I volunteered for a year with the Multinational Force and Observers' Civilian Observer Unit (MFO), tasked with peacekeeping between Egypt and Israel in the Sinai. I returned to an embassy posting in AmEmb MOS, Moscow, Russia—the former Union of Soviet Socialist Republics. My final posting before I retired in 2012 was at the US Embassy in Beijing, BEJ.

All over the world, I met dignitaries, shopkeepers, and scores of others, rich or poor, who were eager to learn the truths contained in *The Urantia Book*. While in Islamabad, in what was the poorest part of town, I introduced the book to a young girl who started translating it so she could share it with her family. Soon we had a group of eighteen young Pakistanis who wanted to know more. At least one of them learned English by reading the book. I could tell comparable stories from at least a dozen other faraway cities and towns.

Now, it is time to dust off the cosmic passport you might not have known you had and take this journey with me on the highway to eternity. Part 1 will discuss the cosmic mind and how it provides our reality response for determining the Truth of Reality. We have a reliable, updated road map—a spiritual GPS—that will prevent us from deviating off course and not misdirect us to dead ends that make no sense. Ol' Blue is a trusted GPS meant to guide all those hungry for the truth and answers to all that still puzzles them. *The Urantia Book* road map, like a GPS, constantly updates for each individual so the person can confirm and personally experience for themselves the direction is true north—toward Paradise.

Sincere yet doubting Thomases (atheists or secularists) have been known to take advantage of *The Urantia Book* to discover a spiritual route they never knew existed. Scientists who expect the signs along the way to be consistent with current scientific knowledge may discover the next mile marker could contain a GPS position update incompatible with their current belief system. I encourage them to check in with their discerning inner compass (thought adjuster) before going further down the path.

The Urantia Book spiritual GPS also serves those who are spiritually inclined or God-conscious. The truth bells will go off as your personal religious experiences are confirmed with the Truth of Reality, as faith sons and daughters grow spiritually while traveling upward and inward on this divine highway to Paradise. I know whereof I speak; *The Urantia Book* can and will stand up to honest criticism. I guarantee it!

In sharing my story, I'm reminded of a retired marine gunnery sergeant, a Vietnam vet. When the "gunny" would visit his grandkids, the little ones would climb up on his lap, surrounded by the older siblings, as soon as he took a seat. The first question out of their mouth was "Grandpa, tell us another story about Vietnam." The gunny would always begin by saying, "What I am about to tell you may not be 100 percent true or completely accurate, but it is the way I remembered it." The Gy.Sgt. would then, once again, mesmerize his grandkids with another story of his time in Nam.

My Purpose

I am just one person in the groundswell popularity of the Urantia community, yet I hope to do my small part to grow the fellowship of students of the Urantia revelation. By helping people to personally experience and recognize the truths revealed in *The Urantia Book*, it is my fondest hope that they become inspired to share this epochal revelation with others who are as eager for truth as they are.

Since being declared in the public domain in 2001, sales of the book have skyrocketed. Urantia Foundation reports sales or downloads of more than 100,000 copies each year from various sites, and the book has been translated into twenty-seven languages, including braille. As part of the book's growing popularity, several companion guides have been written, including my own: *Up Close and Personal with the Urantia Book: Expanded Edition.*[1] *The Urantia Revelation* is uniquely different. Here I will make the case for the veracity and value of both the scientific and religious revelations within *The Urantia Book* and how they interact to create additional value.

This book is divided into three parts. The first two focus on the prescient scientific facts and the revisiting and clarification of historic truths revealed in the original Urantia text published in 1955 and all subsequent printings. Part 1 focuses on the scientific revelations that were eventually discovered and verified in the years after the publication of the original *Urantia Book*, often decades afterward. Part 2 focuses on the religious and spiritual ramifications, which are equally revelatory. Part 3 shows how *The Urantia Book* entwines the proven laws of science with the importance of a living spiritual relationship with God, culminating in a personal philosophy of living that works. Creating a life in which ideals are made practical in the service of our fellows is the true meaning of a living philosophy, an art of living that is increasingly allowing us to be expressive of our true selves, the individuals we are meant to be.

Taken together, parts I and II illustrate each side of the COSAR Principle—the integration of science and religion.[2] The meaningful collaboration of science with religion—the truth of both realities—can best be achieved by revelation. To attain full and expansive awareness of the Truth of Reality revealed in *The Urantia Book*, one must be able to marry both the S (science) and the R (religion or personal-spiritual) factors of the COSAR Principle into his or her own personal and unified picture of reality. Neither the S nor the R can by themselves reveal truth, but together they most certainly can. The S approach, of course, refers to the field in which hypotheses are refined into theories, which are then confirmed or denied through experimentation and only accepted as fact when repeated experiments produce identical results.

The undeniable reality of science contradicts and even refutes Western religious tradition, marginalizing religious claims that have little chance of empirical support, such as the existence of the soul, or even the existence of a higher being. But taken by itself, divorced from spiritual living, it becomes lifeless. The existence of the soul, of beings more evolved than humans, and even of intangible realities of human experience, such as love, free will, truth, beauty, and goodness, may be called into question. They are likely to be relegated to subjective fabrications and opinions of the human mind. Even that human, conscious, and material mind is increasingly equated by a mechanistic and materialistic science with nothing more than the functioning of the human, material, and electrochemical brain.

To be fair, at the opposite pole is the fundamentalism of those who are extremely religious but believe themselves truly faithful. These people make preposterous claims devoid of scientific rationale to the point of denying physical reality to promote primitive mythologies, such as the belief that the Earth is only slightly more than six thousand years old. This is problematic in that science uses solid empirical data to easily disprove such claims. The illogical intractability of the extremely religious only serves to widen the gulf between themselves and scientists whose perspectives appear materialistic and adhere to similarly dogmatic positions that science can or will eventually find answers to everything.

The New Atheists correctly insist there's no scientific evidence that a personal God exists, a denial of religion and spirituality with the sweeping force of a surprise roundhouse blow. Less strenuous are the arguments of religion's supporters who perceive that the current scientific viewpoint is devoid of any possibility of God, a personal, loving heavenly Father, or even creative intent and purpose in the cosmos (intelligent design).

Both viewpoints foster unhealthy confrontation, encouraging volatility, imbalance, and mutually destructive obstacles to truth. A hard R position is unacceptable to educated people searching for truth, just as a hard S position is uncomfortable for people of faith, regardless of their religion or belief system.

The Urantia Book successfully bridges the gulf between these two opposing aspects of intellectual and spiritual nature. It synthesizes the sciences of nature and the theology of religion into a consistent and logical philosophy of the universe that metaphysics has failed to achieve. This promising philosophical unity might subsequently be strengthened by revelation within *The Urantia Book*. As a religious revelation of epochal significance, *The Urantia Book* authoritatively reveals the personal (R) and impersonal (S) side of the deity by providing an unbroken and coordinated explanation of both science and religion with the Truth of Reality. It provides a viewpoint that grounds the facts of cosmology yet reaches down with the Hand of God to show a personal God who loves his children, while depicting the same responsible and loving Father as He who designs a universe destined to be lived in by untold countless numbers of those same personalities.

Religion and science, then, are not two antagonistic views of reality. They are differing viewpoints on two aspects of one reality, those aspects being the personal and impersonal natures of God.

Part 1 states the case for the veracity of the scientific details revealed in now known or about to be known scientific discoveries. The extraordinarily high percentage of correct assertions regarding the prescient scientific facts and the revisiting and clarification of historic truths, which were either not known or not accepted by the scientific mainstream until decades later, makes a case for paying attention to what *The Urantia Book* says scientifically.

Part 2 explains the religious or spiritual aspects of *The Urantia Book*. It focuses on Earth's, Urantia's, five epochal revelations, including, for the first time, a full and accurate account of the life of Jesus—his boyhood, adolescence, and young adulthood, heretofore unknown; his personal relationships and struggles; and, of course, his teachings and resurrection. Stated otherwise, the fourth epochal revelation in *The Urantia Book* is a restatement of the life example and personal teachings of Jesus in modern phraseology, for every year of his life, including the missing years. Finally, a personal account of Jesus of Nazareth as the Son of Man and Jesus, after baptism, as the Son of God and Son of Man follows.

Since *The Urantia Book* addresses the evolution of religious institutions, part 2 will also. And, more important, in alignment with Ol' Blue's teachings, we will put the individual person in direct and personal contact with God, back in the driver's seat of spiritual progression and inner life.

The demise of the Roman Empire dragged civic literacy down with it, leaving the Roman Catholic Church to selfishly guard against the spread of this skill. For almost a thousand years, priests and scribes did their bit to consolidate ecclesiastical power over Europe. Not even kings were able to read and write but needed to dictate to a church-trained scribe who, of course, recited the contents of every missive to their superiors. There is no greater tyrant than a "man of God" who could with a word charge anyone with heresy, and Ecclesiastical authorities made best use of that power. What the church wanted became synonymous with what God wanted; disobedience or even questioning church policies risked excommunication or worse. Free will became the devil's influence and was therefore subjugated by the church's strict insistence on obedience. The Renaissance arrived on a breeze of hope, but its appetite for knowledge was edged with a keen resistance to restrictions deemed acceptable or not by the priesthood, with ecclesiastic intransigence to relinquish any authority and ever crueler punishments for heresy. The church's reluctance to adapt may have contributed to a gradual decline in its influence, which some perceive as evident today.

Knowledge is power, and the idea that, by understanding nature, humankind could control it turned into a clarion call to action and the fuel to drive intellectual pursuits such as science. Scientists strive to learn the laws of the universe through repeated experiments with identical results, squeezing God out of the equation. Since then, the balance of power has shifted steadily toward a secular and materialistic world where faith is relegated to the sidelines. The Urantia Book promises to reset the balance between science and faith:

> *Modern secularism has been fostered by two worldwide influences. The father of secularism was the narrow-minded and godless attitude of nineteenth- and twentieth-century so-called science—atheistic science. The mother of modern secularism was the totalitarian medieval Christian church. Secularism had its inception as a rising protest against the almost complete domination of Western civilization by the institutionalized Christian church. 195:8.2 (2081.2)*

We will allow *The Urantia Book* to further speak for itself regarding the difficulties presented in striving to reconcile the scientific and religious viewpoints:

> *A logical and consistent philosophic concept of the universe cannot be built up on the postulations of either materialism or spiritism, for both of these systems of thinking, when universally applied, are compelled to view the cosmos in distortion, the former contacting with a universe turned inside out, the latter realizing the nature of a universe turned outside in. Never, then, can either science or religion, in and of themselves, standing alone, hope to gain an adequate understanding of universal truths and relationships without the guidance of human philosophy and the illumination of divine revelation. 103:6.5 (1135.7)*

And twenty-nine papers later, the following appears:

The materialistic scientist and the extreme idealist are destined always to be at loggerheads. This is not true of those scientists and idealists who are in possession of a common standard of high moral values and spiritual test levels. In every age, scientists and religionists must recognize that they are on trial before the bar of human need. They must eschew all warfare between themselves while they strive valiantly to justify their continued survival by enhanced devotion to the service of human progress. If the so-called science or religion of any age is false, then must it either purify its activities or pass away before the emergence of a material science or spiritual religion of a truer and more worthy order. 132:1.4 (1457.3)

Within these pages, I hope to begin to reconcile these viewpoints and even unify them, even as they are so unified in the oneness of the original Deity of the I AM. In making such a humble beginning of such a truce, perhaps we will find common ground from where we can all, regardless of our original stance, journey forward together.

Endnotes

1. JJ Johnson, *Up Close and Personal with The Urantia Book: Expanded Edition* (self-pub., 2009), Amazon.
2. JJ Johnson, "The Urantia Book and the COSAR Principle," video, 2:41, August 9, 2010, http://www.youtube.com/watch?v=VKeL6 XNhT1k.

PART I

Science in The Urantia Book: *The Impersonal Nature of God and the Cosmos*

Religion and science are not antagonistic views of reality; they are two aspects of one reality, those aspects being the personal and impersonal natures of God. We, of course, cannot anticipate the scientific discoveries of a thousand years into the future. In fact, we know that even in a relatively few years, many of science's current conclusions regarding the physical sciences will need revision because of additional scientific developments and discoveries.

The word *prescience* might look like pre + science, but it actually comes from the Latin, *praescientia*, which means "foreknowledge," or knowledge that you know before anyone else does. Only the celestial authors of *The Urantia Book* could have authoritatively provided these prescient disclosures before our scientists actually confirmed them many years later.

In the examples that follow, *The Urantia Book* publication date of 1955 will be used, but it is worth noting that parts 1 and 2 of the book were said to be completed in 1934, and part 3 is dated 1935. These dates are relevant insofar as *The Urantia Book* can be said to have been prescient in two ways: it described scientific facts years or even decades before they were accepted in mainstream science and, similarly, it revisited and clarified historical truths that challenged the status quo but were eventually proved correct.

The revisiting and clarification of historical truths and prescient scientific facts detailed in this part of the book were not verified by our scientific community until well after *The Urantia Book* was published in 1955. For the skeptics, I will use the publication date of 1955 to avoid unnecessary bickering. These examples are not to be treated lightly, and I simply will not allow this to be swept under the rug. No matter how tightly you squeeze your eyes shut this will not go away. When truth comes knocking at your door, why would you slam it shut? I'll report; you decide.

This first part will also document independent scientists not affiliated with *The Urantia Book* who have openly acknowledged that the prescient examples provided are accurate and supported in reputable scientific journals and peer reviews. The examples provided are supported from scientists who are not affiliated with the Urantia community and have no axe to grind.

The prescient scientific facts and revisiting and clarification of historic truths, revealed, disclosed and coordinated in *The Urantia Book* support and, with revelation, validate what I call the **COSAR Principle**. Ol' Blue states it this way:

> *The truth—an understanding of cosmic relationships, universe facts, and spiritual values—can best be had through the ministry of the Spirit of Truth and can best be criticized by revelation. But revelation originates neither a science nor a religion; its function is to co-ordinate both science and religion with the truth of reality. Always,*

in the absence of revelation or in the failure to accept or grasp it, has mortal man resorted to his futile gesture of metaphysics, that being the only human substitute for the revelation of truth or for the mota of morontia personality. 103:7.8 (1138.6)

The scientific achievements and revisions to history revealed in *The Urantia Book* that predate their discoveries decades later might not make one believe in a personal God, our loving Heavenly Father. The impersonal nature of God functioning in our time-space universes is a constant reminder that there is no scientific evidence that a personal God exists.

God is spirit, and we require spiritual insight, a personal religious experience, to be God-conscious through the experience of faith. Living faith, the experience, assurance, and conviction of faith, will be discussed in a later chapter. Religion is a personal experience, and the spiritual fruit one bears is a testimony of one's spirit-led life. This is the distinction between how we validate a personal loving heavenly Father versus the impersonal side of Deity in relation to the cosmos and the origin of our finite universe.

All the scientific revelations I describe in Part 1 have been verified by respected scientists, philosophers, theologians, and academicians unaffiliated with any Urantia organization. They have no axe to grind. These prescient scientific facts can and will stand up to *honest* criticism.

For example, chapters 1 and 2 in particular will include excerpts from the author's correspondence with Nobel laureate Kary Mullis (including a personal invitation to his home) and with Professor Mark A. S. McMenamin, author of *The Garden of Ediacara* (Columbia University Press), as well as excerpts from a chapter written by Sarah Lewis in *The Invention of Sacred Tradition*, edited by James R. Lewis and Olav Hammer (Cambridge University Press). Martin Peng, with a PhD in Applied Physics from Stanford University, studied the materials in chapters 1 and 2 and found the content to be correct, thoughtful, comprehensive, and well organized.

Enough Is Plenty

It is not within the scope or intent of part 1 to provide the documentation details of the research and findings of the dozen plus examples given. Reputable sources will be provided, and *The Urantia Book* references that support the scientific findings will be supplied to unequivocally validate their discoveries after the *The Urantia Book* was published in 1955. Those who want more will not be left out to dry. A link will be made available for those who would like to take a deeper dive and really immerse themselves in one or all of the thought-provoking examples given. Moreover, I wholeheartedly encourage you to check out the reference site and weigh in with your insights gained from reading this book. We need all the help we can get.

In many ways, I have served more as a collector and editor rather than as an original researcher in making my case for *The Urantia Papers*. In fact, the research and discoveries in all of part 1 have been peer-reviewed in major scientific journals.

Endnote

Humanity has long sought to create a coherent philosophy that explains both itself and the universe, drawing from science, religion, and metaphysics. However, these efforts have been hindered by the inability to bridge the critical gulf between the material and spiritual realms—what *The Urantia Book* refers to as the "morontia gulf." This gap arises from a lack of understanding about the morontia mind and material, which exist as transitional realities between the physical and the spiritual. Revelation provides the only means to fill this conceptual void, offering the necessary insights to construct a logical and satisfying philosophy of the universe. With such guidance, humanity can better understand its place and purpose in the cosmos.

Chapter 1
The Precambrian Supercontinent

From Revelation to Discovery: The Precambrian Enigma

When I first opened *The Urantia Book*, I had no idea it would hold answers to questions I hadn't yet asked. One of the book's most striking claims leaped out at me early in my reading: its detailed description of a Precambrian supercontinent, said to have existed over a billion years ago. At the time, I had only a layperson's understanding of geology, but the clarity and confidence of this revelation caught my attention.

Years later, I stumbled across the work of Dr. Mark McMenamin, whose research confirmed what *The Urantia Book* had described decades earlier. It was a moment of both validation and awe. How could a book written in the 1930s describe a scientific reality that geologists wouldn't uncover until the 1970s? This wasn't just a coincidence—it was a demonstration of what *The Urantia Book* claimed to be: a revelation designed to bridge the gulf between science and religion.

The discovery of Rodinia was more than a scientific milestone. It reminded me that our universe is deeply interconnected, a grand design that we are only beginning to understand. And it reaffirmed my belief that science and spirituality are not enemies but complementary tools for uncovering the truth of reality. In this chapter, we'll explore how decades before its discovery *The Urantia Book* revealed the story of what McMenamin calls Rodinia and what this means for those of us seeking to reconcile the impersonal facts of science with the personal truths of faith.

The Unbroken Truth of Reality

The history of the mid-twentieth century discloses some startling and fascinating biological, cosmological, and scientific information. The scientific community only recently confirmed several of these facts. Except for a few, most researchers or scientists lack the courage to openly accept or investigate the earlier material, specifically that found in *The Urantia Book*.

The Urantia Book's accuracy on the subject of this chapter is a thunderbolt for science, confirming its revelatory substance beyond question. This is no minor detail; it's a bombshell that science is only now verifying—with astonishment.

In 1970 science discovered for the first time a Precambrian supercontinent that existed one billion years ago.[1] As noteworthy as this is, perhaps even more remarkable is that this newly discovered scientific fact was unequivocally disclosed in exquisite detail in *The Urantia Papers*, which was written in 1935 and published in 1955 as *The Urantia Book*.[2] In *The Garden of Ediacara*, author Mark A. S. McMenamin points to now-known facts of two supercontinents: Pangea and Rodinia.[3] McMenamin's astonishment at *The Urantia Book*'s accuracy, specifically regarding the Precambrian supercontinent Rodinia, is grounded in the surprising precision of its statements in *The Urantia Book*. It authoritatively discloses this in 1935, long before plate tectonics became accepted in the scientific community. *The Urantia Book* posits that the supercontinent existed around one billion years ago; not very long from that time geologically, it began to separate into continents. This breakup, according to *The Urantia Book*, played a role in the emergence of complex life, an insight that McMenamin marvels at because modern science could only validate it a full generation later. Mind you, no one had *The Urantia Book* in mind when it did so!

Here's what Professor McMenamin says: "This book was unknown to me until it was brought to my attention by JJ Johnson in October 1995. I obtained a copy of the book from the Smith College library and noted the 1955 (eighth edition 1984) publication date. What could possibly explain such precocious insight from such an unexpected corner? Perhaps it has to do with a lively, unconstrained, but nevertheless informed imagination. John K. Wright has noted how outrageous hypotheses 'arouse interest, invite attack, and thus serve useful fermentative purposes in the advancement of geology.' But what about outrageous religions?"[4]

A few paragraphs later, Mark reasserts what I assume to him is a pretty outrageous statement to make so authoritatively: "Assuming for the moment that space voyagers are not responsible for life's origin and history on this planet, one wonders how the *Urantia Book* authors arrived at the concept of a Proterozoic supercontinent, and the link between breakup of this supercontinent and the emergence of complex life in the ensuing rift oceans, 30 years before most geologists accepted continental drift and nearly four decades before scientists had any inkling that Rodinia existed."[5]

By 1935 mainstream science still regarded the idea of continental drift with skepticism; Alfred Wegener's theories, discussed later in this book, were viewed with suspicion. Yet, *The Urantia Book* confidently discusses plate tectonics as the driver behind the formation and breakup of supercontinents. This idea, now foundational in geology, was virtually unheard of when the book was written. Rodinia's breakup indeed created oceanic spaces conducive to marine life development, a process confirmed by fossil evidence of diverse life flourishing in those ancient seas.

McMenamin metaphorically links this era with Eden, naming his book *The Garden of Ediacara* to convey how the breakup of Rodinia and the emergence of the Ediacaran organisms set the stage for life's blossoming. This "garden" of life, like Eden, holds a symbolic significance as the cradle of evolution.

This specific discovery of the Earth's geological history features two significant supercontinents that impacted the development of life in profound ways. Each of these supercontinents emerged and eventually broke apart through tectonic shifts, shaping Earth's environment and the life-forms that inhabited it. These three revelational facts are not theories; they are facts.

The Life Carriers in *The Urantia Book* describe the ancient geological forces shaping Earth with an unusual authority. Their descriptions capture processes, like the slow tectonic drift of Rodinia, that would later be recognized as essential to the Cambrian explosion, the swift emergence of diverse organisms. This prophetic alignment, as McMenamin notes, suggests a GPS-like precision, giving humanity a cosmic road map long before the science was available to validate it.

These prescient scientific facts and the revisiting and clarification of the historic truths in Paper 57 are verifiable and supported by comparing the referenced documentation using independent reliable and acceptable sources from reputable scientists, scholars, academics, historians, and researchers. This has all been peer-reviewed too! The authoring of the correct description of this now-accepted prescient scientific fact in *The Urantia Papers* is beyond the scope of conventional experience.[6] It affects the man and woman in the street—and I dare say with the same impact as Einstein's relativity.

Rodinia was Earth's first known supercontinent, formed during a time when life on Earth was almost exclusively single-celled. Around 750 million to 600 million years ago, Rodinia began to break apart. This breakup is particularly significant because it coincided with the emergence of multicellular life-forms, marking the dawn of complex animal life. The rift valleys and newly formed shallow seas created by Rodinia's fragmentation offered ideal environments for early multicellular organisms to thrive. These shallow waters were nutrient rich and relatively stable, creating conditions where life could evolve and diversify at an accelerated rate.

The connection between Rodinia's breakup and the emergence of animals is one of the key revelations that *The Urantia Book* presented two-plus decades before science could confirm it. Geologists now understand that the breakup of Rodinia helped set the stage for the Ediacaran biota, some of Earth's first large multicellular organisms, and later, the Cambrian explosion around 540 million years ago, when a burst of diverse animal body plans emerged within a brief geological window.

Pangea came much later, forming around 300 million years ago. Unlike Rodinia, which influenced early animal evolution, Pangea's environmental impact had more to do with shaping the diversity and distribution of land-dwelling species. Its formation led to a drier, more variable climate across its vast landmass, which prompted adaptive radiation and the diversification of reptiles, eventually paving the way for the age of the dinosaurs. The breakup of Pangea, around 175 million years ago, ultimately shaped the modern continents and has been a major driver in the distribution of species that we see today. This is all outlined in *The Urantia Book* and then detailed in McMenamin's book.

McMenamin had no idea that the *Urantia Book* existed; the remarkable "discovery" that the book reveals could have driven him to call it pseudoscience, thereby hiding this disclosure, but Mark took the high road and admitted to his incredulity in the pages of his book. What a man of terrific integrity! In my dealings with scientists over the years many (or most) either ignore the Truth of Reality when it hits them in the choppers, or they put it in the intellectual broom closet to hope that it will be ignored.

The significance of Rodinia's breakup lies in its timing and the life-altering effects it had on Earth's biological landscape. As Rodinia fragmented, tectonic activity increased, leading to volcanic eruptions that injected carbon dioxide into the atmosphere, gradually warming the planet. This warming helped end the Snowball Earth conditions of extreme glaciation. As the glaciers receded and seas expanded, shallow marine environments emerged. These seas offered ample sunlight and nutrients, creating fertile "gardens" where simple multicellular organisms could evolve into more complex life-forms.

This breakup-driven environmental transformation is pivotal because it gave rise to the conditions necessary for the **Cambrian explosion**, a period that introduced complex ecosystems and most of the major animal groups still present today. Therefore, the breakup of Rodinia was not only a geological event but also a milestone in biological evolution, as the conditions it produced accelerated the diversification of life.

From McMenamin's perspective, *The Urantia Book*'s statements on Rodinia and the connection to animal emergence demonstrate a remarkable foresight. This is not one but three fantastic combined facts: the existence of Rodinia, plate tectonics as the mechanism for supercontinental movement, and the timing of multicellular organisms. These integrated prescient insights suggest an almost cosmic road map that links geophysical changes to biological evolution. One should automatically see these three as interconnected parts of a grand design, in a similar manner that the Discovery Institute sees an intelligent designer operating in the cosmos when looking at Urantia's biological evolution—especially regarding the human anatomy.

Before I discuss my interactions with McMenamin, let me offer a philosophical consideration of the book with a few thoughts that Professor Sarah Lewis has made in the book she contributed to, *The Invention of Sacred Tradition*.

The *Urantia Papers* as published in *The Urantia Book* is a composite replete revelation that begins with God as the I AM. This cannot be proven or disproven.[7] A revelation originates in neither a science nor a religion; its function is to coordinate both science and religion with the Truth of Reality. Science and Religion are not two antagonistic views of reality; they are views of two aspects of one reality, those aspects being the personal and impersonal natures of God. The Coordination of Science and Religion (COSAR) with the truth of reality is

14 | EXPLORING THE URANTIA REVELATION

best achieved by revelation. I refer to and provide examples of this enhanced relationship as the COSAR Principle.[8] The prescient (pre-science) statements in this report support and validate the COSAR Principle, as science now has validated "facts" from a supposed religious book!

Recognizing the revelatory disclosure that predates the scientific facts before they were known and accepted into the scientific mainstream compels an honest and truth-seeking person to want to learn more. Are there more revelations like this one? (The answer is yes; see the next three chapters). A logical question one should ask is, how does God coordinate his *impersonal* Deity levels as an energy creator with his *personal* nature as a universal Loving Father so that we can religiously experience and gel with our personal insights from the sciences?

Now I go back to my interactions with Dr. McMenamin. Mark and I stayed in touch by email beginning early 2007 during my posting with the US State Department inside the Beltway while supporting the secretary of state, Condoleezza Rice, on her trips abroad. For the next decade, Mark and I exchanged emails highlighting current research projects that made headlines. Mark mentioned he took a lot of heat for recognizing *The Urantia Book* regarding the Precambrian supercontinent, even though his colleagues accepted the science in his *The Garden of Ediacara* book, but he was prepared to stand his ground. I called Mark after returning from one of my trips abroad with the secretary of state, for possibly getting together if our time worked out. He was cleaning out his barn during the phone chat, and the hookup never happened. My hectic overseas travel supporting Secretary of State Rice and Mark's busy teaching schedule prevented us from getting together. I bring this up to point out that Professor McMenamin currently is one of a few scholars who openly acknowledges truth whatever the source. Mark did not inform me he provided favorable reviews of *The Urantia Book* accounts of the supercontinent and continental drift in *The Garden of Ediacara*. This was brought to my attention by a retired attorney friend of mine, Dick Johnson, who happened to see a write-up of another *Urantia Book* student, Matthew Block. Matthew researches published sources from both within and without the Urantia community. While researching secondary material, Block happened to stumble onto Professor McMenamin giving me credit for turning him on to Ol' Blue in his book. It was truly a delight to know he was willing to acknowledge prescient science in Paper 57. One of the purposes I aim to achieve with this book is to encourage others who are in a professional position to openly acknowledge the truths they find in *The Urantia Book* that support their science.

Expanding upon This Chapter

For those who want to dig a little deeper into the scientific and philosophical details of this depiction of the Precambrian continent, continental drift, and the Cambrian explosion, my colleague Bob Debold has a more detailed essay, "The Precambrian Supercontinent" (https://deboldgroup.com /Aquatic/Documents/Bobs-Chapter%201.pdf), along with a number of essays on various topics the *Urantia Book* delves into. Bob adds detail beyond this chapter: he fleshes out how this topic relates to my COSAR principle, suggesting that *The Urantia Book* harmonizes scientific and spiritual insights into

16 | EXPLORING THE URANTIA REVELATION

a unified worldview, capable of addressing intellectual and spiritual curiosity alike.[9]

Central to Bob's argument is Mark McMenamin's recognition of *the Urantia Book*'s striking accuracy on the Precambrian supercontinent, Rodinia. Bob conducts a more in-depth examination of this phenomenon, exploring revelatory details that illuminate its connection to the emergence of complex life. Bob delves deeper into McMenamin's amazement at the book's prescient statements, interpreting them as validation of its revelatory nature.

Another theme Bob emphasizes is how *The Urantia Book* not only anticipated scientific discoveries such as plate tectonics and continental drift, but also integrated them with spiritual insights, a capability he argues gives it a "cosmic-GPS" quality. Bob further emphasizes this metaphor by explaining how revelation can serve as a directional guide, helping humanity align scientific exploration with spiritual truths.

Bob also discusses the Cambrian explosion and connects this event to the breakup of Rodinia, proposing that such revelations are cosmic milestones, aligning human understanding with divine insights. He argues that recognizing these revelations can open "cosmic knowledge portals," encouraging humanity to synthesize science and spirituality in their quest for truth. For those who truly want to drink deeply from the well of truth, I recommend you take a look at Bob's essay.

As I continued my journey with *The Urantia Book*, I found myself drawn to its account of humanity's origins and the grand narrative of our spiritual and biological evolution. The book's portrayal of Adam and Eve as celestial beings on a mission to uplift the genetic and spiritual potential of humankind intrigued me deeply. Their story wasn't just a myth or allegory—it became for me a revelation of purpose and design that resonated with my own questions about the nature of progress, both personal and collective.

I began to wonder, *What if our potential isn't limited by the mistakes of the past but is instead an invitation to rise above them? What if their mission, though interrupted, left behind seeds of greatness waiting to be cultivated?* In the next chapter, we'll dive into the fascinating story of Adam and Eve—exploring the interplay of science and revelation to uncover what their genes, and their mission, mean for us today.

Endnotes

1. Chen Wu et al., "Precambrian Tectonic eEvolution of the Qaidam Block, Northern Tibet: Implications for the Assembly and Breakup of Proterozoic Supercontinents," *Earth-Science Reviews* 259 (December 2024): https://doi.org/10.1016/j.earscirev.2024.104985; Mark McMenamin, *The Garden of Ediacara* (New York: Columbia University Press, 1998), 173–88; and Johnson, *Up Close and Personal,* 5. McMenamin says, "Cases such as this one . . . are an exercise in humility for me as a scientist."
2. Urantia Book. 57:8.1 (660.3)
3. McMenamin., *Garden of Ediacara,* 174–76
4. McMenamin., *Garden of Ediacara,* 175.
5. McMenamin., *Garden of Ediacara,* 175.
6. Sarah Lewis, "The Peculiar Sleep: Receiving *The Uranthia Book,*" in *The Invention of Sacred Tradition,* ed. James R. Lewis and Olav Hammer (Cambridge: Cambridge University Press, 2011), 199–212; Ken Glasziou, "Who Wrote the Urantia Papers?," Urantiapedia (website), 2001, https://urantiapedia.org/en/article/Ken_Glasziou /Who_Wrote_the_Urantia_Papers; and Meredith Sprunger, "Affidavit of Dr. Meredith J. Sprunger Regarding the Origin of *The Urantia Book,*" The Urantia Book Fellowship (website), October 24, 1998,

18 | EXPLORING THE URANTIA REVELATION

http://Urantia-book.org/mullinshistory/sprunger_affidavit.htm. Sarah Lewis writes, "Therefore *The Urantia Book* is forced to stand alone."

7. Wikipedia, s.v. "Joe Friday," last modified March 19, 2025, 15:01, https://en.wikipedia.org/wiki/Joe_Friday; and Wikipedia, s.v. "Rodinia," last modified April 5, 2025, 9:23, http://en.wikipedia.org/wiki/Rodinia#Paleogeographic_reconstructions. From the Rodinia page is the statement "The idea that a supercontinent existed in the early Neoproterozoic arose in the 1970s." Sarah Lewis. "The Peculiar Sleep: Receiving *The Urantia Book*," in *The Invention of Sacred Tradition*. 210.

8. Johnson, "Urantia Book and COSAR Principle."

9. Bob Debold, "The COSAR Concept as the Truth of Reality," Debold Group (website), January 2025, https://deboldgroup.com/Aquatic/JJsCOSAR-TOR.html.

Chapter 2
The Genes of Adam and Eve

Discovering the Story Behind Our Story
That My Story Accentuates

In the early years when I was attending reading groups in Hawaii and elsewhere, I found myself often revisiting pages I had previously read, drawn to *The Urantia Book*'s extraordinary ability to illuminate the questions that had long puzzled me. One section in particular struck me with its boldness and clarity: the story of Adam and Eve. Growing up, I had always thought of their story as a simplistic myth, one that painted humanity as flawed from its inception. It seemed designed more to inspire guilt than understanding; the atonement concept surely exaggerates that. But *The Urantia Book* offered something entirely different—a cosmic perspective that reframed Adam and Eve's role, not as the originators of sin, but as pivotal figures in a divine mission to uplift humanity.

It reminded me of the countless times in my own life I had felt the story was incomplete, as though there was a missing piece to our collective story. As a child, I sensed that the fire-and-brimstone teachings of itinerant preachers couldn't possibly represent the fullness of God's nature. And later, during my travels and study, I found myself drawn to questions of human potential and spiritual destiny. What if we weren't as burdened with original sin as we were led to believe? What if our history wasn't just a tale of failure but a story of unrealized potential?

When I encountered *The Urantia Book*'s account of Adam and Eve, I felt as though I had been handed a key to understanding both our past and our future. It described a cosmic framework for human evolution that didn't negate science but built upon it, weaving together biology and spirituality in ways I had never imagined. It was a revelation that not only touched on the larger story of humanity but also resonated deeply with my own journey—a quest to reconcile my inner thirst for truth with the scientific and spiritual realities of existence.

The Adam and Eve narrative mirrored my personal search for purpose and truth. Just as they were sent to elevate humanity, I realized that my own spiritual awakening—my Birth Day—was a call to elevate myself and those around me. Their mission, though interrupted, became a metaphor for my own life's work: to integrate knowledge and faith, to uplift through understanding, and to recognize the divine potential within each of us.

This chapter explores the interplay between science and revelation in the Adam and Eve story, uncovering how *The Urantia Book* not only redefines their mission but also invites us to participate in the ongoing work of spiritual and cosmic evolution. It is a reminder that, like Adam and Eve, we are part of a greater narrative—a story still unfolding, shaped by our choices and our willingness to align with the Truth of Reality.

Interplay Between Science and Revelation in Adam and Eve Story

My intention with this book—to demonstrate that science and religion are both an aspect of a higher truth and that both scientific and religious revelations within *The Urantia Book* will expand our view of history and our spiritual destiny—is especially relevant to the Adam and Eve (A&E) biblical legend.

The story of A&E, traditionally grounded in religious lore, receives a transformative interpretation in *The Urantia Book*. Through an intersection of genetic science and cosmic revelation, I explore this narrative with a depth that reimagines our understanding of human origins. Dr. Bruce Lahn's[1] genetic research on microcephalin,[2] which reveals significant genetic developments approximately 37,000 years ago, aligns with dates cited in *The Urantia Book*, prompting renewed inquiry into the synthesis of science and religion.

This chapter combines broadly both a philosophical perspective and a scientific focus to present a cohesive understanding of how the story of A&E serves as a powerful case study in reconciling science and spirituality. By examining Lahn's findings alongside *The Urantia Book*'s accounts, we explore how revelation may expand our perception of truth, affirming that science and religion are not adversaries but complementary paths toward understanding.

Whereas the previous chapter presented a set of material facts (Precambrian supercontinent) that the revelation identified fifty years before science came to know them as accurate, the story of A&E as a cosmic and spiritual component of Urantia's reality demonstrates a far greater need for science and religion to take the blinders off.

Let me go beneath the surface on this thought. *The Urantia Book* presents the story of A&E as more than an allegory of humanity's fall; it's a cosmic and historical narrative with deep implications for how we understand human potential and spiritual growth. Unlike the traditional biblical account, which centers on a single act of disobedience leading to a moral downfall, *The Urantia Book* reinterprets Adam and Eve's role as an evolutionary and spiritual mission. They came to Earth, not as the very first humans, but as divine beings sent to uplift the human race genetically and spiritually. Their "fall," then, isn't a one-time act of disobedience but a disruption in a planned, progressive enhancement of humanity—a mission cut short, leaving future generations with a diminished but still viable spiritual and material potential.

This perspective reveals a dual inheritance: both the biological limitations and spiritual challenges from the partial failure of A&E's mission and the enduring possibility to complete the growth they began. This concept profoundly challenges the traditional narrative and suggests that humanity's evolutionary potential is not merely about overcoming sin but also about actualizing latent capacities for spiritual and cosmic growth for every individual of normal mind.

To draw a parallel, just as science uncovered the reality of a Precambrian supercontinent long after *The Urantia Book* mentioned it, this expanded story of A&E offers another layer of cosmic truth waiting to be understood in the fullness of time. But the expanded story calls for a partnership between science and religion. To appreciate the full picture, science must be willing to explore beyond the purely physical evolution of human beings, while religion must recognize that spiritual truth doesn't negate biological reality but completes it.

The cosmic reality of Adam and Eve's mission highlights humanity's potential as an ongoing project, an unrevealed destiny, a promise that humanity may yet fulfill. This requires an open-minded integration of scientific insights about human origins, biology, and potential with spiritual revelations about purpose and destiny. Taking off the blinders means setting aside rigid interpretations and allowing science and religion to complement each other—each offering unique insights into the unified truth of human existence and cosmic destiny.

In other words, just as the truth of a supercontinent once seemed beyond belief but is now widely accepted, the idea of human potential as something both materially and spiritually expandable might someday be seen as equally foundational to understanding our place in the universe.

The Urantia Book's Cosmic Perspective on Adam and Eve

The Urantia Book presents A&E not as mere biblical figures but as advanced beings tasked with uplifting human civilization. The A&E order of celestial helpers is designed for the purpose of genetic and cultural enhancement, and its mission is to integrate spiritual and biological advancement within humanity. This mission on Urantia, however, was complicated by the default A&E perpetrated, leading to unintended consequences. This perspective challenges traditional narratives by framing A&E as part of a larger cosmic order, embodying a role designed to catalyze human evolution rather than creating humanity outright, as biblical legend has it.

This expanded revelation in *The Urantia Book* complements the scientific focus on how specific genetic markers align with the narrative and timeline provided by *The Urantia Book*. The mutation in the microcephalin gene, introduced around 37,000 years ago, corresponds with *The Urantia Book's* claim of A&E's arrival at that nearly precise time. Twenty-first-century science has confirmed a rapid spread of this mutation, especially outside sub-Saharan Africa, which aligns with the geographical and cultural influence of Adam and Eve's lineage.

Lahn's Genetic Research and Its Implications

Here's a brief layperson's look into how the science of DNA and genes connects to this cosmic panorama. Dr. Bruce Lahn, a geneticist at the University of Chicago and an investigator with the Howard Hughes Medical Institute (HHMI), conducted pioneering research in the early 2000s on the evolution of the human brain. His studies focused on two genes, microcephalin and the abnormal spindle-like microcephaly associated protein (ASPM), both of which are crucial in regulating brain size. Mutations in these genes can lead to microcephaly, a condition characterized by a significantly reduced brain size.

Lahn's research explored whether the human brain is still undergoing evolutionary changes. By analyzing the genetic sequences of microcephalin and ASPM across diverse human populations, his team sought to identify signs of recent positive selection—genetic changes that confer a survival or reproductive advantage. The motivation was to understand the genetic underpinnings of human brain development and its evolutionary trajectory.

In 2005 Lahn's team published findings indicating that specific variants of microcephalin and ASPM had arisen relatively recently in human history and had rapidly increased in frequency, suggesting ongoing adaptive evolution. For instance, a variant of microcephalin was estimated to have emerged around 37,000 years ago and is now present in approximately 70 percent of the global population.[3] Similarly, a variant of ASPM appeared about 5,800 years ago and is found in about 30 percent of people today.[4]

Lahn's discovery regarding the microcephalin gene is central to the A&E revelation in *The Urantia Book*, specifically Papers 62, 74, and 78.[5] The prescient revelation of not only the timeline of A&E but also the outcome after they defaulted on their mission is remarkable. Microcephalin plays a key role in brain development, and the appearance of a new variant at that time suggests that something unprecedented occurred in human history. This genetic change is corroboration of A&E's genetic upliftment, supporting *The Urantia Book*'s notion of a biological enhancement introduced by the Adamic pair.

The time frames of 37,000 and 1.1 million years in Lahn's DNA research, as it relates to Papers 62, 74 and 78 in *The Urantia Book*, are remarkable. On November 17, 2006, I emailed Professor Lahn regarding his article. It is apparent he is on the right track with the DNA analysis but the wrong train of thought with his speculation that the Neanderthals are the source of the original copy of the D allele.[6]

The microcephalin gene plays a critical role in the growth of the brain; it sits on the Y chromosome in pair number 8. The Y chromosome is known as the male-determiner chromosome, but current research is demonstrating it is much more

26 | EXPLORING THE URANTIA REVELATION

than just a sex determiner. This new contemporary knowledge undoubtedly signals why the *Urantia Papers* refer to "Adams plasm." (Remember, this was 1935 when it was written.) Clearly, the revelation's GPS reveals another truth path—that tracing the male chromosome will bear fruit. The revelators anticipated precociously the discovery and structure of DNA two decades before the publishing of the papers into a book.

Clear and demonstrative resonance is between Lahn's findings and *The Urantia Book*'s prescient dating. Approaching this evidence philosophically suggests that the scientific validation of these timelines may indeed prompt skeptics to reconsider the potential harmony between scientific discoveries and revelatory truths.

I encourage skeptics to do so because further research would provide empirical support for information that appears in *The Urantia Book*, which many have dismissed as purely speculative or religious. When scientific findings, such as those from geneticist Bruce Lahn's research on human evolution, align closely with dates and events described in the book—particularly those that were outlined decades before such discoveries were possible—it challenges the assumption that these revelations lack factual grounding. What could possibly cause one to write so authoritatively about an event (Adam's plasm introgressed[7] into humanity) when no language or concept existed to describe it?

Philosophically, this alignment encourages a reevaluation of the book's content not merely as myth or symbolic teaching but also as a potential source of actual historical or prehistorical insight. This overlap between scientific evidence and revelatory text blurs the assumed hard line between empirical knowledge and spiritual revelation, suggesting that the two may not be as incompatible as often assumed. It invites skeptics to entertain the possibility that revelatory knowledge could offer glimpses of truth about the cosmos and human history, with science acting as a tool that slowly unveils these truths over time. This convergence may encourage a more open-minded approach, fostering a view that science and spiritual revelations can coexist and even enrich each other.

COSAR Principle—Coordination of Science and Religion

I emphasize the COSAR (Coordination of Science and Religion) principle, a core theme in the book, arguing that both scientific and spiritual insights are facets of a greater reality.[8] I underscore how, through revelation, *The Urantia Book* coordinates these fields, helping individuals reconcile the rift between the two.

The philosophical approach to the A&E story highlights the integration of science and religion as essential for an enriched understanding of human origins. I suggest that truth-seeking requires openness to both empirical evidence and spiritual insight and that revelation bridges these realms. The story of A&E exemplifies this process, illustrating how spiritual truths often precede scientific understanding.

In part 2, chapter 7, the COSAR principle comes together in a beautiful way. In the "Second Epochal Revelation—the Edenic Teachings," the history of Adam and Eve takes the prescient scientific facts and chapter 7 to provide a coordinated and unbroken explanation of both science and religion with the Truth of Reality.

Philosophical and Religious Implications

Let's explore the philosophical and religious ramifications of integrating ancient lore, scientific data, and revelatory insights. I encourage readers to adopt a broader perspective that allows faith and reason to coexist harmoniously. *The Urantia Book*'s cosmic framework shows that A&E's mission was intended to foster human development in a way that naturally aligned with evolutionary progress, challenging rigid, literal interpretations of creation stories.

This approach invites readers to view human ancestry through a cosmic lens, where A&E's role represents an archetypal pattern across inhabited worlds. My analysis implies that the purpose of revelation, as illustrated by *The Urantia Book*, is to elevate human consciousness, guiding individuals toward a superconscious understanding of reality where spiritual and scientific truths converge.[9]

The Urantia Papers, published as *The Urantia Book* in 1955, is an epochal revelation.[10] It cannot be proved or disproved.[11]

In contrast to the traditional Christian doctrine of original sin, where A&E's disobedience brought sin into the world, *The Urantia Book* describes their mission as one of biological and cultural upliftment for humanity. Their "default" wasn't a moral failing that cursed all of humanity, but rather a setback in their intended mission to advance human genetics and spiritual awareness. This perspective shifts the emphasis away from inherited sin and toward a view of humanity as inherently evolving and progressing, with challenges but also great potential.

The Urantia Book suggests that Adam and Eve are part of a larger, universe-wide plan, part of a systematic process through which divine beings aid in planetary evolution. This changes the narrative from a purely Earth-centric story to one where humanity's development is part of a much larger, orchestrated cosmic process. It invites believers to consider humanity's place in the universe differently, viewing it as one piece within a grand, interconnected plan rather than a singular, isolated event.

The book describes Adam and Eve as bringing "biologic uplift" to the human race through genetic enhancement, aiming to increase intelligence, health, and spiritual receptivity. This concept can reshape traditional interpretations of Adam and Eve as merely the first humans or moral archetypes into a perception of them as active agents of evolutionary progress. It implies a divine intention to advance humanity not only spiritually but also physically and intellectually.

By framing A&E's mission as a well-intentioned but challenging task within a flawed world, *The Urantia Book* expands the idea of divine mercy. Their "default" is seen as part of the learning and development of both humanity and the universe, rather than a catastrophic event requiring immediate redemption. This narrative can lead to a reinterpretation of redemption, suggesting it as an ongoing process of growth, supported by divine love and patience rather than focused on overcoming a single fall from grace.

The Urantia Book teaches that Adam and Eve's mission involved gradual, generational improvement rather than a single, transformative event. This emphasis on slow, cumulative progress over sudden perfection aligns with an evolutionary perspective on spiritual and cultural growth that may resonate with or challenge traditional beliefs about the nature of salvation and divine intervention.

In sum, *The Urantia Book* offers a story of Adam and Eve that emphasizes spiritual evolution, cosmic citizenship, and

30 | EXPLORING THE URANTIA REVELATION

the gradual development of humanity under divine guidance. This expanded narrative may prompt believers to consider new ways of understanding divine purpose, human origins, and the relationship between humanity and the cosmos, potentially fostering a more universal perspective on spiritual growth and community.

Scientific Validation of Revelation

The story of A&E now can be affirmed as an evidence-based argument for the credibility of revelation in *The Urantia Book* because it shows that scientific findings in genetics validate its claims. The rapid spread of the microcephalin mutation, which emerged in populations outside of sub-Saharan Africa, aligns with the *Urantia Book's* narrative of A&E's influence on global populations. Such evidence, discovered decades after *The Urantia Book* was published, substantiates its revelatory disclosures, compelling one to recognize its potential as a source of credible insights on human origins.

The scientific validation of revelation plays a crucial role in bridging the long-standing gap between science and religion, opening the door to a more harmonious understanding of human origins and our place in the cosmos. For centuries, science and religion have been seen as opposing forces— one dedicated to empirical evidence and the other to spiritual truths. However, when revelations, such as those in *The Urantia Book*, align with scientific discoveries, it suggests that these two perspectives may not be as incompatible as they seem. Instead, they might offer complementary insights into reality, with science exploring the "how" and revelation addressing the "why" behind existence.

In the case of *The Urantia Book*'s expanded story of Adam and Eve, scientific findings in genetics—like the rapid spread of the microcephalin gene variant—provide a compelling layer of evidence that aligns with its narrative. This genetic mutation, which is associated with brain development and emerged outside of sub-Saharan Africa, echoes *The Urantia Book*'s account of Adam and Eve's genetic influence on global populations. Such evidence, which came to light decades after the publication of *The Urantia Book*, adds credibility to its revelatory claims, suggesting that its insights may hold truth not just in a spiritual or allegorical sense but in a literal, historical context as well.

By demonstrating that revelatory truths can withstand scientific scrutiny, science enhances the credibility of religious texts, potentially making them more accessible and meaningful to those who may approach them with skepticism. It offers a pathway for religious ideas to engage with the scientific community and encourages a collaborative exploration of human origins and spiritual destiny. That enriches both fields, allowing science to add context and evidence to spiritual truths, while revelation provides a greater purpose and meaning to the discoveries of science.

Moreover, scientific validation of revelation fosters an open-minded approach to spiritual teachings, a mindset that considers the possibility of divine insights woven into the fabric of human history and progress. It invites a reevaluation of religious texts, not as relics of ancient beliefs but as potential sources of knowledge that may contain real insights into the mechanisms of creation and evolution.

Ultimately, the integration of science and revelation helps pave the way for a more unified worldview that respects both

32 | EXPLORING THE URANTIA REVELATION

the tangible findings of science and the transcendent truths of spirituality. In the context of *The Urantia Book*, this unity creates a compelling framework for understanding human development, encouraging a view of history that includes both the evidence-based timeline of human evolution and the guiding influence of divine purpose. The scientific validation of such revelations can lead to a broader and more nuanced understanding of who we are and why we are here, bridging the gaps between faith, reason, and discovery.

Approaching new ideas with an open mind by temporarily suspending disbelief is not entirely uncommon, but it appears to be a defining trait of innovators who have reached the pinnacle of human achievement. For example, Nobel laureate Dr. Kary Mullis, renowned for his invention of PCR (polymerase chain reaction), identified several striking scientific correlations with the accounts found in *The Urantia Book*. Mullis observed that many details in *The Urantia Book* anticipated later scientific discoveries, such as the timing of genetic variations. These correlations lend support to my COSAR principle, highlighting the potential of revelatory insights to foresee and align with emerging scientific breakthroughs.[12]

Expanding upon This Chapter

For those who want to dig a little deeper in the scientific and philosophical details of the depiction of Adam and Eve, my colleague Bob Debold has a website that has a number of essays on various topics *The Urantia Book* delves into. One of the essays, "Adam and Eve: 'Eight Feet Tall & Purple,'" provides an expanded exploration of the scientific, philosophical, and cultural dimensions of Adam and Eve's story as depicted in *The*

Urantia Book.[13] It delves into scientific correlations with revelation, such as Bruce Lahn's research on the microcephalin gene variant and its alignment with *The Urantia Book*'s timeline for Adam and Eve's mission. The essay also examines their role as biologic uplifters, emphasizing their genetic strategy, including backcrossing, and the far-reaching consequences of their mission's failure on human potential. On a philosophical level, it discusses truth, consciousness, and the evolutionary path to understanding, introducing a model that incorporates both the superconscious and subconscious. Debold further advocates the COSAR principle. Finally, the essay recontextualizes the Adam and Eve narrative within its broader cultural, ethical, and cosmic significance, reflecting on humanity's spiritual development and the impact of traditional beliefs on Western thought. Overall, Bob's essays on the topics in this book employ a more detailed, interdisciplinary approach by incorporating specific scientific evidence, philosophical discussions on truth and consciousness, and a comprehensive view of the historical and cultural impacts of the Adam and Eve narrative.

Halbert Katzen's essay, "UBtheNEWS: Adam and Eve Report,"[14] offers expanded insights beyond focusing on key scientific and cultural correlations with *The Urantia Book*. It examines genetic discoveries, such as the previously discussed microcephalin gene and Y-chromosome mutations. The essay also links the spread of nontonal languages to Adam's lineage, suggesting genetic and cultural influences on language development. Additionally, it traces migration patterns of Adam and Eve's descendants to regions like South America and Northern Africa, aligning with genetic and cultural studies. By citing modern research, including work by Stanford and Bruce Lahn, the essay provides specificity and credibility, further reinforcing the alignment between *The Urantia Book*'s narrative and scientific findings.

As I delved deeper into the story of Urantia in *The Urantia Book*, it became clear that our ancient history is far more profound than I ever imagined. The threads of humanity's spiritual and cultural development seemed to stretch back so far that it's been hard to get my mind around the revelation that in situ spiritual help began five hundred millennia ago—that is, 500,000 years ago! One revelation in particular captivated me: the idea that the early attempts at worship, scattered across the world, were not random but reflected a deeper, divine influence guiding humanity toward unity and progress.

During this exploration, I first learned about Göbekli Tepe—a site more ancient and mysterious than humanity previously thought. It may begin to provide clues as to what happened after Adam and Eve and before the Sumerians showed up. How had these early humans, long before history marks civilization's beginnings, built something so advanced, so spiritually resonant? What drove them to create this "temple to the stars," and what truths might it reveal about our ancestors' search for the divine? In the next chapter, we'll uncover how *The Urantia Book* sheds light on these ancient efforts and how Göbekli Tepe stands as the oldest symbol (so far) of humanity's earliest expressions of faith and creativity.

Endnotes

1.   Catherine Gianaro, "Lahn's Analysis of Genes Indicates Human Brain Continues to Evolve," *University of Chicago Chronicle*, September 22, 2005, https://chronicle.uchicago.edu/050922/brainevolution.shtml.

THE GENES OF ADAM AND EVE | 35

2. Wikipedia, s.v. "Microcephalin," last modified December 19, 2023, 2:59, http://en.wikipedia.org/wiki/Microcephalin#Evolution.

3. Gianaro, "Lahn's Analysis." "For microcephalin, the new variant class emerged about 37,000 years ago and now shows up in about 70 percent of present-day humans. . . . 'In a very short period of time, this class of variants arose from a single copy to many copies. That implies that this must have happened because of positive selection,' Lahn said, pointing out that it is statistically unlikely for a haplogroup this young to have such high frequency as a result of mere random genetic drift."

4. Gianaro, "Lahn's Analysis."

5. *The Urantia Book*, 74:0.1 (828.1). Adam and Eve arrived on Urantia, from the year AD 1934, 37,848 years ago. It was in midseason when the Garden was in the height of bloom that they arrived.

6. Gianaro, "Lahn's Analysis"; *The Urantia Book*, 74:0.1 (828.1); and Patrick D. Evans et al., "Evidence That the Adaptive Allele of the Brain Size Gene Microcephalin Introgressed into Homo Sapiens from an Archaic Homo Lineage," *Proceedings of the National Academy of Sciences of the United States of America* 103, no. 48 (November 7, 2006): 18178–83, https://doi.org/10.1073/pnas.0606966103. The latter article has this information: "We provide evidence that haplogroup D may have originated from a lineage separated from modern humans for ≈1.1 million years and introgressed into the human gene pool by ≈37,000 years ago."

7. Wikipedia, s.v. "Introgression," last modified November 22, 2024, 21:19, https://en.wikipedia.org/wiki/Introgression; and Wikipedia, s.v. "Interbreeding Between Archaic and Modern Humans," last modified April 20, 2025, 20:54, http://en.wikipedia.org/wiki/archaic _human_admixture_with_modern_humans. Introgression refers to the movement of genetic material (such as genes or chromosomes) from one population or species into the gene pool of another population or species through interbreeding. This can occur naturally or through *human-mediated activities* such as hybridization or genetic engineering. Introgression can result in the transfer of beneficial traits from one population to another, but can also lead to the loss of

36 | EXPLORING THE URANTIA REVELATION

genetic diversity and the emergence of new genetic disorders. This is from the article on interbreeding: "The results show that haplogroup D introgressed 37,000 years ago (based on the coalescence age of derived D alleles) into modern humans from an archaic human population that separated 1.1 million years ago (based on the separation time between D and non-D alleles), consistent with the period when Neanderthals and modern humans co-existed and diverged respectively."

8. Johnson, *Up Close and Personal*, 15, 16.

9. *The Urantia Book* describes the superconscious as a creative and functional realm within the mortal mind where religious growth occurs, distinct from the subconscious and conscious domains of the human mind. It emphasizes that the realization of unconscious religious growth is evidence of this superconscious domain. See 100:1.9 (1095.4). Moreover, it reveals that the divine Thought Adjuster—the fragment of God—resides within this superconscious area, serving as the inner guide for spiritual progression. This implies that the mind, as it interacts with the Adjuster, transcends purely biological processes and may, in part, operate within space itself, aligning with the idea that mortal mind is not entirely bound by material constraints but interfaces with cosmic realities. This conjecture suggests a fascinating interplay between the spatial and spiritual dimensions of human cognition.

10. In *The Urantia Book*, *epochal revelation* is defined as "a significant and transformative disclosure of divine truth that is intended to advance the spiritual, intellectual, and moral progress of humanity on a planetary scale." Epochal revelations are given at pivotal moments in human history to guide collective understanding and steer human progress in alignment with divine purpose. They are intended not just for individuals but also for society as a whole, providing a framework for civilization to evolve and flourish. Examples include the bestowal of the Planetary Prince, the arrival of Adam and Eve, the teachings of Melchizedek, the life of Jesus, and the modern *Urantia Book* itself, which is considered the fifth epochal revelation. These revelations correct misconceptions, introduce new truths, and prepare humanity for further stages of development in alignment with the cosmic plan.

In contrast, personal revelation through the cosmic mind or the Thought Adjuster is an intimate, individualized experience of divine guidance intended to help a person make moral and spiritual progress. The cosmic mind is the mechanism through which universal spiritual insights are available to human beings, enabling them to understand truth, beauty, and goodness in their lives. Meanwhile, the Thought Adjuster, a fragment of the Universal Father that indwells each person, works within the individual to prompt higher thinking, personal growth, and alignment with God's will. Personal revelation from the Thought Adjuster is deeply personal, tailored to each person's unique circumstances, spiritual readiness, and life path, and it provides insight and guidance for daily choices and moral decisions.

The primary difference between epochal revelation and personal revelation lies in scope and purpose. Epochal revelation is designed to advance an entire civilization or generation, providing a broad, structured truth to shape societal evolution. Personal revelation, on the other hand, is an ongoing, individualized relationship with the divine, helping each person grow in understanding, make meaningful choices, and cultivate a personal connection with God. While epochal revelations bring substantial new truths and spiritual light to the collective, personal revelation through the Thought Adjuster enriches the inner life of each individual, helping the person to realize spiritual potential and path toward God. Together, these forms of revelation foster the growth of both individuals and society in harmony with cosmic values and divine purpose.

11. As Sarah Lewis states in "The Peculiar Sleep: Receiving *The Urantia Book*," "Therefore the *Urantia Book* is forced to stand alone," 210.

12. Kary Mullis, "The Urantia Book," KaryMullis.com, accessed December 21, 2024, www.karymullis.com/urantia.html.

13. Bob Debold, "Adam and Eve: 'Eight-Feet Tall & Purple,'" Debold Group (website), July 2024, https://deboldgroup.com/Aquatic/Documents/Bobs-Chapter%202.pdf.

14. Halbert Katzen, "UBtheNews: Adam and Eve Report,"Urantia Book Study Aids (website), accessed January 19, 2025, https://ubannotated.com/ubthenews/topics/adam_and_eve/.

Chapter 3
Göbekli Tepe

Moving Urantian History Closer to the Truth of Reality

My journey through *The Urantia Book* often felt like a treasure hunt, each revelation uncovering a hidden gem about humanity's past and our place in the universe. One of the most fascinating discoveries came years after I first encountered the book, during a conversation with a fellow truth-seeker who asked, "Have you heard of Göbekli Tepe?" I hadn't. But as the person described the ancient archaeological site—a temple predating Stonehenge by thousands of years—I couldn't help but feel a thrill of recognition that once again, the revelation will be vindicated.

I had always been fascinated by the origins of human civilization. How had our ancestors, with no written language or apparent technological sophistication, constructed monuments that rivaled the ingenuity of modern architecture? More important, why? These questions echoed the themes I had encountered in *The Urantia Book*, where human history was presented not as a random march of progress but as a carefully guided journey, filled with interventions and turning points meant to lift us toward higher planes of understanding.

When I began reading about Göbekli Tepe, I couldn't shake the feeling that this site—this ancient sanctuary buried for millennia—would prove to be a missing piece of Urantia's story that would connect with the time after Adam and Eve but before the Sumerians. Göbekli Tepe wasn't just a temple—it was a bridge, a meeting point between the evolutionary religions of early humanity and the seeds of revealed truth that the remnants of the Calagastia 100[1] and Adam and Eve's progeny deposited onto the story of Urantian humanity.

As I dug deeper into Göbekli Tepe, it became clear that my own journey mirrored the story of this ancient site. Just as the people who built it were driven by an urge to connect with the divine, my search for truth had always been rooted in a desire to understand our relationship with the cosmos and our Creator. Göbekli Tepe wasn't just a place—it was a testament to the enduring human need to seek, to believe, and to express faith through creativity and collaboration.

This chapter explores how *The Urantia Book* provides a framework for understanding the spiritual significance of sites like Göbekli Tepe. It connects the dots between humanity's early, scattered attempts to grasp the divine and the eventual arrival of epochal revelations that illuminated the greater truth of reality. For me, Göbekli Tepe became more than an archaeological wonder; it became a symbol of the universal quest to know and be known by God—a quest that continues to shape not only our history but our future.

A Doorway to Our Forgotten Past

Göbekli Tepe in Turkey is no ordinary archaeological dig. It's throwing our ideas about human history into a bit of a tailspin.[2]

Adam and Eve's time on this planet spanned between 37,848 years ago (from 1934) to Adam's death 530 years later (37,318 BCE). Eve expired nineteen years earlier. In this chapter I discuss a recent archaeological find in Turkey, an extraordinary dig that many are considering is reshaping human history. Named Göbekli Tepe, it contains carved and polished circles of stone, terrazzo flooring, and double benches. All the circles feature massive T-shaped pillars that evoke the monoliths of Easter Island. It raises more questions than answers because it upends most, if not all, conventional wisdom regarding human origins, though not necessarily for *Urantia Revelation* students. The revelation provides a backdrop and foundation to understand much of the site's apparent paradoxes.

A full understanding of the A&E revelational legacy on this planet requires knowing some perspectives of what transpired beginning nearly 460,000 years prior to their intervention assignment here on Urantia. Adam and Eve's historical significance plays a salient role in humanity's progression to today's twenty-first-century doings, even though they were here for a very short five centuries.

Imagine a hilltop site, thousands of years older than the pyramids or Stonehenge, filled with massive stone pillars, each carefully carved and arranged in circular formations. And here's the kicker: this site was built long before humans were supposed to have settled down or learned to work with stone on such a grand scale. Yet, here it is, standing as a silent testament to something that doesn't quite fit into our textbooks.

If you're familiar with *The Urantia Book*, this might not be such a shock. According to the book, humanity's history runs much deeper than our modern theories give it credit for. From its perspective, a fascinating backstory fills in the missing details of places like Göbekli Tepe. So, let's take a stroll through this ancient site and see how it might be rewriting the story of us all.

In this section we present an overview and summary of the status of the planet just prior to milestone number 4 as follows—essentially what was facing Adam and Eve when they were repersonalized after the long journey from Jerusem, the headquarters of Urantia's local system of Satania.[3] The following four milestones are significant to this narrative:

1. One million years prior to 1934: the advent of the first two humans.
2. Five hundred thousand years prior to 1934: the arrival of the Planetary Prince, including six Sangik (colored) evolutionary races.
3. Two hundred thousand years prior to 1934: the commencement of the Lucifer rebellion.
4. Thirty-eight thousand years prior to 1934: the arrival of A&E.

The long period of human evolution (about 950,000 years) from when the first humans emerged from the primate tree[4] to Adam and Eve's arrival requires an understanding of how a religious legend might consider the pair as our first parents. It is difficult for us humans to wrap our minds around a few millennia of history, let alone tens of thousands. This chapter penetrates the ground a little deeper beyond the previous one in respect to the thirty millennia from A&E to the Sumerians. Göbekli Tepe dates to nearly seven millennia before the Sumerians and is a cannon shot across the bow of humanity's conventional wisdom—both scientific and religious. It has opened a knowledge portal that may provide

EXPLORING THE URANTIA REVELATION

more anomalies than Alice experienced traversing the white rabbit's sanctuary.

You Can't Get the Picture When You Are in the Frame

Our summary narrative in chapter 2 of humanity's origins covered a broad sweep of 500,000 years prior to 1934. Göbekli Tepe is a conundrum regarding just how it came into existence, what it did, and who and why someone constructed it in the first place. After all, it is dated to somewhere between ten and twelve thousand years *after* A&E died. Göbekli Tepe creates a paradigm shift that will forever transform one's vision of history. Stanford University's head of archaeology summed it up: "Many people think that it changes everything. . . . It overturns the whole apple cart. All our theories were wrong."[5]

The history related in *The Urantia Book* covers the Adamites and the cultural legacy they left behind, including how they influenced civilizations far and wide. But before them were beings with advanced knowledge living among early humans. This story isn't just about archaeology—it's a peek into a world where genetics, culture, and spirituality blended in ways that might surprise even the most seasoned historians. Göbekli Tepe, it seems, might just be the missing chapter that brings some of these ancient puzzle pieces together—especially for those who are not *Urantia Book* students.

For example, Graham Hancock, a contemporary author and researcher who has written extensively on ancient civilizations and lost civilizations, discusses Göbekli Tepe in his book *Magicians of the Gods*. Hancock speculates that Göbekli

Tepe was built by a lost civilization, an advanced civilization that existed before the last Ice Age, around twelve thousand years ago. He believes that this civilization was wiped out by a global cataclysm, possibly a comet impact or a solar flare.

Listening to the Joe Rogan's interview with Graham Hancock demonstrates why Hancock maintains a respectful following. Although Hancock opens the door to expanding knowledge, without the revelation's entire cosmology for understanding the rebellion of Lucifer as it relates to A&E, one will find the speculations on the right path but destined to turn down a cul-de-sac. Within these pages, I will summarize the full history of the human race, starting nearly a million years ago, returning Graham to solid ground with conclusions that back up his research as insightful but limited. By providing prescient scientific facts and revisiting and clarifying historic truths that our esteemed researchers have dug up, *The Urantia Book* proves why it should be taken more seriously. What follows should pique the attention of any truth-discerning anthropologist worth his or her salt.

Some Details

In 1994 some archaeologists stumbled upon what would soon be known as one of the world's oldest temples. This wasn't your typical dig site with simple tools and primitive art. No, what they found were towering pillars, carved with intricate images of animals and symbols, some weighing over fifteen tons. These stone circles were, by all appearances, places of gathering and perhaps worship. But here's the part that gets archaeologists scratching their heads: the site dates back nearly twelve thousand years, to a time when humans supposedly hadn't yet figured out how to farm, let alone build temples.

You might think, *Maybe they just lived nearby, and this was their community hangout.* But no traces of homes, firepits, or regular village life were found. It seems folks gathered here for a specific reason, possibly something spiritual or ritualistic. And when the time was done, they didn't abandon it to the elements—they buried it, almost as if they wanted to preserve it for a future generation to discover.

Only 5 percent to 10 percent has been excavated to date, so even a layperson should be amazed at what archaeologists are finding. The deeper they dug, the more ornate and elaborate the findings became. Think about that. One would imagine older and presumably less sophisticated discoveries should be found deeper. But the opposite is true regarding this unique mystery site known as Potbelly Hill. To say the least, Göbekli Tepe is an enigma wrapped in a conundrum. Read on, and we'll provide some revelatory Truth of Reality to this apparent mystery.

Shifting Our Understanding of Human History

If we're following the usual story, civilization as we know it didn't get rolling until people settled down to farm and raise animals. In other words, the first farmers gave rise to the first cities, which then led to temples and organized religion. But Göbekli Tepe seems to have flipped that script on its head. Here, it appears the desire to gather and build something sacred came before people learned to plant crops or domesticate animals. It's almost like the urge to come together and worship was what set us on the path to civilization.

Archaeologist Klaus Schmidt, who led the dig at Göbekli Tepe, called it a game changer. He suggested that instead of agriculture leading to religion, maybe religion led to agriculture. Imagine that: people coming together to build something monumental, realizing they needed steady food sources to keep things going, and then, out of necessity, planting the first seeds. It's a theory that gives us a fresh perspective on what really drove us to settle down in the first place.

The Urantia Book's Take

The Urantia Book has its own way of explaining these early milestones in human history. According to its teachings, civilizations didn't just pop up randomly; a guiding hand has always been in play and respectful of free will—except for the rebellion. The book introduces the concept of beings known as the Adamites and the Andites, who carried knowledge and genetic qualities intended to boost human development.

The Adamites, present about 38,000 years ago, weren't about dominating the native folks—they were here to uplift and share. Over time, their influence spread out from the cradle of civilization in Mesopotamia, creating what we might recognize today as the seeds of art, music, writing, and even agriculture.

This view helps explain why a place like Göbekli Tepe might exist. It suggests that these early monuments weren't random flukes but part of a grander, purposeful influence on humanity. And when you think about it, the massive effort and skill required to build Göbekli Tepe line up well with the idea of an advanced, intentional influence behind the scenes.

46 | EXPLORING THE URANTIA REVELATION

And that influence was undoubtably the superior races still existent on Earth but slowly diminishing in numbers.

A Cultural Conundrum

Göbekli Tepe isn't just a mystery because of its age or size. The craftsmanship here suggests a deep understanding of both the natural and spiritual worlds, with carvings depicting everything from animals to abstract symbols. But what makes it truly unique is how the site changes over time. The older structures are larger, more ornate, and more impressive, while the newer ones show a gradual decline in craftsmanship. It's as if the people who built Göbekli Tepe were at their peak early on, and then something happened to lead them into decline.

What's more, it seems that the whole site was deliberately buried around 8,000 BC. There's no evidence of a mudslide or natural disaster—this was a planned burial, almost like a time capsule left for future generations. Archaeologists are still scratching their heads over why anyone would go to the trouble of burying such a magnificent structure. But if we take *The Urantia Book*'s perspective, this decline might reflect a gradual fading of the advanced influence that first inspired Göbekli Tepe, as well as a protective gesture to preserve its significance.

Piecing Together a Lost World

Who were these early builders, and what inspired them? For archaeologists, trying to make sense of Göbekli Tepe has been like putting together a puzzle with half the pieces missing. Without any signs of villages, farming, or everyday life nearby, it's hard to place Göbekli Tepe into a familiar category of ancient sites. Typically, these kinds of large stone structures show up where people have settled into farming communities with enough free time and resources to build them. But Göbekli Tepe doesn't fit that pattern.

The Urantia Book offers an intriguing possibility: maybe these builders were influenced by a civilization that was already advanced in both spiritual and practical knowledge. According to its teachings, the Adamites and Andites spread their influence throughout regions like Mesopotamia, Eurasia, and even Africa, carrying their knowledge of agriculture, architecture, and spiritual practices. They were a peaceful people, often sending out their excess population as teachers rather than conquerors, sharing what they knew with less developed tribes.

Could it be that Göbekli Tepe is a remnant of that influence, a place where people gathered to connect with the spiritual and cultural legacy of the Adamites? Maybe they came together here, drawn by a sense of purpose or higher calling, and built something magnificent to reflect that inner drive. If so, it's no wonder this site doesn't resemble the typical hunter-gatherer or early farming settlements we'd expect—it's a reflection of something entirely different.

The Tale of the Amadonites, Nodites, and Sangiks

Long before the familiar names of Sumerians or Egyptians made their way into the pages of history books, there were folks with names that would sound mighty peculiar today—like the Amadonites, Nodites, and Sangiks. Well, maybe the Nodites would not, as the land of Nod appears in the Bible!

48 | EXPLORING THE URANTIA REVELATION

Each group had its own quirks, gifts, and challenges, and together, they set the stage for a complex human story, the likes of which we're still piecing together—even *Urantia Book* students. Picture these groups as different threads, each bringing a unique color to the tapestry of early humanity. They weren't just hunting and gathering; they carried traditions, shared knowledge, and faced trials that would shape the very core of civilization.

The Amadonites were a loyal bunch, descendants of one of the earliest, bravest humans known as Amadons, who held tight to a vision of life shaped by moral integrity and a sense of duty to something greater. They were the kind to stick around when things got tough, keeping alive the ancient traditions passed down from a spiritual leader named Van.

The Nodites had a more complicated past. These folks were the offspring of beings who'd once been part of a grand celestial plan but took a hard turn during the rebellion led by the notorious Caligastia—the onetime Planetary Prince. They became an independent group, proud and sharp, yet still holding on to fragments of their former spiritual understanding. Together, the Amadonites and Nodites powerfully influenced the early human scene, blending their knowledge and traditions in surprising ways.

Then came the Sangiks, who were altogether different. They weren't a single race but a diverse family of races, each with distinct traits, including different skin colors that somehow set the stage for future human diversity. You might think of them as the vibrant newcomers on the block, bringing new energy, new ideas, and a spark of creativity that hadn't quite been seen before. From red to yellow to blue, the Sangiks were like a burst of colorful energy, pushing humanity forward in unexpected ways. They may not have had all the spiritual insights of the Amadonites or the complex legacy of the Nodites, but they carried a strength and adaptability that made them the perfect candidates for the next steps in human civilization.

Gathering Place for the Ages?

Imagine Göbekli Tepe as a meeting place for these diverse groups, a spot where the old ways of the Amadonites, the mystical heritage of the Nodites, and the raw potential of the Sangiks could all come together. It wasn't just a random collection of stones; it was a place of connection—a crossroad for sharing, learning, and growing. The site itself, with its towering pillars and intricate carvings, suggests it wasn't built by one group alone but was likely a collaborative effort. Each group brought its unique touch, and together, they created something that has managed to baffle and inspire us thousands of years later.

From the perspective of *The Urantia Book*, these groups were all important players in a grand plan, carrying both the wisdom and the struggles of early humanity. The Amadonites and Nodites likely passed down stories, perhaps even using the symbols carved at Göbekli Tepe to teach and remind each generation of their origins. Meanwhile, the Sangiks, with their unique racial diversity, might have provided the creative spark and energy needed to complete such an ambitious project. In this sense, Göbekli Tepe was more than a monument; it was a canvas where each group painted their mark on the shared journey of humanity.

Carving the Legacy in Stone

Looking at those animal carvings and abstract designs, it's easy to imagine that the people of Göbekli Tepe weren't just carving stone; they were carving out a legacy. They were leaving markers that told stories, expressed beliefs, and perhaps even passed down warnings or hopes for the future. The Nodites might have brought a taste for the mystical, a memory of celestial origins, while the Amadonites contributed their moral resilience and unshakable faith. The Sangiks, with their fresh perspectives, may have been the ones to find meaning in symbols, to see the art in animal figures, and to use the carved stone as a language all its own.

And so, Göbekli Tepe became a kind of open book, each carving a chapter of their shared story, which no single group could tell on its own. It was as though these early humans, with all their differences, knew that together they could create something that would stand the test of time. Maybe they sensed that this project wasn't just for their generation but for the ages—that one day, people from far-off lands and times would look at their work and wonder, *Who were they, and what were they trying to say?*

The Mystery and the Message

Today, when we look at Göbekli Tepe, we see more than stone. We see the fingerprints of the Amadonites, the Nodites, and the Sangiks, and we sense the story of humanity's early strides toward civilization. It's easy to get swept up in the mystery of it all, to wonder how they managed such a feat and what knowledge they might have had that we've since lost. But in the end, maybe that's the message: that even from the earliest days, we humans have been reaching out, striving to connect, and working to leave something meaningful behind. Göbekli Tepe is a testament to our shared history, a reminder that humanity has always been more than the sum of its parts—more than just hunter-gatherers or early farmers. It's a symbol of our potential to come together, to build, and to believe in something greater than ourselves.

Art and Symbols with Deep Meaning

The carvings and art at Göbekli Tepe are another layer to the mystery. They're intricate and clearly symbolic, suggesting a worldview that linked the material and spiritual realms. Among the carvings are depictions of dangerous animals like snakes and lions, symbols that seem to carry a weight of meaning we can only guess at today.

For those who study *The Urantia Book*, these carvings might reflect the teachings and experiences of early human spiritual leaders who sought to bridge the gap between earthly life and a higher cosmic order. Accordingly, the animals might not just represent physical threats or everyday experiences but also symbolic markers of the journey from a primal, survival-based existence to a more enlightened, spiritually aware society.

And then there's the headless man carved onto one of the stones, a figure that seems to suggest ideas about life, death, and possibly an afterlife. If we lean into *The Urantia Book*'s narrative, such an image might symbolize humanity's evolving understanding of life's mysteries—a reminder that we're more than just physical beings. This idea of being on a spiritual journey aligns well with *The Urantia Book*'s teachings

52 | EXPLORING THE URANTIA REVELATION

that humanity was always intended to progress toward higher knowledge, both of the material world and of spiritual truths.

Decline and Burial: Protecting a Sacred Legacy?

One of the most puzzling aspects of Göbekli Tepe is its decline and eventual burial. Over time, the monuments become less sophisticated, almost as if the builders were losing their grip on the advanced skills that had first inspired the site. Scholars theorize that the later generations may have been less connected to the knowledge and motivation that drove their ancestors, leading to a gradual fading of this early burst of creativity and skill.

And then, for reasons we may never fully understand, the site was carefully buried. This wasn't just a case of a few stones being tossed over the site; it was a deliberate, extensive process that required significant effort. The builders—or their descendants—might have felt the need to protect Göbekli Tepe, preserving it as a kind of sacred time capsule, or they may have buried it as they moved toward new religious practices that didn't align with the old ways.

According to *The Urantia Book*, this kind of transition—where older spiritual practices give way to new ones—was part of the evolving journey of early humanity. Perhaps those who buried Göbekli Tepe were marking the end of one era and the beginning of another. As humanity shifted toward a more settled, agricultural lifestyle, new gods, new beliefs, and new ways of understanding life emerged. And sometimes, when new gods arrive, it's time to lay the old gods to rest.

Göbekli Tepe and Genetic Legacy

Another layer of Göbekli Tepe's mystery ties into what *The Urantia Book* describes as a genetic uplift to humanity. According to the book, Adam and Eve were real beings sent to provide a genetic boost to early humans, meant to enhance intelligence, health, and spiritual awareness.

In the book's account, the blending of the Adamic genetic line with native populations led to a group known as the Andites, who were said to possess advanced abilities and cultural inclinations that distinguished them from other groups. The book even suggests that the Andites had a strong influence over the spread of early civilization, arts, and science across Europe, Asia, and beyond. Göbekli Tepe's grandeur and symbolism might reflect the influence of these early Andite cultures, showing us a glimpse of their spiritual and intellectual world.

When Archaeology Meets Ancient Stories

For archaeologists, a site like Göbekli Tepe is a massive puzzle—an outlier that doesn't match the usual progression of human development. Scholars like Klaus Schmidt, who led excavations there, have been stumped by how early humans, without any sign of agriculture or permanent homes, could have constructed something so advanced.

But *The Urantia Book* suggests that early humanity didn't progress in a straight line. Instead, bursts of advancement—what it calls spiritual interventions—nudged humanity forward. These interventions introduced new genetic lines, cultural practices, and spiritual teachings. Göbekli Tepe might very well be a relic of one of these transformative moments, a place where human potential was inspired and uplifted.

Paradigm Shift Waiting to Happen

If Göbekli Tepe teaches us anything, it's that human history is a lot more complex than we thought. Maybe civilization didn't begin because we humans learned to farm and settle down. Maybe it began because we had a drive to connect with something beyond ourselves, something sacred. This site challenges us to look at our origins with fresh eyes and consider the possibility that spiritual aspiration was a significant catalyst for our first communities.

The Urantia Book provides a perspective that complements this idea. It proposes that we're more than just products of evolution and survival—we're beings on a journey, constantly nudged forward by influences both seen and unseen. Göbekli Tepe might be a testament to this journey, showing us that our ancestors weren't simply primitive hunters and gatherers. They were seekers, builders, and dreamers who reached for something higher.

Lessons from the Past for Today's World

What can we take from all this? For one, Göbekli Tepe is a reminder that we humans have always been a bit more ambitious, creative, and spiritually minded than we often give ourselves credit for. Modern science sometimes tells us we're just a bundle of survival instincts, but sites like Göbekli Tepe remind us there's more to our story. We've always been drawn to the mysterious, the transcendent, and the sacred.

And if we consider *The Urantia Book*'s teachings, there's a message here about the cycles of civilization. According to the book, human societies rise and fall, but they also evolve, influenced by spiritual insights and genetic developments. Göbekli

Tepe might be an ancient echo of that cycle—a place that rose, reached its peak, and eventually gave way to something new. Today, as we grapple with our own challenges, there's wisdom in remembering that our journey as humans is far from linear. We may rise and fall, but each phase brings us closer to understanding our potential and our place in the universe.

Passing Down Ideas: The First Memes in Stone

Imagine a gathering of early humans at Göbekli Tepe. There are no books, no written languages, not even a shared spoken tongue across all groups, but there's a need to remember, to pass down ideas, to connect generations. And so, they use what they have: stone and symbols. They carve shapes, animals, and patterns that mean something to them and, in a sense, these carvings become the very first memes of humanity—ideas passed down not by speech or writing, but by images and shared understanding—social DNA, if you will.

These folks weren't sitting around talking about the latest in philosophy or art theory, but they were leaving a lasting mark. Maybe one carving meant "strength," another represented "protection," and maybe a particularly strange pattern was a reminder of a wild tale from their ancestors. Whatever the case, each symbol, each design, was a bit of knowledge that could be passed from one generation to the next. It was as if they knew they couldn't just rely on memory; they needed something solid, something durable, to remind future generations of who they were and what they believed. And so, they put their memes in stone, where they've stayed for us to see, many thousands of years later.

Memory Bank of Culture and Belief

Think of Göbekli Tepe as a memory bank. Each stone circle, each carved animal, is like a vault holding the beliefs, fears, and dreams of its builders. The people who came to this place may have looked at those carvings the same way we look at old family photo albums. A young child might have pointed to a symbol and asked an elder, "What does that one mean?" And in that moment, a story would come alive, passed from old to young, bridging the gap between the past and the present. This wasn't just a place for rituals—it was an early classroom, a place for sharing ideas, for passing down wisdom, and for building a culture.

It's funny to think that we do the same thing today, just in a different way. When we share ideas online, create art, or write down our thoughts, we're participating in the same tradition as those early builders. We're trying to make sure that something of who we are and what we value will be there for others to find. Göbekli Tepe was their way of saying, "We were here, and this is what we knew." Each carving was a little piece of their lives, recorded not on paper or pixels but in the most lasting way they could manage—solid stone.

Symbols That Survived

Some of the drawings at Göbekli Tepe are pretty mysterious. Why a headless man? Why snakes and big, fierce animals? Some researchers suggest that these could have been warnings or teachings, like a visual guide to things that were dangerous or sacred. But they weren't just practical; they were also symbolic. Animals could mean power, cunning, or courage—qualities they admired or maybe even feared. This was their language, a language without words but full of meaning. You could almost say these symbols had a life of their own, influencing how people thought and acted long after the original builders had passed on.

Here's the wild part: these memes survived, engraved in stone, even as people changed, cultures shifted, and new generations walked the land. Those carvings kept whispering their stories, maybe in ways that grew more mysterious over time. Göbekli Tepe is like a message from the past, a collection of symbols and ideas that have lasted longer than any of us can imagine. And in a way, it shows us that ideas—those little seeds of thought—can have an immortality if we find the right way to share them.

Humanity's First Cultural Network

When you think about it, Göbekli Tepe was a lot like a network. Each time someone added a carving, it was like adding a post to the network, contributing to a conversation that would stretch on for centuries. The symbols weren't just personal; they were communal, a way for people to connect across time and space. This early network didn't use wires or screens but was just as powerful because it created a shared understanding. And isn't that what culture is?

So, while we may never know the exact meaning behind every carving at Göbekli Tepe, we can appreciate what those symbols represent—a moment when people decided that their ideas, their beliefs, and their stories were worth preserving. They took the leap to build something that could outlast them, something that could carry their spirit forward. In a world without written words or shared languages, they

58 | EXPLORING THE URANTIA REVELATION

created a universal language in stone, showing us that the drive to connect, to communicate, and to leave a mark is as old as humanity itself.

Wrapping Up Our Journey

In the end, Göbekli Tepe leaves us with more questions than answers, and maybe that's a good thing. It opens a door to a lost past, one where humans gathered not just for survival, but for something deeper. It's a site that challenges us to rethink what we know about ourselves, and it suggests that the story of humanity is far richer than we've imagined.

So next time you hear about Göbekli Tepe, think of it not just as a historical site but also as a symbol of our ancient urge to seek, to build, and to connect with the divine. And remember, the journey isn't over—we're still uncovering the truths that shape us, still seeking the wisdom that might one day help us build something as enduring and inspiring as those stone circles on a Turkish hillside.

You may think that this chapter waxed poetic more than practical. If you do, you are partly correct, for much of the speculation regarding Göbekli Tepe is being done in real time with perplexed archaeologists and others. What we do know as revelation readers is that Göbekli Tepe has geography that aligns with the intersections of very advanced peoples and very primitive ones. We know that Göbekli Tepe shows up with radiocarbon dating prior to the Sumerians who, so far, demonstrate the first history of civilization. An archangel opines:

And all this explains how the Sumerians appeared so suddenly and mysteriously on the stage of action in

Mesopotamia. Investigators will never be able to trace out and follow these tribes back to the beginning of the Sumerians, who had their origin two hundred thousand years ago after the submergence of Dalamatia. Without a trace of origin elsewhere in the world, these ancient tribes suddenly loom upon the horizon of civilization with a full-grown and superior culture, embracing temples, metalwork, agriculture, animals, pottery, weaving, commercial law, civil codes, religious ceremonies, and an old system of writing. At the beginning of the historical era, they had long since lost the alphabet of Dalamatia, having adopted the peculiar writing system originating in Dilmun. The Sumerian language, though virtually lost to the world, was not Semitic; it had much in common with the so-called Aryan tongues. 77:4.7 (860.2)

Two paragraphs later, she writes that these superior peoples called Adamites and the even more ancient Nodites intermarried and in many cases lost some of the history as it was roughly twenty millennia before them:

The Sumerians well knew of the first and second Edens but, despite extensive intermarriage with the Adamites, continued to regard the garden dwellers to the north as an alien race. Sumerian pride in the more ancient Nodite culture led them to ignore these later vistas of glory in favor of the grandeur and paradisiacal traditions of the city of Dilmun. 77:4.9 (860.4)

Göbekli Tepe is an enigma of human history—a monumental site in Turkey, built over 11,000 years ago by hunter-gatherers who, against all expectations, possessed the architectural prowess to construct massive, intricately carved stone pillars arranged in circular enclosures. The site predates the advent of agriculture, cities, and writing by thousands of years, contradicting the conventional narrative that complex societies and monumental architecture only emerged after farming and settled life. Instead, Göbekli Tepe suggests that spiritual or ritual motivations may have driven early humans to organize labor, develop advanced engineering skills, and create social hierarchies long before agriculture transformed their way of life. Its existence raises profound questions: Were religious or symbolic purposes the true catalyst for civilization? Or was there a lost cultural knowledge that these early builders inherited?

However, without acknowledging the disrupted Adam and Eve mission described in *The Urantia Book*, archaeologists may struggle to fully resolve the mysteries of Göbekli Tepe. *The Urantia Book* presents a cosmic context for human civilization, proposing that divine influences and celestial administration played direct roles in humanity's early development. The catastrophic failure of the Adamic mission—a plan to biologically and culturally uplift early humans—left a fragmented and confused legacy on Earth. Unless new artifacts are discovered that shed further light on the site's purpose, scholars may remain confined within a materialist framework, missing a broader spiritual and cosmological perspective that could explain the site's astonishing complexity and sophistication.

As time passes, multiple speculative interpretations build up around the enigma, each trying to explain it from different perspectives. The more theories that emerge without definitive evidence, the more confusing the puzzle becomes.

Academic and scientific institutions may become entrenched in certain explanations or resist alternative perspectives, making it difficult for genuinely new ideas to be considered. In the absence of a clear resolution, an enigma can become a breeding ground for myths, pseudo-history, and conspiracy theories, further clouding its true nature.

Göbekli Tepe is a prime example—originally a remarkable archaeological find, it has become a focal point for wildly diverse theories ranging from ancient advanced civilizations to extraterrestrial influence, each adding layers of confusion to its true story.

An interested truth-seeker can find out much, much more. If you by chance are a new or nonreader of the revelation, I commend Bob Debold's website (https://deboldgroup.com/Aquatic/DBG-Page3.html#gobekli), where he has a deeper dive into this enigma. If you explore the website, your understanding of the historical context of *The Urantia Book* would be greatly enriched, particularly regarding insights on Göbekli Tepe. Let it be a companion in your quest. Bob's research in conjunction with *The Urantia Book* elevates this chapter to a whole new level.

In his essay *Göbekli Tepe: A GPS for Understanding Rare Discoveries*, Bob Debold delves into the profound implications of the Göbekli Tepe archaeological site on human history, viewing it through the revelatory insights of *The Urantia Book*. Debold's approach goes beyond traditional archaeological analysis, exploring the site's intricate architecture and carvings not just as relics of ancient craftsmanship, but as potential echoes of strategies once implemented by Adam and Eve in their effort to uplift early humanity. Recognizing that Adam and Eve's biological downgrade to human status allowed them

62 | EXPLORING THE URANTIA REVELATION

only roughly five hundred years to influence Urantia, Debold examines how their truncated mission might have left cultural and symbolic imprints that endured for millennia, possibly influencing the ritualistic and monumental construction evident at Göbekli Tepe.

Göbekli Tepe, situated nearly 25 millennia after the departure of Adam and Eve, stands as a silent testament to a forgotten chapter of human development—one that defies conventional theories of civilization's rise. Debold suggests that the site may be a distant cultural artifact connected to the legacy of Adamic influence, filtered through generations of scattered, evolving tribes. By integrating the revelatory cosmology of *The Urantia Book* with archaeological evidence, Debold opens a pathway for understanding Göbekli Tepe not merely as an archaeological anomaly but as a faint echo of a higher, yet disrupted, purpose in human history. His analysis challenges readers to consider that the enigma of Göbekli Tepe cannot be fully resolved without acknowledging the deeper, divine context that *The Urantia Book* offers.

I also urge you to look at Halbert Katzen's "UBtheNEWS: Göbekli Tepe Report" (https://ubannotated.com/main-menu /animated/topical-studies/gobekli-tepe/). Halbert takes a similar but varied approach to what Bob does. Halbert poses a number of questions and then proceeds to respond to them, taking the Urantia revelation as his fulcrum. His questions include *How did people this primitive cut, carve, move, and build with enormous stones in excess of 15 tons? And why did this civilization decline over a period of several thousand years and then intentionally bury the site around 10,000 years ago?* Halbert says, "The Urantia Book answered these questions forty years before we discovered this mysterious site existed. The history of humanity provided by the authors of *The Urantia Book* recounts that a genetically superior and well-developed herder-farmer civilization existed in this area over 30,000 years ago. They also explain why this particular civilization experienced a prolonged genetic degradation and, therefore, cultural decline. Additionally, *The Urantia Book* says that, due to population pressures, inferior and more barbaric tribes drove out this more peaceful and advanced civilization."

Halbert's UBtheNEWS website represents decades of meticulous effort, tracking and documenting emerging discoveries that intersect with the insights presented in *The Urantia Book*. Exploring UBtheNEWS in relation to many of the topics addressed in my book provides valuable context and depth to the arguments and perspectives discussed in these chapters.

The more I explored *The Urantia Book*, the more I realized it wasn't just another spiritual text—it was a revelation that spoke with stunning authority across multiple domains. Nowhere was this more evident than in its scientific disclosures, which described key aspects of cosmology, biology, and planetary history decades before modern science caught up. Each discovery—the Precambrian supercontinent, the genetic implications of Adam and Eve, the deep history of early civilization—added weight to the idea that the book was more than an inspired work; it was a road map, guiding humanity toward a fuller understanding of the truth of reality.

But something even more profound was unfolding. If *The Urantia Book* could reveal scientific truths with such precision, what did *that* say about its depiction of God? If science and spirituality weren't opposing forces but rather two aspects of the same reality, then perhaps the most significant revelation was not about the cosmos itself, but the loving, personal nature of its Creator. Part 1 explored the impersonal aspects of God through science, but Part 2 will take us deeper into the personal dimension—how God's presence is not just written in the fabric of the universe but also intimately woven into the hearts and destinies of His children.

Endnotes

1. The "Caligastia 100" refers to a group of one hundred specially trained volunteers who accompanied Caligastia, the Planetary Prince of Earth (Urantia), as part of a divine mission to guide early human civilization approximately half a million years ago. These volunteers, chosen from the ascendant mortal citizens of Jerusem (the capital world of the local system), were uniquely modified for their work on Earth, temporarily separated from their Thought Adjusters (the divine fragments of God) and endowed with new semi-physical bodies adapted to the planet's environment. They were organized into ten autonomous councils, each tasked with specific areas of advancement, including education, agriculture, industry, and religion. The Caligastia 100's mission was to uplift and civilize early human tribes, but their efforts were tragically disrupted by the rebellion of Caligastia, who chose to defect from the divine order, aligning with Lucifer in a widespread celestial insurrection. This rebellion is often associated in religious biblical legend with the figure of the devil, a distorted and symbolic representation of Lucifer's defiance against divine authority. Their story is a foundational narrative within *The Urantia Book*, illustrating themes of divine guidance, free will, and the consequences of betrayal.

2. Patrick Symmes, "Turkey: Archeological Dig Reshaping Human History," *Newsweek*, last modified March 13, 2010, https://www.newsweek.com/turkey-archeological-dig-reshaping-human-history-75101.

3. Satania is a local system within the greater universe structure described in *The Urantia Book*, consisting of approximately one thousand inhabited worlds, including Earth (Urantia). As one of the ten thousand systems within the constellation of Norlatiadek, which itself is part of the larger local universe of Nebadon, Satania is governed by a System Sovereign, who is responsible for the administration and spiritual welfare of its inhabited planets. At the time of the Lucifer Rebellion, this role was held by Lucifer, a high-ranking and once-trusted System Sovereign who initiated a rebellion against the divine administration of Nebadon. Satania became the epicenter of this insurrection when Lucifer, along with his primary lieutenant, Satan, and the Planetary Prince Caligastia of Earth, openly defied the divine order. Lucifer's manifesto rejected the authority of the Universal Father and the local universe governance of Michael (Christ), leading to a cosmic crisis that directly affected indirectly all the inhabited worlds within Satania, and directly thirty-seven of those whose planetary princes joined the rebellion. The rebellion is a pivotal event within *The Urantia Book*, illustrating the struggle between divine law and authority and the misuse of free will in the universe's spiritual hierarchy.

4. *The Urantia Book*, Paper 62: "The Dawn Races of Early Man," 62:0.1 (703.1)–62:7.7 (710.6).

5. Graham Hancock, "Unveiling Göbekli Tepe's Hidden Secrets," interview by Joe Rogan, video, 0:58, Feb 24, 2024, https://www.youtube.com/watch?v=DSSaL65HSH0. Patrick Symmes, "Turkey: Archeological Dig Reshaping Human History," *Newsweek*, February 18, 2010, https://www.newsweek.com/turkey-archeological-dig-reshaping-human-history-75101.

Chapter 4
A Baker's Dozen[1]

Spiritual Engagement

The feeding of the five thousand is a profound moment in Jesus's ministry, recounted with remarkable consistency across the synoptic gospels. *The Urantia Book* presents it as a multilayered event, rich with spiritual lessons, human dynamics, and cosmic implications. The detailed account in Paper 152 not only affirms the miraculous nature of the event but also offers a nuanced perspective on its limited impact in advancing the gospel. While the material-minded crowd was drawn to the spectacle, their spiritual receptivity was lacking, underscoring a timeless truth: material wonders rarely inspire enduring spiritual transformation.

This is a cautionary tale for proponents of *The Urantia Book* who seek to validate its revelatory nature through its prescient scientific statements. Whereas the book contains numerous examples of scientific accuracy ahead of its time, from descriptions of continental drift to the structure of the atom, relying solely on these to garner belief is a flawed strategy.

Scientific accuracy does not necessarily lead to spiritual conviction. History is replete with instances where technological or scientific breakthroughs failed to inspire moral or spiritual growth. The miracle of feeding five thousand, though awe-inspiring, failed to cement faith in the kingdom of God for most of the crowd. Similarly, presenting *The Urantia Book's* prescient science as proof of its divine origin risks appealing only to intellectual curiosity rather than fostering deeper spiritual engagement.

Moreover, science evolves. What is validated today may be reinterpreted tomorrow. If one's faith in the book hinges solely on its scientific claims, that faith may falter when faced with shifts in scientific paradigms. Revelation's primary purpose is to illuminate spiritual truths, not to serve as a textbook for transient scientific knowledge. To conflate the two risks obscuring the book's deeper message.

Yet, although scientific validation may not be a reliable strategy for conversion, it can serve another crucial purpose: opening minds. For the skeptical or the materially minded, *The Urantia Book's* authoritatively accurate scientific statements can act as a gateway to deeper inquiry. By demonstrating a level of credibility in the physical sciences, the book may invite readers to suspend disbelief and explore its spiritual cosmology with an open mind. This is a critical step, creating space for the Spirit of Truth to operate and for the individual to engage in reflective thinking.

Reflective thinking—accessing the cosmic mind through the superconscious—is where genuine spiritual transformation begins. When readers move beyond intellectual curiosity and engage with the book's robust cosmology, they encounter profound insights into the nature of God, the purpose of life, and the human potential for progressive growth. In this reflective state, the teachings of *The Urantia Book* can resonate deeply, awakening the spirit-born individual to the realities of the Father's love and the path to eternal progression.

What can be accomplished, then, by leveraging *The Urantia Book's* scientific content is not conversion but provocation to

68 | EXPLORING THE URANTIA REVELATION

think beyond conventional paradigms, which can lead individuals to question materialistic assumptions, explore spiritual dimensions, and ultimately embark on a journey of personal growth. For those who choose to delve deeper, the book's teachings offer a framework for integrating science, philosophy, and religion in a harmonious pursuit of truth, beauty, and goodness.

For the open-minded individual, the spark of curiosity generated by the scientific material can ignite a transformative journey, where the robust spiritual cosmology of *The Urantia Book* connects with inner capacities for truthseeking and spiritual growth. And in that connection lies the true power of revelation: not in proving itself, but in guiding souls toward the eternal adventure of discovering the Father's love. Melchizedek emphasizes this: "The fact of religion consists wholly in the religious experience of rational and average human beings. And this is the only sense in which religion can ever be regarded as scientific or even psychological. And this fact is proof that revelation is revelation because it synthesizes the apparently divergent sciences of nature and the theology of religion into a consistent and logical universe philosophy, a co-ordinated and unbroken explanation of both science and religion."[2]

Seamless Continuity

Melchizedek's statement in *The Urantia Book* offers a fascinating way to think about science and religion—not as rivals but as two pieces of the same puzzle. It suggests that revelation bridges the solid facts of science with the deeper truths of religion. The book claims this connection creates a unified view of the universe, where what we study in the lab and what we feel in our hearts work together to tell the same story.

Take, for example, the way *The Urantia Book* describes the universe. On the scientific side, it explains the physical setup—galaxies, gravitational forces, and the vast systems that organize the cosmos. But then it adds a spiritual layer, saying all this structure is not random but guided by a divine purpose centered on Paradise, the dwelling place of God outside of time and space. It's as if science gives you the map, but religion tells you why the journey matters.

The book doesn't shy away from hot topics like evolution. It embraces the idea that life developed through natural processes like genetic variation and environmental adaptation. But here's the twist: it says evolution is part of a bigger plan, overseen by divine beings called Life Carriers. It's like watching a movie and realizing the plot is even deeper than you thought—every twist and turn has meaning.

Even when it dives into complicated stuff like energy and matter, *The Urantia Book* keeps tying things together. It talks about energy transforming into matter in ways that sound a lot like modern physics, but then it says this process reflects the creativity of God and his delegated creators, artisans, and administrators. Imagine learning about atoms in science class and realizing they're part of a divine art project. Suddenly, even the smallest things feel significant.

What's marvelous is that the book doesn't just throw out a bunch of facts and hope you figure it out. It uses philosophy as a kind of middle ground, helping science and religion play nice. For instance, it explains time and space not just as physical realities but as tools God uses to organize the universe. It's a fresh way to think about the clock ticking in your kitchen—time isn't there to stress you out; it's part of a cosmic design.

The idea of morontia worlds is another example. These are described as intermediate places where people grow spiritually after death. It's a bridge between the physical and the spiritual, a way to show how life keeps going in a way that makes sense both scientifically and religiously. It's kind of like having a study guide for what comes next in the grand scheme of things.

Ultimately, *The Urantia Book* pushes us to see science and religion as teammates. It doesn't pit one against the other but shows how they can work together to give us a bigger picture of reality. Science asks, "How does this all work?" while religion wonders, "Why does it matter?" The book steps in to say, "Hey, both of you are asking the right questions—let me show you how the answers fit."

For anyone of any intellectual stature trying to make sense of both the natural world and the big questions of life, *The Urantia Book* offers a perspective that's both intellectually and spiritually satisfying. It's like having a cosmic playlist where every song—whether scientific or spiritual—flows seamlessly into the next.

Let me describe one more integrative concept that the book has in store for us. The concept of morontia substance, as described in *The Urantia Book*, opens up fascinating possibilities for future scientific discoveries. The revelation that the superuniverse of Orvonton contains one hundred octaves of wave energy, of which science on Urantia identified only sixty-four by the book's publication year of 1955, suggests that our understanding of energy is far from complete. This vast and largely unexplored spectrum provides a tantalizing hint that morontia substance—an intermediate form between physical matter and pure spirit—might someday be discovered as our ability to probe higher and lower energy frequencies expands.

Currently, our scientific tools allow us to study a relatively narrow band of these energy octaves, ranging from radio waves on the low-frequency end to gamma rays on the high-frequency end. The visible spectrum, which constitutes only a single octave (the forty-sixth), is a tiny sliver of the energetic reality described in the revelation. What lies beyond the limits of our current instruments—above gamma rays and below radio waves—remains a frontier of untapped potential. If morontia matter exists in an energetic frequency beyond the reach of our current instruments, its discovery might depend on a significant expansion of our understanding of quantum and subquantum energy phenomena. It's possible that breakthroughs in energy detection and manipulation could reveal entirely new states of matter, with properties that align with the morontia description—something that bridges the gap between what is tangible and what is spiritual.

Morontia substance might also exist in a higher-dimensional framework that intersects with, but is not entirely contained within, the dimensions of physical matter and energy we currently study. As science delves deeper into theories of multidimensionality, such as those suggested by string theory and other advanced physics models, we may find tools to detect and interact with these intermediate substances. Perhaps morontia matter operates in octaves where energy manifests in ways we can't yet imagine—where it exhibits properties like partial tangibility or dual responsiveness to physical and spiritual forces.

On the lower end of the spectrum, humanity has only begun to explore the richness of radio and subradio frequencies. There may be forms of morontia-like energy operating at these octaves

72 | EXPLORING THE URANTIA REVELATION

that could provide insights into the foundational connections between energy, matter, and consciousness. Could the morontia realm represent a series of energy frequencies that directly interface with both biological and spiritual mechanisms? If so, the study of these frequencies could revolutionize our understanding of life itself, linking physical phenomena like DNA and neural activity to higher-order spiritual influences.

The possibility of discovering morontia substance also carries profound philosophical implications. Imagine the impact on human thought if science was to identify an entirely new category of reality—one that bridges the physical and the spiritual, proving their interconnectivity. Such a discovery would not only validate aspects of *The Urantia Book* but also catalyze a new era of unity between science and religion. It could pave the way for deeper exploration of human consciousness, spirituality, and the ultimate meaning of existence.

In this light, the hundred octaves of wave energy revealed in *The Urantia Book* stand as an invitation for humanity to broaden its scientific horizons. They suggest that the ultimate truths of the universe are not limited to what we can currently measure but extend into realms where science and spirituality converge. Perhaps one day, as our instruments and understanding evolve, we will uncover morontia substances and take another step toward realizing the unity of all creation.

I offer one final personal note before I delve into the baker's dozen.

Science Is Gaining on It

In a 2001 article entitled "High-Energy Astronomy: 60 New Octaves of Discovery Space," Dr. David J. Helfand, a professor of astronomy at Columbia University in New York City, suggested that the electromagnetic spectrum spans approximately one hundred octaves.[3] His estimation considers both the highest-energy gamma rays and the lowest-frequency radio waves observed. In a 2022 email exchange with Dr. Helfand and Bob Debold, he reaffirmed this approximation.[4]

Whereas Dr. Helfand's estimate is based on current observational data and the capability of detection instruments, other scientists provide different figures, depending on the specific ranges they consider and the definitions they apply. For instance, some sources suggest the electromagnetic spectrum spans about eighty-one octaves, while others propose around fifty. These variations highlight the evolving nature of scientific understanding and the influence of technological advancements on our perception of the electromagnetic spectrum.

Dr. Helfand's approximation is a reasoned estimate. As scientific knowledge progresses and detection methods improve, this estimate may be refined, leading to a more comprehensive understanding of the full extent of the electromagnetic spectrum. Although this particular scientific topic can be segmented today in a secular box devoid of any religious or spiritual overtones, as soon as the revelational cosmology of morontia (i.e., "more real") is considered, the possibilities of immense proportion are opened up.

Predictions or Prescient Statements?

Since its publication, a number of dedicated students, most with scholarly and institutionally respected credentials, have analyzed the science in the *Urantia Book*.[5] The two sources

74 | EXPLORING THE URANTIA REVELATION

referenced analyze and evaluate over two dozen scientific statements in *The Urantia Book*. They compare them with science's versions, show the agreement between the two, and outline what more can be anticipated. At the time of analysis, statements that agree with science and those that partly agree constitute about one-third of all the predictions considered. This should be considered remarkable. A number of statements have yet to agree, but this is to be expected.

A **prediction** looks forward, aiming to foresee future outcomes based on current knowledge. A **prescient statement** looks insightful in hindsight, standing out because it reveals truths unknown or unproven when it was made. Both are valuable in their contexts, but prescient statements often carry an air of mystery or foresight that predictions lack. The statements in *The Urantia Book* about scientific matters, such as the existence of the Precambrian supercontinent, are not predictions per se. Instead, they are presented as authoritative descriptions or assertions about reality, regardless of whether those facts were known, accepted, or provable at the time the book was written. Their prescience emerges only in hindsight, as advancements in science confirm these previously unknown assertions. The book does not explicitly present statements as conditional or speculative forecasts. Instead, it conveys information as if it were established fact, even when the broader scientific community had no basis for agreement at the time. The authoritative tone of *The Urantia Book* does not suggest an attempt to predict; rather, it conveys knowledge that the authors claim is already true, even if unrecognized by contemporary science.

If one accepts the revelatory claims of *The Urantia Book*, then its scientific statements would be less about forecasting and more about disclosing facts that are true but not yet known or understood. This aligns with its purpose of integrating science, philosophy, and religion into a unified worldview.

Baker's Dozen

I provide below a small sample of topics, a baker's dozen, to briefly highlight how they relate to the COSAR principle. My expanded edition of *Up Close* highlights these scientific concepts that predate the validation of our science and before accepted into the scientific mainstream.[6]

I most gratefully acknowledge my indebtedness to Dick Bain and his fellow teammates and Urantia scientists who carry on in keeping all of us abreast of the science content in the *Urantia Papers* as it continues to validate our natural science. I regularly follow Mr. Bain's updates on Urantia websites with keen interest.

Continental Drift and Plate Tectonics

The layer of Earth where eight billion people live is the lithosphere, a collection of rigid slabs called tectonic plates, that are constantly shifting and sliding into each other.[7] They fit together like pieces of a puzzle, but their shifts and movements, which have formed Earth's spectacular mountain ranges, valleys, and coastlines, also cause earthquakes, volcanic eruptions, tsunamis, landslides, and other geological hazards. As the unifying theory of geology, the discovery of plate tectonics was revolutionary in helping us understand how over the centuries the earth's topography was formed and how it continues to change during our lifetime.

76 | EXPLORING THE URANTIA REVELATION

Though continental drift had been proposed by Alfred Wegener in 1912, his theory, drawn from geology, geophysics, zoogeography, and paleontology, drew the wrath of scientists from all these disciplines. These reactions eventually shut down serious discussion of the concept, which was almost universally rejected by geologists until a half century later. In the 1960s, measurements of the ocean floor showed that sea floor spreading was taking place. Geologists finally acknowledged it as the mechanism that was pushing continents apart and causing continental drift. Only then did the scientific community recognize the continents as giant floating plates drifting about on the earth's surface. This phenomenon was labeled *plate tectonics*. Years earlier, however, *The Urantia Book* could not have been clearer on this point:

> 750,000,000 years ago the first breaks in the continental land mass began as the great north-and-south cracking, which later admitted the ocean waters and prepared the way for the westward drift of the continents of North and South America, including Greenland. The long east-and-west cleavage separated Africa from Europe and severed the land masses of Australia, the Pacific Islands, and Antarctica from the Asiatic continent. 57:8.23 (663.1)

Scientists now agree that *The Urantia Book* embraced continental drift at a time when it was decidedly out of vogue in the scientific community. In fact, long after *The Urantia Book* was published in 1955, geologists revised and pushed back to six hundred million to eight hundred million years the commencement of plate tectonics breakup, finally matching the dates in *The Urantia Book*.

The Star of Bethlehem

This example is special. Around Christmastime, the Star of Bethlehem gets a great many Google hits from interested folks fascinated by this mysterious legend. Below is an explanation of this historic account that simply will not go away.[8]

The conjunction of Jupiter and Saturn is yet another scientific revelation from *The Urantia Book* ultimately confirmed by much more recent scientific discoveries. The information in *The Urantia Book* is revelatory, while Jet Propulsion Laboratory in California used state-of-the art methods to confirm it.

The Urantia Book clearly states that the conjunction of Jupiter and Saturn in the constellation of Pisces occurred three times in the year 7 BC—on May 29, September 29, and December 5. However, only in 1976 did the Jet Propulsion Laboratory (JPL) corroborate what *The Urantia Book* had revealed decades earlier. In association with the US Naval Observatory, a team of JPL scientists calculated the positions of all major bodies in the solar system during a span of forty-four centuries, from 1411 BC to AD 3002. The calculations were made possible by a new technique of simultaneous numerical integration. It took a state-of-the-art Univac 1100/81 nine days of computer time, using a method of calculation inconceivable just a few decades earlier.

Even more remarkably, the dates taken from the JPL output in 1976 and published in 1986 match with uncanny accuracy the data in *The Urantia Book*, published in 1955. We

78 | EXPLORING THE URANTIA REVELATION

now know that approximately every twenty years, a great con-junction occurs between Jupiter and Saturn due to the orbital period of the two planets—11.86 years in the case of Jupiter, 29.45 years for Saturn. What was refutable up until 1976 and not brought to light until 1986 was the precision of the three dates in the same year almost two thousand years ago. Using JPL data, Roger W. Sinnott found that the dates for the three conjunctions occurred on May 29, September 30, and December 5, 7 BC. Two of these dates are exactly the same as revealed in *The Urantia Book*; one is off by a single day.

What is equally important about *The Urantia Book*'s scientific revelation (now proven to be both precise and accurate) is its religious significance. Not only could the precision of the triple, three-times-in-one-year conjunction no longer be discredited, but *The Urantia Book* also indicated that the Star of Bethlehem was not a star visible on the night of Jesus's birth, but rather a reification of three astrological events into a religious myth.

The three conjunctions listed in *The Urantia Book* provide a reasonable basis for the legend of the Star of Bethlehem, which astronomers and Biblical scholars alike have been searching for, and both can now wholeheartedly accept. *The Urantia Book* couldn't be clearer:

These priests from Mesopotamia had been told sometime before by a strange religious teacher of their country that he had had a dream in which he was informed that "the light of life" was about to appear on earth as a babe and among the Jews. And thither went these three teachers looking for this "light of life." After many weeks of futile search in Jerusalem, they were about to return to Ur when Zacharias met them and disclosed his belief that Jesus was the object of their quest and sent them on to Bethlehem, where they found the babe and left their gifts with Mary, his earth mother. The babe was almost three weeks old at the time of their visit.

A few pages later is this:

These wise men saw no star to guide them to Bethlehem. The beautiful legend of the Star of Bethlehem originated in this way: Jesus was born August 21 at noon, 7 B.C. On May 29, 7 B.C., there occurred an extraordinary conjunction of Jupiter and Saturn in the constellation of Pisces. And it is a remarkable astronomic fact that similar conjunctions occurred on September 29 and December 5 of the same year. Upon the basis of these extraordinary but wholly natural events the well-meaning zealots of the succeeding generation constructed the appealing legend of the Star of Bethlehem and the adoring Magi led thereby to the manger, where they beheld and worshiped the newborn babe. Oriental and near-Oriental minds delight in fairy stories, and they are continually spinning such beautiful myths about the lives of their religious leaders and political heroes. In the absence of printing, when most human knowledge was passed by word of mouth from one generation to another, it was very easy for myths to become traditions and for traditions eventually to become accepted as facts.

The Star of Bethlehem and the Pisces constellation are of keen interest to astronomers and Christians alike, but as yet no independent astronomers have acknowledged this prescience as it relates to our current science. My consistent outreach highlights that even mainstream scientists are starting

80 | EXPLORING THE URANTIA REVELATION

to recognize these events, which defy conventional scientific explanation. I've contacted the Jet Propulsion Laboratory in California and the Naval Observatory on numerous occasions but, you guessed it, have gotten no response.

Tycho Brahe's Nova of 1572

Tycho Brahe's Nova of 1572 is one of only eight supernovae ever to be visible to the naked eye.[9] Although the Danish astronomer Tycho Brahe wasn't the first to observe it, he won the prize of having it named after him, no doubt because he described it so accurately.

Regardless of who gets credit, the observation of this Milky Way supernova almost 450 years ago remains one of the most important events in the history of astronomy. It immediately revised ancient models of the heavens and accelerated a revolution in astronomy, most notably challenging the Aristotelian dogma of the unchangeability of the stars.

It wasn't until *The Urantia Book*, however, that it was suggested Tycho Brahe's Nova was due to the explosion of a double star. This was finally confirmed by scientists when the Einstein Observatory, the first fully imaging X-ray telescope put into space, sent back the relevant data in 1967.

Collapse of a Star During a Supernova

The Urantia Book unequivocally states the following:

> *In large suns—small circular nebulae—when hydrogen is exhausted and gravity contraction ensues, if such a body is not sufficiently opaque to retain the internal pressure of*

support for the outer gas regions, then a sudden collapse occurs. The gravity-electric changes give origin to vast quantities of tiny particles devoid of electric potential, and such particles readily escape from the solar interior, thus bringing about the collapse of a gigantic sun within a few days. It was such an emigration of these "runaway particles" that occasioned the collapse of the giant nova of the Andromeda nebula about fifty years ago. This vast stellar body collapsed in forty minutes of Urantia time.

The supernova collapse of a star due to neutrino outflux was not proven until the SN1987A supernova was monitored by instruments that could detect the neutrinos reaching the earth from the supernova. The "tiny particles devoid of electric potential" can only be neutrinos, as the particles were later named.

The next six summaries are fully described in a compendium that covers over two dozen prescient but authoritative revelatory statements that since 1935 have been found by science to be true.

Black Holes

The Dark Islands of Space. These are the dead suns and other large aggregations of matter devoid of light and heat. The dark islands are sometimes enormous in mass and exert a powerful influence in universe equilibrium and energy manipulation. The density of some of these large masses is well-nigh unbelievable. And this great concentration of mass enables these dark islands to function as powerful balance wheels, holding large neighboring systems in effective leash. They hold the gravity

> *balance of power in many constellations; many physical systems which would otherwise speedily dive to destruction in near-by suns are held securely in the gravity grasp of these guardian dark islands. It is because of this function that we can locate them accurately.* 15:6.11 (173.1)

The existence of black holes, while theorized, was in doubt until 1971 when astronomers determined that the star in Cygnus X1 has a companion smaller than the earth but with more mass than a neutron star and that this companion would have to be a black hole. The "dark islands of space" fit the concept of black holes. The name *black hole* was coined in 1968.

Motions of the Moon

The Urantia Book reveals the moon is moving away from the earth. This was not confirmed until the 1970s when lasers were bounced off reflectors left on the moon by US astronauts; the lasers were able to measure the change in distance over time between the moon and the earth.

X-Rays from the Sun

The Urantia Book asserts that the earth's sun and other stars radiate X-rays. Scientists did not detect them until 1948.

Mystery of the Mediterranean Basin

The Urantia Book states that the Mediterranean Sea was isolated from the Atlantic Ocean for millions of years, a fact discovered by geologists in 1970.

Crab Nebula

The Urantia Book describes a small remnant star at the center of the nebula. This star, which is a pulsar, was first detected in 1967.

Age of the Solar System

According to *The Urantia Book*, the earth is 4.5 billion years old. As late as 1950 the age of the Earth was accepted by scientists as about 2 billion years, but more recent radioactive element dating has established the age of the earth as 4.55 billion years.

Temperature of Deep Space

The Urantia Book tells us that space has a temperature, that it is not devoid of heat. This was not confirmed until 1965 when noise due to the temperature of space was first detected by Arno Penzias and Robert Wilson of Bell Telephone.[10]

The Great Kentucky Volcanic Eruption

The Urantia Book informs us of a great volcanic eruption about 325 million years ago in the area of modern Kentucky. In the 1980s, volcanic ash in the area was dated to about 310 million years ago.[11]

Planetary Atmospheres

The density of the atmosphere on Venus and Mars was not confirmed until spacecraft could actually visit these planets and measure their density, well after *The Urantia Book* reported that Venus has an atmosphere considerably denser than Earth's, while Mars has an atmosphere considerably less dense. Venus's atmosphere is roughly 90 times that of Urantia[12] and Mars is 1 percent of Earth.[13]

Endnotes

1. Alison Eldridge, "Why Is a Baker's Dozen 13?," *Encyclopedia Britannica*, March 29, 2017, https://www.britannica.com/story/why -is-a-bakers -dozen-13.
2. *The Urantia Book*, 101:2.1 (1105.5).
3. David J. Helfand to Bob Debold, May 27, 2022, author's collection. A copy is available from the author upon request.
4. David J. Helfand, "High-Energy Astronomy: 60 New Octaves of Discovery," *Space Publications of the Astronomical Society of the Pacific* 113 (October 2001): 1159–61, https://iopscience.iop.org/article/10 .1086/323414/pdf.
5. Irwin Ginsburgh and Geoffrey L. Taylor, "Scientific Predictions of The Urantia Book," The Urantia Book Fellowship, accessed January 5, 2025, https://archive.urantiabook.org/archive/science/ginsss2.htm; and Richard Bain et al., eds., *Science Content of the Urantia Book* (Mason City, IA: Brotherhood of Man Library, 1991), https: //ubhs.hosted-by-files.com/docs/A/ai1991ssss_bainr_37.pdf. *Science Content of the Unantia Book* may also be accessed at TruthBook (website), 1991, https://truthbook.com/Urantia-book/science-studies /science-content-of-the-Urantia-book/.
6. Johnson, *Up Close and Personal.*
7. Halbert Katzen, "Pangaea to Plate Tectonics Report," UBtheNews (website), last modified April 21, 2007, https://ubannotated.com /wp-content/uploads/2018/03/Pangaea.pdf; and McMenamin, *Garden of Ediacara,* 175–76.
8. Johnson, *Up Close and Personal,* 12.

9. Halbert Katzen, "UBtheNews: Tycho's Nova Report," Urantia Book Study Aids (website), accessed January 12, 2025, https://ubannotated.com/ubthenews/topics/tychosnova/.

10. Wikipedia, s.v. "Discovery of Cosmic Microwave Background Radiation," last modified May 2, 2025, 00:36, https://en.wikipedia.org/wiki/Discovery_of_cosmic_microwave_background_radiation.

11. "UBtheNEWS: Kentucky Volcano Research Page," *UBannotated*, accessed May 19, 2025, https://ubannotated.com/ubthenews/topics/ubthenews-kentucky-volcano-research-page/.

12. "Venera 7," *Wikipedia*, last modified May 19, 2025, https://en.wikipedia.org/wiki/Venera_7#:~:text=The%20probe%20transmitted%20information%20to,%C2%B1%20220%20psi)%20was%20calculated.

13. Richard Bain et al., eds., *Science Content of the Urantia Book* (Mason City, IA: Brotherhood of Man Library, 1991), https://ubhs.hosted-by-files.com/docs/A/ai1991ssss_bainr_37.pdf., and "Atmosphere of Mars," *Wikipedia*, last modified May 19, 2025, https://en.wikipedia.org/wiki/Atmosphere_of_Mars.

Chapter 5
Recent Discoveries and the Yet to Be Discovered

I have used more than my share of the Amazon forest in the printing of these extra pages to bring home my point. At the expense of getting on the wrong side of my editors, I made my case to leave these gems in.

Ground-Dwelling Sloth

The January 2009 discovery of a ground-dwelling sloth in Hispaniola, specifically the new species *Parocnus dominicanus*, was a significant paleontological finding that shed light on the diversity and adaptation of ancient sloths in the Caribbean. The evidence was first uncovered when divers found the sloth's bones in a flooded cave on the island of Hispaniola, which is now home to the Dominican Republic and Haiti. The cave, known as Padre Nuestro, was once dry and provided a unique preservation environment for the sloth remains.

Parocnus dominicanus was smaller than a black bear and exhibited distinctive anatomical features, particularly in its forelimbs. These features included unique muscle attachments that likely provided enhanced mobility and strength, suggesting that this species was adapted for terrestrial locomotion in lowland environments, unlike its tree-dwelling relatives. The sloth's forelimb anatomy indicated a great range of motion, which may have been advantageous for navigating the forest floor.

The discovery was crucial for understanding the variation in the fossil record and the evolutionary history of sloths, highlighting the diversity of sloths that once inhabited the Caribbean, with some species being as large as elephants. This newly identified species was about 10 percent to 15 percent smaller in all measurements compared to previously known sloth species.

The researchers speculated that *P. dominicanus* and other ground sloths in the Caribbean disappeared around four thousand years ago, coinciding with the arrival of humans in the region about five thousand to six thousand years ago. This overlap suggests that humans and sloths coexisted for approximately one thousand years. However, it remains unclear whether the sloths were widely hunted or if their extinction was primarily due to habitat changes spurred by human activity.

In *The Urantia Book*, a resident Life Carrier describes in some detail how the animals today we commonly expect to be relatively small at one time were decidedly huge. This was of course unknown by 1935. Only recently has this become conventional wisdom via fossils.[1]

Consider the following from *The Urantia Book*:

These first two ice invasions were not extensive in Eurasia. During these early epochs of the ice age North America was overrun with mastodons, woolly mammoths, horses, camels, deer, musk oxen, bison, **ground sloths***, giant beavers, saber-toothed tigers,* **sloths as large as elephants***,*

88 | EXPLORING THE URANTIA REVELATION

and many groups of the cat and dog families. But from this time forward they were rapidly reduced in numbers by the increasing cold of the glacial period. Toward the close of the ice age the majority of these animal species were extinct in North America. (emphasis added) 61:5.7 (699.8)

For a short time all the land of the world was again joined excepting Australia, and the last great world-wide animal migration took place. North America was connected with both South America and Asia, and there was a free exchange of animal life. **Asiatic sloths**, *armadillos, antelopes, and bears* **entered North America**, *while North American camels went to China. Rhinoceroses migrated over the whole world except Australia and South America, but they were extinct in the Western Hemisphere by the close of this period. (emphasis added) 61:4.3 (698.5)*

In general, the life of the preceding period continued to evolve and spread. The cat family dominated the animal life, and marine life was almost at a standstill. Many of the horses were still three-toed, but the modern types were arriving; llamas and giraffelike camels mingled with the horses on the grazing plains. The giraffe appeared in Africa, having just as long a neck then as now. In South America sloths, armadillos, anteaters, and the South American type of primitive monkeys evolved. Before the continents were finally isolated, those massive animals, the mastodons, migrated everywhere except to Australia.

Saber-Toothed Cat in North America

In 2021 scientists identified a giant saber-toothed tiger that roamed North America between five million and nine million years ago. Weighing up to nine hundred pounds, the species hunted prey that likely weighed one thousand to two thousand pounds, such as rhinos.

"One of the big stories of all of this is that we ended up uncovering specimen after specimen of this giant cat in museums in western North America," John Orcutt, assistant professor of biology and coauthor of the study, said. "It's been known that there were giant cats in Europe, Asia and Africa, and now we have **our own giant saber-toothed cat in North America during this period as well**," added Jonathan Calede, assistant professor of evolution, ecolology, and organismal biology and the other author[2] (emphasis added).

Calede continued, "There's a very interesting pattern of either repeated independent evolution on every continent of this giant body size in what remains a pretty hyperspecialised way of hunting, or we have this ancestral giant saber-toothed cat that dispersed to all of those continents. It's an interesting paleontological question."[3]

***The Urantia Book*'s identification of the existence of saber-toothed tigers in North America seventy years before science discovered it is another example of the COSAR principle**. Following is the proof in the pudding from a revelatory source:

> *The dog family was represented by several groups, notably wolves and foxes; the cat tribe, by panthers and large saber-toothed tigers, the latter first evolving in North America. The modern cat and dog families increased in*

90 | EXPLORING THE URANTIA REVELATION

numbers all over the world. Weasels, martens, otters, and raccoons thrived and developed throughout the *northern latitudes. 61:3.13 (697.8)*

Mammalian life had been little changed by the great glacier. These animals persisted in that narrow belt of land lying between the *ice and the Alps and, upon the retreat of the glacier, again rapidly spread out over all Europe. There arrived from Africa, over the Sicilian land bridge, straight-tusked elephants, broad-nosed rhinoceroses, hyenas, and African lions, and these new animals virtually exterminated the saber-toothed tigers and the hippopotamuses. 64:4.7 (721.5)*

And there's more to come.

Yet to Be Discovered

Many scientific revelations found within *The Urantia Book* have not yet been verified by the scientific community but are expected to be in the near future. I'll conclude part 1 with a discussion of these statements of fact that are currently under investigation and worth keeping on your radar. The discussion is a lead-in to the chapters within part 2 that demonstrate *The Urantia Book's* religious revelations are equally valid.

Antigravity

Antigravity is mentioned twenty-one times in *The Urantia Book.*[4] I have firsthand knowledge of a specific antigravity project. I was in the U.S. Ambassadors' office in Beijing discussing this antigravity prospect shortly before Jon Huntsman

RECENT DISCOVERIES AND THE YET TO BE DISCOVERED | 91

Jr.'s departure.[5] Ambassador Huntsman, who left a few months before I did, was running on the Republican platform for the presidential nomination in 2012. Huntsman had a quick wit and also had quite a history. He dropped out of high school a few months shy of graduation to play in a rock band called Wizard. The good ambassador went on to graduate from the University of Pennsylvania and has seven honorary doctorate degrees.[6]

During my visit in the ambassador's office, Jon asked what I planned to do upon my retirement. I indicated I would be returning to Phoenix, Arizona, and remain active with the Urantia community there. Also, I was involved in an antigravity project at the time, and we had several patents. This got his attention, which prompted further questions. To make a long story short, Huntsman's secretary kept popping her head in his office to inform him that the ambassador from Pakistan was waiting for his scheduled appointment. After waving the secretary off several times, he finally said, "Tell the ambassador he is being held up by antigravity."[7] A few days prior to his departure at a going away event, I asked Ambassador Huntsman if he remembered the book I brought to his attention a month back. He replied, "*The Urantia Book?*" The man had a photographic memory—I'm not sure how good he was in the rock band Wizard.

The concept of "equal force presence" is the approach the inventor is taking to build a system that will achieve this lofty goal. A Divine Counselor mentions this in the *Urantia Book* in a discussion of the Infinite Spirit:

> *Antigravity can annul gravity within a local frame; it does so by the exercise of equal force presence. It operates*

only with reference to material gravity, and it is not the action of mind. The gravity-resistant phenomenon of a gyroscope is a fair illustration of the effect of antigravity but of no value to illustrate the cause of antigravity.

You can review the detail of how these insightful plans are designed by examining the patents.

Apparatus and Method for Gyroscopic Propulsion

1. US US7383747B29. Priority 2002-03-01 • Filed 2006-10-16 • Granted 2008-06-10 • Published 2008-06-10.[8]
2. US US6705174B210. Priority 2001-03-28 • Filed 2002-03-01 • Granted 2004-03-16 • Published 2004-03-16.[9]

An antigravity search in Google results in over 200,000 hits. To my knowledge this project terminated primarily due to lack of funding. I became familiar with the project, as this originated in Phoenix, Arizona. I remain optimistic that eventually someone with the resources will build a demonstrable prototype to prove this concept. This is just too important to let this concept fall into oblivion. Humankind can benefit tremendously from advances like this.

Atlantis and Eden

Atlantis as it relates to the Garden of Eden account is in Paper 73.[10] See also the December 7, 2019, *Spirit of Truth* podcast.[11]

Fred Harris came to Boulder, Colorado, in August 2019 raising awareness about his recent project: The Eden—Atlantis project. Fred and others are currently generating a buzz about a third expedition in search of the original location of the Garden of Eden. Based on research by Robert Sarmast, this third voyage to the Mediterranean will be led by Captain Bob Bates.

The video "Discovery of the Garden of Eden—Urantia Book Verified" covers the discovery of the area.[12] Finally, see the article "The Eden/Atlantis Connection—Much More than a Legend?"[13]

As it has on numerous occasions, current scientific discovery continues to confirm the dates, places, and events originally disclosed in the *Urantia Papers* nearly a century ago. One such recent discovery highlights a possible connection between the legend of the lost continent of Atlantis and the first Garden of Eden. The map shown here is featured in *Discovery of Atlantis* by Robert Sarmast. It pinpoints the lost continent of Atlantis in the exact location that *The Urantia Book* describes as the first Garden of Eden. The similarities between Plato's Atlantis and *The Urantia Book*'s Garden of Eden, compiled by Robert Sarmast (2003),[14] provide tantalizing evidence that the island of Cyprus is a remnant of the peninsula—"a virtual underwater continent."[15]

The Eden-Atlantis mystery continues to capture the attention of Urantia students and curiosity seekers from all walks of life. You will enjoy checking out the various sites that describe what Sarmast has found and documented.

Gradual Decline of Dinosaurs Before Chicxulub

According to *The Urantia Book*, the extinction of dinosaurs is presented in a way that differs significantly from mainstream scientific theories, including the Chicxulub impact hypothesis. The book suggests that dinosaurs experienced a gradual decline over millions of years due to their inability to adapt effectively to changing environmental conditions and the competition from more advanced and adaptable species. This narrative aligns with the concept of a slow decline rather than a catastrophic event.

The Urantia Book mentions that the remnants of the dinosaurs persisted until approximately **35,000 years ago**, a timeline that is far more recent than the scientific consensus of 66 million years ago for the mass-extinction event. The book frames the extinction of dinosaurs as part of the natural, evolutionary progression on Earth, where more primitive creatures are replaced by more advanced forms of life. This perspective aligns with the book's overarching theme of evolutionary creation but diverges from the catastrophic model of extinction events in paleontology.

For well over six decades since its publication, science hasn't even had a hint that anything other than a huge meteor hit caused the sudden extinction. However, new research suggests the gradual decline of the dinosaurs and pterosaurs presumably came before the impact of the Chicxulub asteroid and the global mass extinction at the end of the Cretaceous period.[16] In a new study, published in the journal *Nature Communications*, an international team of scientists, which includes one from the University of Bristol, shows that the animals were already in decline for as much as ten million years before the final death blow.

Dr. Wolfgang Stinnesbeck of Heidelberg University and Professor Eberhard Frey of the State Museum of Natural History Karlsruhe also indicate that bird species spread and diversified at the same time the dinosaurs disappeared. Their results were published in the journal *Geological Society of America Bulletin.*

While conducting paleontological research in northeastern Mexico, the scientists came upon sedimentary rock deposited toward the end of the Cretaceous period that evidenced an enormous diversity of fossils, including the tracks of birds, dinosaurs, and pterosaurs. "Most of the imprints come from at least five different species of birds; dinosaur tracks, however, are rare. Only a single footprint comes from a predatory dinosaur," explains Professor Stinnesbeck. The finds therefore indicate a gradual decline of the dinosaurs with a simultaneous increase in the diversity of birds even before the end of the Cretaceous period. "Until now, it was generally assumed that the dinosaurs died out first and bird species diversified afterward," states the researcher. "Our data, however, substantiate the theory that birds ascended before dinosaurs became extinct."[17]

Some scientists who continue to dispute this emerging theory reason, "This idea has been around for years. It's kind of like saying, 'Bob got shot with a bazooka, but he had a cold at the time, so he died of multiple causes.'" The meteor strike at Chicxulub, Mexico, which is associated with the mass extinction event at the end of the Cretaceous period, is dated to approximately **66 million years ago**. This event marks the boundary between the Cretaceous and Paleogene periods (formerly known as the K-T boundary). While the metaphor has merit, the point we make is that even the decline, which is now a fact, was unknown until the twenty-first century. Yet, once again, the revelation provides us clues to find the Truth of Reality should we suspend disbelief.

96 | EXPLORING THE URANTIA REVELATION

I am fully confident that science will begin to home in on the dinosaurs' last breath thirty-five million years ago very soon.

Fabien Condamine, a French National Centre for Scientific Research (CNRS) researcher from the Institut des Sciences de l'Evolution de Montpellier and lead author of the *Nature Communications* article, says, "The data are getting better all the time. The decline in dinosaurs in their last ten million years makes sense, and indeed this is the best-sampled part of their fossil record as our study shows."

For full report on how *The Urantia Book* predates and previews current science, it is a must to see Halbert's UBtheNEWS: Dinosaur Extinction research page.[18]

For a complete list of Urantia Book Study Aids, visit https://ubannotated.com/ubthenews/reports_list/.

The So-Called Big Bang Never Happened!

Perhaps I've saved the best for last—the big bang. Michael Wisenbaker has waited a long time for science to catch up with his perspective of *The Urantia Book*'s authoritative description of a revolving, nonexpanding universe. The big bang has always been a hot topic, but when one maintains that the universe is pulsating (expanding some then contracting some), or respiring in some sense, you might get the rolling of eyes. Add to that *revolving* (like a wheel) and most think you are talking about some science fiction story. That is what Michael did in 1991; he said the Truth of Reality is exactly that. It is precisely what *The Urantia Book* reveals. He evaluated contemporary science, which by the late twentieth century was uncovering data that cast doubt on the big bang hypothesis,

RECENT DISCOVERIES AND THE YET TO BE DISCOVERED | 97

and he meticulously demonstrated how this emerging evidence aligned with *The Urantia Book* model. Wisenbaker was clearly on the right path—when you stick to revelation, you can't go wrong. Truthfully, the big bang never happened.[19]

I keep in regular touch with Michael. In his email dated May 17, 2022, he states, "I have done nothing more to my 30-year-old work which I believe stands on its own, particularly as it deals with 'Inflation.'"[20] Michael's email dated April 28, 2021, reflects his belief that his original work has stood the test of time. Michael said, "The Big Bang theory of the origin and evolution of the universe began to develop major problems throughout the 1970's and 1980's as new astronomical observations became inconsistent with more and more of its theoretical underpinnings: generally, the astronomical observations simply did not square with a system controlled only by gravitational forces. Such observations have resulted in the current 'crisis in cosmology' which begs for the Big Bang theory to be replaced with another cosmological model."[21]

So, Michael took on the challenge and began a deep dive into the data at the time to see how *The Urantia Book*'s model lines up with it. And boy, does it!

In Michael's 1991 magnus opus, he reviews current problems in astrophysics data in the 1980s that was then beginning to point to *The Urantia Book*'s cosmology if one took the time to look at the revelation's model closely. Michael criticizes inflation as a theoretical fix for the big bang model's horizon problem[22] (why distant parts of the universe appear uniform) and flatness issue[23] (why the universe's geometry is near flat). He critiques the missing-mass hypothesis (dark matter) as an ad hoc (fabricated) solution to explain discrepancies in galactic rotation curves and large-scale structure. Clearly, Michael paved the way for future students to take more advanced data that would further support *The Urantia Book*'s cosmos model of an oscillating (respirating), revolving, and geographically finite universe. This has happened, and we will get to that.

The troubling observational and theoretical problems of the 1970s and 1980s increasingly challenged the big bang model. It also began having more and more difficulty reconciling the latest observational details found by astronomers with the fundamental assumption that on the galactic and cosmic scales gravity was the sole player. In other words, the theory failed to explain convincingly how matter had become organized in clusters of galaxies and superclusters in the time allotted since the big bang.

Also, for the universe to be structured in a manner consistent with current observations, more than 90 percent of its matter would have to be in the form of some unknown, unseen, but unbelievably massive dark matter, which would not only have to be present in such a huge quantity that it would account gravitationally for the size and behavior of the new clusters and superclusters but also have to be of such a bizarre quality that it could not possibly be detected by even the most sophisticated technology. For instance, gravity working alone would have taken something like 100 billion years to create the supercluster 2.5 billion light-years across that was recently discovered by American and German observers. This was a time scale at least five times longer than permitted by even the most generous of the big bang models. For well over forty years, it has become a fact the standard model is well-nigh incapable of an outcome from an explosion of energy in a spherical manner.

Wisenbaker concludes his analysis of the big bang with a

RECENT DISCOVERIES AND THE YET TO BE DISCOVERED | 99

calculation by Roger Penrose, the distinguished Cambridge mathematician. In his book *The Emperor's New Mind* Penrose posits a metaphor called the "Creator's Pin."[24] By that he concludes that the probability of the universe we live in is less than 1/10. The number is so small the denominator could not ever be written down—or envisioned! If the Creator was pinpointing the universe we live in, He would have to choose between that many possibilities. The pin couldn't be small enough, nor would it make sense to even try. (That's assuming the area to pick from, phase space, even existed.)

Michael only had the data from the Hubble telescope launched in 1990. Since then, the James Webb Space Telescope (JWST) launched on 2021 is now retrieving data with greater precision and distances. The JWST is primarily designed for infrared astronomy, allowing it to peer through cosmic dust and observe the faint light of distant galaxies and stars. Believe it or not, it is 1.5 million kilometers from Earth, whereas the Hubble orbits Earth at about 570 kilometers, within the Earth's shadow, subject to light pollution and thermal interference. While Hubble truly revolutionized our understanding of the universe, JWST's infrared focus, larger mirror, advanced cooling, and sensitivity to the earliest light make it a transformative tool for uncovering, closer to the Truth of Reality, the origins of galaxies, stars, and planets.

As we follow the findings of the JWST,[25] updates continue to baffle those who scoffed at *The Urantia Book*'s model as pseudoscience. For those like Michael, we "know" the next set of data will move science closer to the Truth of Reality. The "Jimmy Webb" was launched on an Ariane 5 rocket from French Guiana on December 25, 2021. What an end-of year holiday season gift to humankind! Our local Urantia study

100 | EXPLORING THE URANTIA REVELATION

group here in Phoenix, Arizona, affectionately call it the Jimmy Webb when studying related sections of *The Urantia Book*.[26]

The Urantia Book provided its readers with hope long before the Hubble. Check out these two prescient statements:

Although the unaided human eye can see only two or three nebulae outside the borders of the superuniverse of Orvonton, your telescopes literally reveal millions upon millions of these physical universes in process of formation. Most of the starry realms visually exposed to the search of your present-day telescopes are in Orvonton, but with photographic technique the larger telescopes penetrate far beyond the borders of the grand universe into the domains of outer space, where untold universes are in process of organization. And there are yet other millions of universes beyond the range of your present instruments. 12:2.2 (130.4)

In the not-distant future, new telescopes will reveal to the wondering gaze of Urantian astronomers no less than 375 million new galaxies in the remote stretches of outer space. At the same time these more powerful telescopes will disclose that many island universes formerly believed to be in outer space are really a part of the galactic system of Orvonton. The seven superuniverses are still growing; the periphery of each is gradually expanding; new nebulae are constantly being stabilized and organized; and some of the nebulae which Urantian astronomers regard as extragalactic are actually on the fringe of Orvonton and are traveling along with us. 12:2.3 (130.5)

We can talk about how being hopeful due to Michael's work gets real by fast-forwarding to 2024 and looking at George Park's newest essay, "On the Evidence for the Revelatory Presentation of Cosmology: Findings from *A New Model of the Universe* and New JWST Findings."[27] The essay "On the Evidence," along with its complement "A New Model of the Universe," presents a detailed analysis suggesting that data from the JWST seriously challenges the expanding-universe lambda cold dark matter model (ΛCDM) and supports a return to a *static* universe model.[28] *The Urantia Book* describes a universe with a revolving structure centered on Paradise. It rejects the idea of universal expansion, attributing redshifts[29] to time-space distortions and gravitational effects. The revelatory model emphasizes a geographically finite *stable* cosmic framework governed by both physical and spiritual laws. I use *stable* over *static*, as it seems more descriptive in a pithy way. Static misses the point.

George provides the reader with revelatory statements, philosophical rendering, and supporting math. I highly recommend even the mathematically and astronomically faint of heart to give it a go. Regardless, here's a statement by Park that is a good follow-on from Wisenbaker: "Outer space galaxies are not receding at the unbelievable rate of tens of thousands of miles per second. Their 'apparent speed of recession is not real.' The revelators do not tell us what causes the redshift-distance relation. But they do say it is the result of 'numerous factors of error' and other 'time-space distortions.' This last phrase is curious and catches the attention, since it appears to hint at the theory of relativity. Although the revelators are not permitted to share unearned knowledge, they have permission 'for the co-ordination and sorting of present-day knowledge.'"[30]

George presents space respiration as a central cosmological principle in *The Urantia Book*'s framework, emphasizing its role as a cyclical process that governs the finite grand universe. As did Michael, George draws heavily from *The Urantia Book* to assert the reality of space respiration, and he also critiques the shortcomings of conventional cosmological models, particularly the big bang and its proposal of infinite expansion, again as Wisenbaker does. Park integrates current observational evidence, theoretical reasoning, and philosophical considerations to suggest that space respiration provides a more coherent explanation for the universe's behavior.

Michael and George's articles, written more than thirty years apart, both demonstrate the evolving interplay between revelatory cosmology and scientific advancements. Whereas the Wisenbaker material is a conceptual critique, the Park articles employ data-driven arguments, showing how *The Urantia Book*'s ideas might align with or challenge contemporary findings. Although both articles critique the expanding-universe model, Wisenbaker zeroes in on inflation and missing mass as theoretical patches, while the Park articles expand the critique to encompass the broader implications of ΛCDM's failure to align with cutting-edge (JWST) astronomical data. This reflects a natural shift over the three decades from theoretical debates to data-driven challenges.

For example, in discussing the JWST data regarding redshifts greater than expected, Park quotes from a Russian team from the Saint Petersburg branch of Special Astrophysical Observatory, in conjunction with the Department of Mathematics, State Marine Technical University in Saint Petersburg, and the Department of Computer Science, Saint Petersburg State University: "Another inconsistency with the expanding model is the lack of evolution time: "Everything points to the possibility that the actual age of the objects in the Universe is far larger than predicted by ΛCDM cosmology."[31]

George goes on to point out that "the 13.8-billion-year age of the expanding universe is too short, because there are high redshift galaxies with 'disks and bulges, which indicate that they have passed through a long period of evolution.' Both galactic disks and bulges are believed to require billions of years to form. It is also supposed that many galactic mergers over billions of years are required to explain the formation of massive galaxies like the Milky Way." The authors conclude, "These issues indicate that the galaxies at redshifts $z > 15$ discovered by JWST do not have enough time within the framework of the standard cosmological model to evolve into what is observed. There is no age limit in the static model, since it has no identifiable starting point."

The communication capabilities and potential real collaboration today is exponentially more mature from when Michael began the quest for the Truth of Reality of Urantia's cosmic and spiritual understanding of the cosmos. As more data gets exposed and more reputable and concerned folks get involved, the entire revelation might just come center stage in human thinking.

Nevertheless, if you remain a staunch big banger, please don't throw the baby out with the bath water.[32] I respectfully request those thirsty for the Truth of Reality sincerely reflect on the aforementioned essays and presentations and arrive at their own personal insight. For those who have already made up their mind, have a nice day.

Buckle up! Double check that your cosmic passport is current and up to date, download the latest spiritual GPS navigation system (*The Urantia Book*), and prepare for a reality check in the following epilogue to part 1.

Endnotes

1. "Scientists Report Evidence for a New—but Now Extinct—Species of Ancient Ground-Dwelling Sloth," ScienceDaily, October 12, 2021, https://www.sciencedaily.com/releases/2021/10/211012154739.htm. See also Emily Caldwell, "Newly Identified American Saber-Toothed Cat Roamed North America 5–9 Million Years Ago," ScienceDaily, May 3, 2021, https://www.sciencedaily.com/releases/2021/05/210503113933.htm.
2. Caldwell, "Newly Identified American Saber-Toothed Cat"; and Halbert Katzen, "UBtheNews: Saber-Toothed Cats Research Page," Urantia Book Study Aids (website), https://ubannotated.com/ubthenews/topics/saber-toothed-cats/."
3. Caldwell, "Newly Identified Saber-Toothed Cat."
4. Johnson, *Up Close and Personal*, 16.
5. Alison Eldridge, "Jon Huntsman, Jr." *Encyclopedia Britannica*, last modified March 22, 2025, https://www.britannica.com/biography/Jon-Huntsman-Jr.
6. "Jon Huntsman Jr.," Harvard Institute of Politics, accessed January 12, 2025, https://iop.harvard.edu/fellows/jon-huntsman-jr.
7. J. J. Johnson, "Spirit of Truth #11," interview by Derek Samaras, October 26, 2019, in *Spirit of Truth*, podcast, video, 1:38:41, https://www.youtube.com/watch?v=whj3NLIhv0I.
8. Raymond Kelly Tippett, Apparatus and method for gyroscopic propulsion, US Patent 7383747 B2, filed October 16, 2006, and issued June 10, 2008, https://patents.google.com/patent/US7383747B2/en.
9. Raymond Kelly Tippett, Apparatus and method for gyroscopic propulsion, US Patent 6705174 B2, filed March 1, 2002, and issued March 16, 2004, https://patents.google.com/patent/US6705174B2/en.

RECENT DISCOVERIES AND THE YET TO BE DISCOVERED | 105

10. "Paper 73: The Garden of Eden," Urantia Book Fellowship, 2008, https://archive.urantiabook.org/newbook/pdf-Papers-UP/pdf_073 .pdf.

11. Fred Harris, "Spirit of Truth #16," interview by Derek Samaras, December 7, 2019, in *Spirit of Truth*, podcast, video, 24:59, https: //www.youtube.com/watch?v=1MUg0pIFrXM.

12. Invisible Brotherhood, "Discovery of the Garden of Eden—Urantia Book Verified," video, 41:26, June 18, 2022, https://www.youtube. com/watch?app=desktop&v=_ixpRV_79P4.

13. "The Eden/Atlantis Connection—Much More than a Legend?," TruthBook (website), accessed January 12, 2025, https://truthbook .com/quotes-about-life/the-eden-atlantis-connection/.

14. Robert Sarmast, "Atlantis-Eden Parallels," Square Circles (website), 2003, https://squarecircles.com/atlantis-eden-parallels/.

15. Robert Stanley Bates, "The Eden-Atlantis Project," Urantiapedia (website), 2018, https://urantiapedia.org/en/article/Robert_Stanley _Bates/The_Eden_Atlantis_Project.

16. Fabien L. Condamine et al., "Dinosaur Biodiversity Declined Well Before the Asteroid Impact, Influenced by Ecological and Environmental Pressures, " *Nature Communications* 12 (2021): https: //doi.org/10.1038/s41467-021-23754-0.

17. "New Indications of Gradual Decline of Dinosaurs Before the End of the Cretaceous Period," *ScienceDaily*, April 3, 2017, https://www .sciencedaily.com/releases/2017/04/170403135935.htm.

18. Halbert Katzen, "UBtheNEWS: Dinosaur Extinction Research Page," Urantia Book Study Aids, accessed December 27, 2024, https://ub annotated.com/ubthenews/topics/ubthenews-dinosaur-extinction -research-page/.

19. Michael B. Wisenbaker, "Cosmic Design: The Creator's Pin" (paper, Scientific Symposium II, Oklahoma City, OK, May 18, 1991), https://ubhs.hosted-by-files.com/docs/A/az19940705_wisenbakerm _25.pdf.

20. *Inflation* is the idea that the universe expanded exponentially in size during an incredibly short time, solving key problems with the big bang theory, like why the universe appears uniform (horizon

problem) and flat (flatness problem). In essence, inflation is like blowing up a tiny balloon to cosmic proportions almost instantly, smoothing out irregularities and setting the stage for the universe as we see it now.

21. Michael B. Wisenbaker, email message to author, May 17, 2022; and Michael Wisenbaker, email message to author, April 28, 2021.

22. In the early universe, the speed of light limits how far information (e.g., heat or radiation) can travel. Distant regions of the universe would not have had enough time to exchange energy or information with each other before emitting the cosmic microwave background (CMB) radiation. These regions should have developed independently, leading to different temperatures and characteristics. Inflation proposes that the universe underwent an extremely rapid exponential expansion in the first fraction of a second after the Big Bang. Before inflation, the universe was small enough that all regions were in thermal contact, allowing them to reach a uniform state. Inflation then expanded this uniform region to cosmic scales, resulting in the observed uniformity across the sky.

23. The flatness problem is a conceptual issue in the standard big bang model related to the observed geometry of the universe. It arises from the fact that the universe's density appears to be very close to the critical density required for a flat geometry, which seems highly improbable without an explanation.

24. Roger Penrose, *The Emperor's New Mind: Concerning Computers, Minds, and the Laws of Physics* (Oxford: Oxford University Press, 1989) 340.

25. National Aeronautics and Space Administration, "James Webb Space Telescope," last modified May 5, 2025, https://science.nasa.gov /mission/webb/.

26. Grand Canyon Urantia Book Society, accessed January 12, 2025, https://azUrantia.org/.

27. George L. Park, "A New Model of the Universe" (paper, Science Symposium III, online, June 17, 2022), https://www.urantia.org /sites/default/files/docs/A-New-Model-of-the-Universe_George -Park.pdf; —, *On the Evidence* (online, December 2024), https:

RECENT DISCOVERIES AND THE YET TO BE DISCOVERED | 107

//ubannotated.com/wp-content/uploads/2024/12/On-the-Evidence
-V2.pd.

28. For some Urantia students the idea of a *static* universe is anathema to the revelatory descriptions of a revolving, respirating, geographically limited grand universe. This term is being used almost in a metaphorical sense to move the conversation in positive ways. Early thinkers like Aristotle and Ptolemy described a static, geocentric universe, where Earth sat immobile at the center of concentric celestial spheres. This model dominated Western thought until the Renaissance. Isaac Newton's laws of gravity and motion implied a static and infinite universe. However, Newton recognized that without a balancing force, gravity would cause the universe to collapse. In 1917 Albert Einstein developed a cosmological model using his general theory of relativity. To achieve a static universe, Einstein introduced the cosmological constant (Λ), a repulsive force to counteract gravity and prevent collapse. Einstein's static model, however, proved unstable. Small perturbations would either cause universal contraction or expansion, an issue resolved later with dynamic cosmological models. This is one reason the big bang and expansion took hold as the collective scientific paradigm.

29. Redshifts are a phenomenon in astronomy where light from distant celestial objects, such as galaxies, appears shifted toward the red end of the electromagnetic spectrum. This shift occurs because the wavelengths of light are stretched, making them appear longer and redder. Redshifts can be caused by three primary factors: Doppler redshift, resulting from objects moving away from the observer (similar to the change in pitch of a receding sound source); cosmological redshift, due to the expansion of the universe stretching light as it travels across vast distances; and gravitational redshift, where light leaving a massive object is shifted due to the warping of space-time around that object. In cosmology, the observation of redshifts in distant galaxies provides crucial evidence for the expanding universe and is foundational to the Big Bang model of cosmic evolution.

30. Park, "New Model of Universe." See also *The Urantia Book*, 101:4.2.

108 | EXPLORING THE URANTIA REVELATION

31. Nikita Lovyagin et al., "Cosmological Model Tests with JWST," *Galaxies* 10, no. 6 (2022): https://doi.org/10.3390/galaxies10060108.

32. Elena Jones, "Throw the Baby Out with the Bathwater," The Idioms (website), n.d., https://www.theidioms.com/throw-the-baby -out-with-the-bathwater/.

Epilogue to Part I

For too long, science and religion have moved in parallel lines, sometimes crossing briefly yet often speaking past one another. *The Urantia Book*'s insights reach deep into both worlds, presenting a cosmology centered on an immovable Paradise and an intricate spiritual hierarchy tasked with guiding humankind toward perfection. Such claims demand scrutiny, not just by believers but also by skeptics, atheists, agnostics, and mechanistic humanists who have been steadfast in their dedication to reason, materialism, and evidence-based truth.

So, to these individuals, I extend an invitation to a seat at the table. I am inviting voices from across the spectrum: vocal skeptics like Neil deGrasse Tyson, Richard Dawkins, Michael Shermer, and even Howard Stern, who wield their influence with confidence and conviction. Each of these figures has made waves within their own circles, often boldly questioning and refuting traditional religious claims. And yet, their critiques merit testing against the grand vision of reality offered by *The Urantia Book*. Here, I am inviting them to step beyond their familiar territory and openly engage in a discussion that spans the boundaries of knowledge and belief.

The seat at the table isn't just for discussing God's existence or the cosmos. It's about opening a dialogue that tests these ideas against the very truths they have advocated. With science uncovering hints of a transcendent designer, as figures like Stephen Meyer propose, the stage is set for an honest exchange. If these figures hold steadfast to their ideals of truth and reality, then they owe it to their audiences—and indeed to humanity—to explore and challenge what *The Urantia Book* claims to reveal about the deepest questions of existence.

To create a forum for this dialogue, I've reached out to prominent scholars, scientists, and religious thinkers—over a thousand individuals across these domains. Though the response has been sparse, the intent is unwavering: those who are courageous enough to debate and examine these claims are invited to do so at any of the major conferences where ideas intersect and clash. This invitation is both friendly and serious, a call to engage, examine, and consider that there may be more to reality than either science or religion, alone, has revealed.

In the vignettes below, I explain why these individuals, and others like them, have earned a seat at the table.

Neil deGrasse Tyson

In one of Neil deGrasse Tyson's (NDT) interviews, the opening question posed to him was, "Do you believe in God?" As an astrophysicist and science communicator, Neil responded, "There is no evidence that God exists."[1] This one-line knee-jerk response, standing alone, is not accurate and not fair, and it potentially lessens the respect of the scientific community in general and those who are God-knowing and exhibit proof of the existence of a personal God by the experience of living faith in the fruits they bear. With all due respect, I enjoy listening to Dr. Tyson on his many podcast interviews that garner millions of listeners when talking about the stars and universe in a captivating manner. He's a charmer! NDT could charm a junk yard dog off a meat wagon. But I think when Neil was asked about his belief in God, he tap-danced around giving his personal view, if he has one. This reminds me of a politician who, when asked his or her favorite color is, replies, "Plaid." When correspondent Martha Teichner asked the acclaimed astrophysicist if he believes in God, his appropriate direct and accurate response should have been there is no *scientific* evidence a *personal* God exists.

In *The Late Show with Stephen Colbert*,[2] Neil discussed the mystery that keeps him up at night. The interview continues to boil down to the impersonal nature of God that is manifested in the cosmos and the origin of our finite universe and the personal nature of our loving heavenly Father that is experienced in the personal religious experience of every faith son and daughter of God. The proof of his existence of his personal nature is in the spirit fruits each God-conscious person exhibits in his or her daily life. Because God is spirit, it requires spiritual insight to become God-conscious by living faith. This faith is real. It includes the experience of faith, the conviction of faith. The existence of God in the cosmos that NDT alludes to should only require evidence of an *intelligent designer*. Science can never prove the existence of a personal God from his impersonal nature in the origin of our finite universe. Neil said in his interview that if there is evidence, to bring it on. A heartfelt challenge to NDT is hereby given. I request a sincere review of part 1 with the prescient scientific facts and the revisiting and clarification of historic truths coupled with part 2. At that time, based on insight from *The Urantia Book* and the COSAR principle, see if this answers your thought-provoking question of the

112 | EXPLORING THE URANTIA REVELATION

mystery that keeps you up at night to see if you qualify for a seat at the table:

Knowledge is the sphere of the material or fact-discerning mind. Truth is the domain of the spiritually endowed intellect that is conscious of knowing God. Knowledge is demonstrable; truth is experienced. Knowledge is a possession of the mind; truth an experience of the soul, the progressing self. Knowledge is a function of the nonspiritual level; truth is a phase of the mind-spirit level of the universes. The eye of the material mind perceives a world of factual knowledge; the eye of the spiritualized intellect discerns a world of true values. These two views, synchronized and harmonized, reveal the world of reality, wherein wisdom interprets the phenomena of the universe in terms of progressive personal experience. 130:4.10 (1435.2)

I was not aware of the extraordinary extent to which the intelligent design (ID) movement has progressed in the arena of existence of self-evident evidence of an intelligent designer—God. Dr. Stephen Meyer of the Discovery Institute, and the concept of ID, was brought to my attention while I was in the middle of one of my draft manuscripts. Brad Garner, a second-generation *Urantia Book* student who resides here in Phoenix, introduced me to Dr. Meyer's work.[3] Brad and his talented musician wife, Ruthie, also a second-generation Urantia student, are active in the Urantia community and at Urantia conferences. The Gen X, Gen Z, and millennials are an inspiration to the Urantia community and a godsend to the diminishing generation and baby boomers. I sense the fifth epochal revelation torch is being passed on to an able corps of aspiring universe-conscious citizens.

What I learned is that the ID camp is making excellent progress in providing support for ID based on science. However, this can take us only so far. *The Urantia Book* reveals how God's intelligent designer(s) are behind the ID in our finite cosmos. This will be detailed out later in the epilogue.

Professor Richard Dawkins

Dawkins is a British evolutionary biologist, ethologist, and popular-science writer who emphasizes the gene as the driving force of evolution and generates significant controversy with his enthusiastic advocacy of atheism.[4]

Richard Dawkins, the prominent British evolutionary biologist and outspoken atheist, is widely known for his critique of religion, particularly in his best-selling book *The God Delusion*. Yet, in a recent interview, Dawkins expressed an affinity for what he terms "cultural Christianity." Despite his staunch rejection of religious belief, he acknowledged a sense of connection to the Christian cultural heritage of his native Britain. "I do think we are culturally a Christian country. I call myself a cultural Christian," Dawkins remarked, distinguishing between religious faith and a broader cultural identity shaped by Christian traditions. While he reiterated that he does not "believe a word" of the Christian faith, he conveyed an appreciation for Christian hymns, Christmas carols, and the familiar ambiance of Christian customs. "I love hymns and Christmas carols and I sort of feel at home in the Christian ethos," Dawkins stated, emphasizing his recognition of Christianity's cultural imprint on British society.[5]

114 | EXPLORING THE URANTIA REVELATION

Richard Dawkins versus John Lennox

Richard has had many debates over the years and a dedicated following.[6] As with NDT and Stern, I admire his success and the contribution he's made to society as a whole. The thorn in the side with Dawkins is that when he gets outside his wheelhouse during his debates and presumably with authority denies the existence of God. I respect his passion, but his dogmatic approach diminishes his contribution as an evolutionary biologist.

Richard Dawkins is a proponent of atheism, the critique and denial of metaphysical beliefs in God or spiritual beings. Much of Dawkins's work has generated debate for asserting the supremacy of science over religion in explaining the world. He also asserts that laws of probability preclude the existence of an omnipotent creator.[7]

When it comes to debates, Richard is a legend in his own mind. If he doesn't want to end up as a footnote in history, a serious review of my prescient scientific facts and a revisiting and clarification of historic truths in *The Urantia Book* could very well place Dawkins at a seat at the table.

Howard Stern

A staffer on *The Howard Stern Show*, Sal Governale, explained that he had been researching *The Urantia Book*.[8] Here is what Stern said: "U-ran-cha—that's the disease on your balls, Sal."

Howie, let's set the record straight. *The Urantia Book* is not a disease of the testes. Our gonads have nothing to do with U-ran-cha, or Urantia. However, it is a contagious benign virus of love. You have a platform and audience to give *The Urantia Book* the rightful attention it deserves. Take the time to review *The Urantia Book* before or after your afternoon nap and, like Neil and Dawkins, become familiar enough to discern this is praiseworthy and deserves the attention to your audience. It should not be necessary to "open up a serious can of whoop-ass" to set the record straight with your audience regarding your attempt at humor while not being familiar with *The Urantia Book*.[9] To right the ship, consider inviting someone on your podcast to answer your questions, in addition to your followers who may be acquainted with *The Urantia Book*. That has to be said.

Trying not to ruffle the feathers with the topics put forth in this book cannot be avoided. Truth can and will stand up to honest criticism. *The Urantia Book* is not a mere revelation of facts; it is an epochal revelation of Truth.

No matter how tight an atheist squeezes his or her eyes shut, *The Urantia Book* will not go away; it will continue to increase in acceptance by sincere truth seekers of all persuasions who personally experience the cosmic truth, universe beauty, and divine goodness throughout this religious revelation of epochal significance to our strife-torn planet.

If I seem somewhat harsh in my attitude toward the atheist and insincere skeptics, keep in mind that in a later chapter I will hold the feet to the fire for dogmatic Christians and those of other evolutionary religions who fail to recognize the science if it doesn't fit into their belief system.

Invention of Sacred Tradition

In her chapter "The Peculiar Sleep: Receiving *The Uranthia Book*" in *The Invention of Sacred Tradition*, Sarah Lewis provides one of the most thorough independent academic

116 | EXPLORING THE URANTIA REVELATION

assessments of *The Urantia Book* available. Lewis, a lecturer in religious studies at the University of Wales, Lampeter, specializes in new religious movements and has published on *The Urantia Book* alongside studies of the Unification Church and other traditions.

In her chapter (pages 199–212), Lewis begins her analysis by referencing Larry Mullins and Meredith Justin Sprunger's *A History of the Urantia Papers*.[10] Mullins, a longtime student of *The Urantia Book*, has authored eight secondary works on the subject. Lewis draws upon Mullins's work while also citing nine additional sources to support her conclusions. After quoting Mullins on page 199, she states, "The way the Urantia revelation is said to have emerged is quite unlike that found within most other traditions. There is no belief that the message is a reemergence of a previously lost tradition, nor is there any claim that the material emerged from any great figure from history. Indeed, *The Urantia Book* is claimed to have been divulged by higher beings, through a human being, through an unknown method that is not channeling, and relatively recently."[11]

She continues, "If followers of older belief systems are not concerned by their remarkable origins, then neither should critics or supporters feel that the mystery surrounding *The Urantia Book* makes it less worthy. It makes sense of the world for certain people, and in that way, it is considered 'true.'"[12]

Another perspective comes from Martin Gardner, one of the few researchers outside the Urantia Foundation to examine the movement. Although Gardner's work is notable, his strong skepticism may limit the academic credibility of his conclusions.[13]

Lewis acknowledges the difficulty in proving or disproving *The Urantia Book*'s claims: "Of course, it is impossible to prove or disprove the claim that the Urantia Revelation was made through a hitherto never seen means that was not channeling. Equally, it is impossible to prove or disprove that the Revelation was channeled, or whether the Revelation came from a divine source or from human fabrication."[14] She concludes, "The Urantia Revelation is presented without easily recognizable and verifiable support from elsewhere, and therefore *The Urantia Book* is forced to stand alone."[15] The remainder of the chapter explores statistical investigations into authorship, contributing to a balanced and fair academic discussion.

With respect to *The Urantia Book* bridging the gulf between science and religion, I argue that spiritual unity is essential, though philosophical uniformity is not. The COSAR principle suggests that the relationship between science and religion can be understood as complementary, fostering mutual respect rather than conflict.

Highlight for End of Part I

We came up with a big bang theory to produce an explanation for observed phenomena that allowed us to posit a first cause that wasn't God. But that explanation is losing its empirical underpinnings. Increased observations are being found inconsistent with what should be observed if the big bang was the origin of the observable universe.

The Urantia Book presents a cosmos that has an organization centered around an eternal nucleus that is revealed to be the Eternal Isle of Light and Life, the geographic center of infinity that is outside of time and space, which everything else revolves around.

Revelation is required to understand that what is not immediately discoverable has to be revealed. It required *The Urantia Book* to reveal and disclose the missing pieces needed to truly understand this. How can you solve a puzzle if pieces are missing?

Intelligent Design and Our Search for Meaning

This topic deserves special treatment. The idea of intelligent design (ID) has been around for quite some time, though it's often misunderstood. It's not some strange new religion, but rather a way of looking at the world through the lens of science. That might sound odd, especially to those who equate science with hard data and religion with faith, but the truth is, ID is more science than religion—at least 80 percent of it! But when scientists deeply invested in materialism hear about it, they often dismiss it as pseudoscience. Let me take you through why I think that's a mistake.

The guy who's been waving the flag for ID is Dr. Stephen Meyer, the head of the Center for Science and Culture at the Discovery Institute in Seattle.[16] Meyer's not out to push a religious agenda, but he does argue that the complex structures we see in biology, like DNA, point to a deliberate designer. He's gone toe-to-toe with some pretty big names in science, folks like Richard Dawkins and Michael Shermer, who believe everything can be explained through natural processes like evolution. But Meyer's point is, if you look at the incredible intricacy of life—things like the information packed into

DNA—it makes more sense to think some intelligent force is behind it all rather than just blind chance.

Adding a complementary voice from the theological side, Fr. Martin Hilbert—a Catholic priest with a deep grounding in both science and doctrine—has emerged as a thoughtful supporter of intelligent design.[17] Whereas Stephen Meyer approaches the topic from a philosophical and scientific standpoint, Hilbert brings in a theological perspective rooted in Catholic tradition, emphasizing that faith and reason are not at odds but work hand in hand. He views the apparent design in nature as fully compatible with the idea of a purposeful Creator, aligning with Church teachings that affirm God's role as the ultimate author of life. For those interested in exploring how theological insight and scientific evidence can converge in support of intelligent design, Bob Debold's website offers a range of essays that engage deeply with this topic, weaving together Meyer's ideas, Hilbert's theology, and broader reflections on intelligently directed evolution.

The Bridge Between ID and Bigger Things

Here's where it gets interesting. I believe ID can be a bridge to even bigger questions—like "Why am I here?" You see, ID might not take you all the way to believing in a revelation like that in *The Urantia Book*, but it's a step in the right direction. It's like starting the journey across a bridge. Meyer's ideas about a purposeful, intelligent designer can lead us to think about not just any designer, but a personal God with a plan.

For example, Meyer often talks about how finely tuned our universe is. Gravity, electromagnetism—all these forces are dialed in just right for life to exist. Could that be by accident?

Meyer doesn't think so, and neither do I. The fact that the universe seems so purpose-built for life suggests that intention is behind it, not just random chaos. Meyer also makes the point that DNA, with all its complexity, is like a code—a language, really. And what do we know about languages? They come from minds, not accidents.

On the cover of Meyer's *God Hypothesis* book is the subtitle "Three Scientific Discoveries That Reveal the Mind Behind the Universe." Meyer uses evidence from cosmic fine-tuning, biological information and origins, and the beginning of the universe to hypothesize that a transcendent, intelligent mind or God. That is, intelligent design is the best explanation for the observed phenomena. *The Urantia Book* eloquently describes the IDer outside of time and space that Meyer hypothesizes.

Science and Religion—Best Friends?

For a long time, folks have been told that science and religion can't mix, like oil and water. Meyer, though, argues that this isn't true. He thinks the evidence we've gathered through scientific discoveries actually points us toward a belief in God, not away from it. He's not talking about the kind of God who winds up the universe and then walks away, like a deist might believe in. No, he's talking about a personal God, one who's involved in the day-to-day, one who cares about what's happening in His creation.

This idea, that God is both the creator and an active presence in the world, aligns well with the theistic worldview Meyer supports. He's not just pulling this out of thin air. He backs it up with solid arguments, saying that the order and consistency of the universe reflect the nature of a rational, purposeful God. This view holds that God not only created the laws of physics but also maintains and interacts with them, sustaining the world and answering prayers. In Meyer's eyes, all this fine-tuning points to a personal God who's not just watching from afar but is deeply involved with creation.

What Happened to Science?

Here's a question you might be wondering: If intelligent design makes so much sense, why didn't more civilizations develop modern science like we did in the West? Meyer has an answer for that too. He says that while other societies, like those in China, India, and the Islamic world, had impressive achievements in math and engineering, they didn't have the same theological and philosophical outlook that motivated Western scientists to systematically study nature.

Take China, for example. Its worldview, shaped by the concept of yin and yang, focused on harmony and balance. Although that was great for certain things, it didn't encourage the idea that nature worked according to fixed laws that could be tested. Similarly, in the Islamic world, some strains of theology suggested that every event was directly caused by God, which discouraged scientists from looking for natural laws because everything was seen as God's immediate action.

What About India?

In India, things were a bit different. Their philosophical traditions, like Hinduism and Buddhism, were more focused on the inner, metaphysical world—understanding the self and consciousness. That's valuable in its own right, but it didn't lend itself

122 | EXPLORING THE URANTIA REVELATION

to the same empirical approach to studying the natural world that developed in the West. Plus, the hierarchical social structures in India often kept scientific inquiry from spreading widely.

It wasn't until these civilizations came into contact with the West—through trade, colonialism, and intellectual exchanges—that they began to adopt modern scientific methods. Today, countries like China and India are world leaders in technology and science, showing that once the right conditions are in place, any society can thrive scientifically.

Why Materialism and Secularism Took Over

Over time, science in the West became increasingly secular. The success of the scientific method led many to believe that the natural world could be explained entirely through material causes. This idea, called methodological naturalism, pushed the notion of God further and further to the margins of scientific inquiry. Folks began to think that science and God didn't mix, and that kind of thinking dominates today. But Meyer believes this is a mistake, as do I. If we take a closer look at what science is telling us, it actually opens the door back up to God.

Crossing the Bridge to Revelation

So, where does that leave us? Meyer's intelligent-design ideas are like the first few steps across a bridge. But to really understand the full picture, we need to look further. *The Urantia Book*, for instance, offers a cosmic revelation that goes beyond intelligent design, revealing the personal nature of God in a much deeper way. It's not just about designing systems and achieving goals—it's about relationships, spiritual growth, and communion with God.

The Urantia Book paints a picture of God as a personal being who desires a relationship with His creations. He invites us to grow and experience eternal life through our choices and spiritual progress. This idea of personal agency goes beyond just creating the universe—it's about entering into a divine relationship where free will and spiritual growth play central roles.

Bringing It All Together

Meyer's work has brought a fresh perspective to the age-old conversation between science and religion. His arguments for intelligent design challenge the secular framework that has dominated science for so long. By showing that modern scientific discoveries actually point to a personal, intentional designer, Meyer builds a bridge that can lead us to a deeper understanding of the universe and our place in it.

But if we want to cross that bridge, we need to be open to even more. *The Urantia Book* takes us beyond the physical universe, offering a spiritual framework where science, faith, and personal growth come together. It's a big step, but one worth taking. So, let's keep asking questions, keep searching for answers, and remember that the journey to understanding our universe is just as much about what's inside us as it is about the stars above.

In the meantime, I provide the reader a few YouTube videos that may be of interest. First,

Dr. Stephen Meyer returns to Uncommon Knowledge with Peter Robinson to delve into his latest work, *Return of the God Hypothesis: Three Scientific Discoveries That Reveal the Mind*

Behind the Universe. In this expansive and thought-provoking interview, Meyer articulates the core principles of the "God hypothesis," reinforcing his evolving case for intelligent design. He traces the historical role of Judeo-Christian theology in the birth of modern science and examines the profound mystery of DNA—an intricately encoded molecule whose origins, he argues, defy explanation through natural selection alone. The conversation navigates these themes and more, offering a compelling exploration of science, philosophy, and theology.[18]

I also recommend a video where Dr. Stephen Meyer joins Kirk Cameron for a compelling conversation on *Takeaways with Kirk Cameron* on TBN. In this engaging dialogue, Meyer explores how scientific research, the mysteries of the universe, and the concept of fine-tuning all point toward evidence of intelligent design and, ultimately, a Creator. The discussion delves into the remarkable complexity of human DNA, which Meyer presents as clear evidence of a purposeful programmer. Additionally, the conversation addresses a thought-provoking question: Would the discovery of extraterrestrial life challenge a biblical worldview? This thought-provoking exchange offers valuable insights for anyone interested in the intersection of science, faith, and philosophy.[19]

Lastly, Bryan Callen hosts an engaging discussion between Dr. Stephen Meyer and Dr. Michael Shermer, exploring the question of whether science can provide evidence for the existence of God. This thought-provoking dialogue brings together two prominent voices—Meyer, a leading advocate for intelligent design, and Shermer, a well-known skeptic—who present contrasting views on the relationship between science and faith. Of the recommended links, this exchange stands out as particularly worthwhile, offering a balanced and intellectually stimulating exploration of a timeless question.[20] Out of the links offered, this one is most worthy of your time.

The Stephen Meyer YouTube links provide the baseline support for intelligent design. *The Urantia Book* offers a logical basis (a "rationalization") for proponents of Intelligent Design when addressing the arguments of New Atheists. Specifically, it claims that *The Urantia Book* explains that the origin of the evolutionary universes occurs beyond the dimensions of time and space—within a "prefinite" reality. In simpler terms, it suggests that the creative force behind the universe, as described in *The Urantia Book*, exists in a realm that is not bound by the temporal and spatial limitations of the physical cosmos, thereby providing a framework for understanding divine creation beyond materialistic explanations. The prescient scientific facts and revisiting and clarifying historic truths revealed in the examples provided in this book give the New Atheists and all those hungry for the Truth of Reality the curiosity to take in parts I, II, and III of *The Urantia Book* and personally arrive at the conclusion of this option. Revelation-aided philosophy has never been seriously considered by the mainstream before but is the best viable and sound proposition. It also provides support for the atheistic scientist to encourage the Christians to throw out the errors in the Bible and learn anew the difference between the Bible Jesus and the *Urantia Book* Jesus.

The following review of *Return of the God Hypothesis* is by Dr. Michael Denton, former senior research fellow of biochemistry, University of Otago, and author of *Nature's Destiny*:

> Reviewing all relevant evidence from cosmology to molecular biology, Meyer builds an irrefutable "case

126 | EXPLORING THE URANTIA REVELATION

for God" while delivering an unanswerable set of logical and scientific broadsides against the currently fashionable materialistic/atheistic worldview. Meyer builds his argument relentlessly omitting no significant area of debate. The logic throughout is compelling and the book almost impossible to put down. Meyer is a master at clarifying complex issues making the text accessible to the widest possible audience. Readers will be struck by Meyer's extraordinary depth of knowledge in every relevant area. The book is a masterpiece and will be widely cited in years to come. The best, most lucid, comprehensive defense of the 'God hypothesis' in print. No other publication comes close. A unique tour de force.[21]

These foregoing topics need to be addressed in light of *The Urantia Book* and its treatment of the impersonal nature of God, the IDer, behind the creation of the finite universe. Our scientists simply cannot and will not be able to provide scientific evidence of the existence of the impersonal nature of the Intelligent Designer behind the ID of our finite universe. The First Great Source and Center of All Things, the Uncaused Cause, the existential I AM, is the Intelligent Designer (IDer) behind the ID in the finite evolutionary universes of time and space. However, this existential prefinite reality takes place outside of time and space of our finite evolutionary universes.

The IDer personally resides on the eternal Isle of Light and Life, Paradise, which is the geographic center of infinity (before time and space). Space does not exist on any surfaces of Paradise—the material is unlike that of the evolving universes. Space is not infinite; it has boundaries. The boundary of space is the fourth outer-space level. Beyond this outer-space level is the quiescence of the Unqualified Absolute. The absolute of time is eternity. Time is nonexistent on Paradise (2:1.5) (14:1.11) (54:5.13) (65:8.1–3). Paradise is from eternity; there are neither records nor traditions respecting the origin of the nuclear Isle of Light and Life.

To gain maximum comprehension and insight into pre-reality of the IDer from a finite perspective, the following excerpts from the *Urantia Book* are offered:

> There are antecedent and eternal realities, superfinite realities which are ancestral to our time space evolutionary finite universes. Therefore, simultaneous events of eternity must be presented as sequential transactions [since time does not exist on Paradise]. In this original transaction the theoretical I AM [IDer] is the Absolute primal causation in infinity functioning as the infinite, the eternal and the absolute I AM. This philosophic concept of the I AM does afford us some basis for an attempted approach to the partial comprehension of absolute origins and infinite destinies. To our finite mind there simply must be a beginning, and though there never was a beginning to reality, still there are certain relationships which reality manifests to infinity.
>
> The prereality, primordial, eternity situation may be thought of something like this: At some infinitely distant, hypothetical, past-eternity moment, the I AM, the intelligent designer [IDer], may be conceived as both thing and no thing, as both cause and effect, as both volition and response. At this hypothetical

eternity moment there is no differentiation throughout all infinity. Infinity is filled by the Infinite; the infinite encompasses infinity. This is the hypothetical static moment of eternity; actuals are still contained within their potentials, and potentials have not yet appeared within the infinity of the I AM [IDer]. But even in this conjectured situation we must assume the existence of the possibility of self-will. [from pages 102 and 103 in my expanded edition[22]].

Endnotes

1. Neil deGrasse Tyson, interview by Margaret Teichner, *CBS Sunday Morning*, video, 2:15, April 30, 2017, https://www.youtube.com /watch?v=I0nXG02tpDw. See especially 1:17–1:19.
2. Neil deGrasse Tyson, interview by Stephen Colbert, *The Late Show with Stephen Colbert*, video, 9:00, January 6, 2018, https://www .youtube.com/watch?v=TgA2y-Bgi3cc. See especially 8:40–8:50).
3. Stephen C. Meyer, *Return of the God Hypothesis: Three Scientific Discoveries That Reveal the Mind Behind the Universe* (San Francisco: HarperOne, 2021).
4. Anthony G. Craine and Richard Pallardy, "Richard Dawkins," Encyclopedia Britannica, last modified March 27, 2025, https: //www.britannica.com/biography/Richard-Dawkins.
5. Catholic News Agency, "Famous Atheist Richard Dawkins Says He Considers Himself a 'Cultural Christian,'" October 10, 2023, https://www.catholicnewsagency.com/news/257276/famous-atheist -richard-dawkins-says-he-considers-himself-a-cultural-christian.
6. Richard Dawkins and John Lennox, The God Delusion Debate, produced by Spencer Cooper (Feb 8, 2017; University of Alabama, Birmingham), video, 1:46:37, https://www.youtube.com/watch?v=zF5 bPI92-5o.
7. Craine and Pallardy, "Richard Dawkins."

8. Sal Governale, interview by Howard Stern, *The Howard Stern Show*, August 5, 2019, video, 4:12,https://www.youtube.com/watch?v =0-f9YyH1vzM.

9. I take a cue from Dr. Phil when he turned the tables on David Letterman, who was excoriating Dr. Phil with some pretty wild statements. Dr. Phil came on the show "to open a serious can of whoop-ass." Check out this YouTube recording of how Dr. Phil met Letterman's derogatory name-calling: https://www.youtube.com/watch ?v=yqX8fm2YXxo.

10. Larry Mullins and Meredith Justin Sprunger, *A History of the Urantia Papers* (self-pub, CreateSpace Independent Publishing, 2010).

11. Sarah Lewis, "Peculiar Sleep," 209.

12. Sarah Lewis, "Peculiar Sleep," 210.

13. Martin Gardner, *Urantia: The Great Cult Mystery* (Amherst, NY: Prometheus Books, 2008).

14. Sarah Lewis, "Peculiar Sleep," 212.

15. Sarah Lewis, "Peculiar Sleep," 212.

16. "About," Stephencmeyer.org, accessed January 12, 2025, https://stephen cmeyer.org/about/.

17. Martin Hilbert, *A Catholic Case for Intelligent Design* (Seattle: Discovery Institute Press, 2023), Kindle ed.

18. Stephen Meyer, interview by Peter Robinson, March 30, 2021, in *Uncommon Knowledge*, podcast, video, 1:00:12, https://www.youtube .com/watch?v=z_8PPO-cAlA.

19. Stephen C. Meyer, interview by Kirk Cameron, October 9, 2023, video, 24:11, https://www.youtube.com/watch?v=nfNG0y-O6Qc.

20. Stephen Meyer and Michael Shermer, interview by Bryan Callen, *Bryan Callen Show*, June 1, 2023, https://www.youtube.com/watch ?v=QIqzfdDnPjI&t=403s.

21. Michael Denton, review of Return of the God Hypothesis by Stephen Meyer, "Return of the God Hypothesis," Stephencmeyer.org, accessed January 12, 2025, https://stephencmeyer.org/books/return -of-the-god-hypothesis/.

22. Johnson, *Up Close and Personal*, 102–3.

PART II

Religion in The Urantia Book: *The Personal Nature of God—Our Heavenly Father*

If I had to pick a catchphrase to introduce someone to *The Urantia Book*, I reckon I couldn't do better than "Who's your daddy?" Now, before you raise an eyebrow, let me explain. That book isn't just some light read—it's a vast, cosmic journey that'll take you from one end of the universe to the other. It begins with the infinitude of the I AM and moves down to the smallest material particle in the grand universe. And connects it all in between! But let's not get ahead of ourselves. Let's start with a simple fact: right in the opening sentence, a Divine Counselor straight up tells us that we humans are mighty confused by the idea of God. And the whole point of this revelation? To give us bigger, better ideas about the universe and to help us sharpen our spiritual senses. That's what it says on page 1, right there in the foreword (0:0.2).

And guess what? At the end of 2,097 pages, the book wraps it all up by saying, "When all is said and done, the Father idea is still the highest human concept of God" 196:3.35 (2097.3). So, for sure, the book makes it pretty clear—God is our daddy. But in between that first sentence and the last,

131

132 | EXPLORING THE URANTIA REVELATION

you'll find everything under the sun (and beyond) that might interest you about life and the universe.

Maybe you're not into quantum physics—no problem. How about learning what the family has to do with spirituality and morals? Or digging into the first twenty-nine years of Jesus's life? Angels more your thing? Buckle up—actually, you might want to strap on a pilot's harness because this book will take you to places you've never imagined. Curious about abortion? Well, *The Urantia Book* takes a whole different angle, one that goes deeper than anything religion or science has ever said. It offers a spiritual and cosmic "solution" for what happens to a soul that never gets the chance to be born. And life after death? Jesus's resurrection cracked that door wide open, and this book takes it further, explaining "the way, the truth, and the light" in ways that'll open your eyes.

By the time you hit Paper 16, you might feel like your brain is ready to jump right out of your head, or you'll be so charged up you can't wait to see what's next. But here's the real kicker—if your brain starts hurting and you think about tossing the book back on the shelf or hiding it where it'll never see the light of day again, you might want to reconsider. A Universal Censor gives a sharp rebuke near the end of Paper 16 (16:6.9). He says that scientific, moral, and spiritual insights are built right into our cosmic minds. We've all got this potential, all we have to do is ask questions, no matter how simple they are. It's called "reflective thinking." And you know who spent countless hours doing that? Jesus himself, as you'll find out in part 4 of *The Urantia Book*. But the sad truth is, too many folks here on Earth don't take the time to enjoy this kind of deep, courageous thinking. Don't be one of those people who believe that all there is to life is

RELIGION IN *THE URANTIA BOOK* | 133

just material stuff. Dive in, open your mind, and see where it takes you!

Here's the deal. What *The Urantia Book* really drives home is that God is personal. It takes what Jesus taught in his gospel, and moves it up a few notches. Jesus taught our Father is not some far-off, unreachable being. What *The Urantia Book* teaches is that He's got a personality, and that personality reaches out to us through Jesus and beyond. The revelation here isn't just about being saved by faith, though that's important. It's also about realizing that each of us is a personality-son of God, not just a random living organism wandering through the universe until that life ceases. We're a potentially eternal personality contributing to part of something already eternal, and this truth changes how we understand our place in the universe. (And we will come to know that the bestowal of personality is one of the two aspects of prereality that God doesn't delegate to any other being in all the wide universe of universes. The other is the bestowal of the Thought Adjuster.)[1]

So, let me tell a little something in a down-to-earth way about the importance of personality in the grand scheme of things. You see, the big idea behind the fifth epochal revelation—that's the latest in a series of important spiritual messages meant to guide humanity—is to show us the reality of God's personality.

Most folks might think they already know a bit about what personality is. But hold on to your hats, because this book introduces a whole new way of understanding the concept— and it's not what you'd expect. Up until now, we humans might have had a little glimmer of the truth, like holding up a candle in the dark. Sure, that little flame shows us something, but it's nothing compared to what happens when the sun comes up and shines a light on the whole world. That's what this revelation is like—moving from that flicker of a candle to the brightness of the sun.

Before, religionists might have thought that the highest form of reality was spirit—something unseen, a bit mysterious. But here comes this revelation telling us, "Hey, you know what's even more important? Personality." It's saying that personality, who you are deep down, is more real and even more important than spirit. It spells the difference between will and free will—and, well, that's gonna get a whole lot clearer too.

If you're wondering about Jesus and where he fits into all this, he wasn't just telling us that God is spirit. No sir, he also lived it out and showed us the personality of God. Remember when, as recorded in the Bible (John 14:9) and in the *Urantia Book* (157:6.13), Jesus pronounces, "If you've seen me, you've seen the Father"? Jesus didn't just show us what God's spirit is like—he gave us a front-row seat to see what God's personality is all about.

So, the big takeaway from this fifth revelation is that God's personality is the most real thing in the universe—and that's something new for humanity to really wrap its collective head around. It's not just theological hocus-pocus; it's about who we are in relation to a very personal, very real God. And that, my friend, is a truth that's shining like the sun after a long, dark night.

Part 1 of this book laid out a pretty big idea—*The Urantia Book* is like a spiritual GPS. It's full of all sorts of information, a lot of which science only caught up with much later. Not only that, it takes another look at human history, clears up old misunderstandings, and adds context to things we used to

RELIGION IN *THE URANTIA BOOK* | 135

just call myths. But now, in part 2, we're shifting gears to talk about religion and spirituality.

In part 1, we wrestled with the scientific community and agreed there's no scientific proof for a personal God. Yet, even with all the back-and-forth between intelligent-design folks and atheists, it turns out that the best scientific explanation for the universe's origins might just involve some kind of intelligent design. But here's the kicker: *The Urantia Book* isn't just another religion. It's a religious revelation—the kind that bridges that big ol' gap between those who believe in God and those who don't. And it gives us the missing piece: our Father is outside of time and space. That's right, He's not confined to the material world.

Religion is a personal experience, and we each have to find our own spiritual insight. This book isn't here to convince you of my personal experiences, but rather to help you find something as meaningful for yourself. If you're really looking for truth, you'll feel it in your gut when you find it. I'm casting a wide net here—anyone, no matter who they are, can be a sincere seeker of truth. Part 1 might've been more appealing to the science-minded, while part 2 is going to hit home for those with big spiritual questions. Put them together, and you've got a full explanation of science, religion, and the Truth of Reality that might just speak to all of humanity and anything you may be wondering about.

Every once in a while, when talking to someone new about *The Urantia Book*, I hear things like, "Hey, didn't *The Urantia Book* predict the Precambrian supercontinent?" or "Didn't it say Adam and Eve showed up 37,000 years ago?" Actually, *The Urantia Book* doesn't predict anything—it's revealing truth from a cosmic perspective.

If you made it through part 1 and you're still with me, then you're ready to dig into part 2. If you're genuinely after the truth, you won't be disappointed. But if you've already got all the answers, if you're happy with your place in life and aren't interested in things like what Jesus did during those first twenty-nine years of his life, then this may not be for you. For those of you who do want to know more, though, get ready for a ride that goes beyond words.

I'm hoping that what you saw in part 1 will get you just as interested in the religious side of *The Urantia Book*. Let's keep it simple: *The Urantia Book* has already shown it knows its scientific stuff, so why wouldn't the religious truths hold the same weight? I'm just asking you to keep an open mind as we look at the R side of the equation.

In part 2, we're going to look at the five epochal revelations in *The Urantia Book*. You guessed it, *The Urantia Book* is the fifth. These aren't your run-of-the-mill revelations—they're straight from spiritual beings who know Earth's history inside and out. You'll get the answers to the big questions, like how our planet got so mixed up thanks to the Lucifer rebellion and how Adam and Eve showed up about 37,848 years ago to keep things moving along.

So, let's dig into those five epochal revelations. You'll find a whole section on the Dalamatian teachings, the Edenic teachings, Melchizedek of Salem, Jesus of Nazareth, and of course, the *Urantia Papers* themselves. There's a lot to cover, but I'll also be touching on some popular topics like family life, angels, soul survival, free will, and what our future looks like as we ascend to higher levels of existence. We'll also compare a few current scientific beliefs to what *The Urantia Book* says.

It's time to dive deep, so let's get started with the big five revelations and see where they lead us.

Endnote

1. *The Urantia Book*, "Foreword," 0:5.5 (8.5), and 0:5.11 (9.1).

Chapter 6
The Dalamatian Teachings

When we look at the world today, it's easy to forget how long we've been at this business of trying to figure out who we are, where we come from, and where we're headed. It's hard to wrap our minds around the sheer length of human history, let alone cosmic history. But I've come to see that, just as I found *The Urantia Book* and it started clicking for me, way back in the early days of Urantia, some things were beginning to click for humanity too, and some things . . . well, they started to go sideways pretty fast.

Before we dig into the teachings that came from Dalamatia, I've got to set the stage. The revelators, as they tell us, have no favorites. They pick the ones who are willing, not the ones who might seem important. This was true with Melchizedek's work with Abram, and it was true with Caligastia's time on Urantia before things went off the rails with the Lucifer rebellion. And trust me, it was a rebellion like no other—because when it started, it was like hitting a reset button on our spiritual progress.

The Long Path to Adam and Eve

Let's talk about where things were when Adam and Eve were sent to our world. We had been on this planet a long time— by *we*, I mean humanity. As *The Urantia Book* lays it out, we're

139

talking nearly a million years ago when the first two humans popped up out of the evolutionary line (UB 62:0.1). Imagine that. We've been evolving for nearly a million years since the first will-dignity humans appeared, and for 500,000 of those years, we were pretty much figuring things out by ourselves before the Planetary Prince, Caligastia, arrived.

But here's where it gets interesting. You see, when Caligastia showed up, he didn't come alone. He brought with him what we call the Caligastia 100, a group of volunteers who were once human and now advanced and serving a mission on this planet to help us evolve (UB 66:0.2). They were going to help us out in a big way, slowly guiding us toward higher things—better social organization, spiritual insight, and everything we needed to move forward. These were the humanly visible celestial helpers; Caligastia was not.

Their headquarters was in a city called Dalamatia, down near the Persian Gulf. The teachings that came out of Dalamatia were simple but revolutionary for those early humans. They taught basic morality, social structure, and spiritual ideas that were meant to help us begin our ascent toward civilization. For hundreds of thousands of years, things were going pretty well. Sure, we had our ups and downs, but humanity was making progress.

The Caligastia 100

Let's dive into one of the most intriguing parts of Urantia's early history: the story of the Caligastia 100. These weren't your average human beings, but volunteers from Jerusem who had come to Earth—Urantia—with a mission that was supposed to shape the future of humanity. Their story is one of both hope and tragedy, because while they started with noble intentions, their fate was tightly bound to the fall of Caligastia during the Lucifer rebellion.

The Caligastia 100 were selected to serve as the Planetary Prince's administrative staff when Caligastia was installed on Urantia some 500,000 years ago. The volunteers, once mortal beings like you and me, had advanced far along the ascension path. However, none of the Caligastia 100 had yet fused with their Thought Adjusters—the inner fragments of the Universal Father that guide each of us toward our spiritual destiny (UB 66:2.4). This is a crucial point because, as advanced as they were, they were still unperfected beings, capable of making errors—and as we'll see later, some did.

Laying the Foundation of Civilization

When the Caligastia 100 arrived, Urantia was a wild and untamed planet. Humanity was in its infancy, still grappling with basic survival and rudimentary social structures. The role of Caligastia and his staff was to guide the development of early human civilization—not just in a spiritual sense, but in every facet of life: education, law, science, and even practical skills like farming and building.

The idea was to uplift the human races, bringing order and progress to the evolutionary chaos. But they were not here to impose their will. Instead, the Caligastia 100 were supposed to work quietly behind the scenes, offering guidance and support, helping humanity make the leap from primitive tribes to more organized, spiritually aware communities.

To manage this enormous task, the Caligastia 100 were divided into ten autonomous councils, each overseeing a

142 | EXPLORING THE URANTIA REVELATION

different area of planetary administration. Here's a breakdown of what each council was responsible for:[1]

- Food and material welfare
- Animal domestication and utilization
- Science and industry
- Trade and commerce
- Revelation and religion
- Art and culture
- Government and law
- Health and sanitation
- Education
- Race and culture relations

An Advanced Yet Vulnerable Group

As amazing as their mission sounds, it's important to remember that the Caligastia 100 were not perfect beings. Because they had not yet fused with their Thought Adjusters, they were still capable of moral and spiritual error. The fact that they had volunteered for such a risky assignment shows their dedication, but it also meant they were vulnerable to the influences of rebellion when it came.

Their lack of Thought Adjusters likely limited their ability to discern the will of the Universal Father compared to the primitive humans, some of whom may have possessed Adjusters. All were volunteer ascending beings from the local system headquarters, highly advanced and knowledgeable, but they just weren't yet adjuster-fused. They were, as revealed, material helpers constituting the connecting link between the Prince and the world races. We aren't told why, but they were required to detach[2] from their Adjusters before embarking on this Urantian mission. We can only assume that this vulnerability becomes critical when considering how some of them later succumbed to the Lucifer rebellion, following Caligastia into his disastrous path.

Still, before the rebellion, their work was critical to the early progress of human civilization. For 300,000 years, the Caligastia 100 and their councils quietly advanced human society as directed. It's no exaggeration to say that without their efforts, humanity would have remained stuck in a far more primitive state for a much longer time.

But as we'll see next, the good work they started was undone in a tragic twist that would send humanity spiraling into darkness for tens of thousands of years. The rebellion was coming, and with it, the dreams of Dalamatia and the noble mission of the Caligastia 100 would be shattered.

When Everything Went Sideways

But then something happened that no one saw coming—not even the angels. About 200,000 years ago, Lucifer, the system sovereign—basically the head guy of our local planetary system—decided he was done with the way things were being run. *The Urantia Book* tells us Lucifer was no slouch. He was one of the brightest and most powerful beings in the local universe, but somewhere along the way, he got a little too impressed with himself (53:1.3). Have you ever meet someone who's so smart the person thinks he or she knows better than everyone else, even when that's not true? Yeah, that was Lucifer.

He started cooking up ideas about self-government, and,

before long, he declared outright rebellion against the universe government. He said, "Why should we answer to the Universal Father? Why should we follow this long, drawn-out ascension plan when we could just take matters into our own hands?" (UB 53:3.2–53:3.7). He even went so far as to say that the Universal Father didn't exist, that this whole thing about a divine plan was just a trick to keep us all in line. That's some bold talk, and it didn't take long for him to gather a following—including Caligastia, our Planetary Prince.

You might be wondering, *Why would Caligastia join this rebellion?* It's not entirely clear, but the guy seemed to think he'd get more freedom to run things his own way. Once he signed on with Lucifer, everything on Urantia started to unravel. The circuits that connected our planet to the universe were cut off (UB 53:7.3), and humanity—already struggling—was suddenly without its spiritual guidance.

Dalamatian Teachings: A Legacy Disrupted

Before the rebellion, the teachings that came from Dalamatia were slowly shaping humanity into something better. But the rebellion threw all that into chaos. The Caligastia 100, those advanced beings who were working directly with humanity, were split down the middle. Some stayed loyal, but others followed Caligastia into rebellion (UB 53:6.2).

The human races, still very primitive, had no idea what was happening in the cosmic sense. All they knew was that their progress slowed, their spiritual development stalled, and the social order that had been so carefully cultivated started to fall apart. That's the thing about rebellion—it doesn't just affect the spiritual realms; it affects everything down here on the ground too.

Dalamatia was destroyed, the teachings were lost, and humanity regressed. That's the cost of rebellion—what had been a slow and steady climb toward civilization turned into a long period of darkness. And let me tell you, it wasn't just dark for a few years or centuries. We're talking about tens of thousands of years where we were stumbling around, trying to make sense of things.

Adam and Eve's Mission

Fast-forward to about 38,000 years ago, and we find ourselves on the brink of another big change. Adam and Eve were sent to Urantia to try to pick up the pieces, to help us recover from the rebellion and get us back on track (UB 51:3.5). They were meant to uplift our biology, to teach us more about the Universal Father, and to help reestablish a sense of divine order on the planet.

But, as you probably know, things didn't go as planned. Eve made a well-meaning but misguided decision to speed up their mission by directly engaging with the local populations—a decision that led to what we now call "the default." In other words, the problem was **not the apple in the tree but a pair on the ground** (UB 75:3.6–8). Adam and Eve's mission was compromised, and although they did their best to make up for it, their work was never fully realized.

Yet, even in the midst of all these setbacks—the rebellion, the default—some still held on to the truth—people like Van, who remained steadfast even as the world around him descended into chaos (UB 67:3.8). Van and his followers kept alive the core of the Dalamatian teachings, and that kernel of truth was what eventually allowed humanity to start making progress again.

What We Can Learn from Dalamatia

What does all of this mean for us today? For starters, it shows us that even when things go wrong, even when the world seems to fall apart, there's always a way forward. The Dalamatian teachings may have been disrupted, but they weren't destroyed. The truth they carried lived on in the hearts of those who stayed loyal, and, eventually, that truth found its way back into the world.

Just like Machiventa Melchizedek came to help Abraham thousands of years later and just like *The Urantia Book* has come to help us today, there's always a revelation waiting to guide us forward when we're ready to receive it. The revelators don't pick favorites; they always are on the lookout to work with those that desire to serve. And no matter how far off course we get, there's always hope that we can find our way back.

As I look around today, I see echoes of that old struggle between light and darkness. But I also see the steady progress we've made. We're still on that long journey toward understanding who we are, where we come from, and where we're going. And as long as we stay open to the truth, as long as we keep moving forward, I have no doubt we're going to get there.

Inch by Inch, Truth by Truth

Just as the Caligastia 100 were quietly laying the foundation of human civilization, so too was humanity, inch by inch,

THE DALAMATIAN TEACHINGS | 147

making its slow but steady way toward the Truth of Reality. I know this because of my own search for that truth, as outlined in the introduction.

Each of the epochal revelations that have come before *The Urantia Book* has been like a stepping stone, guiding humanity forward, one truth at a time. From the Dalamatian teachings that sought to instill basic morality and social order to the teachings of Adam and Eve that aimed to uplift the biological stock and spiritual consciousness of humanity, every revelation has inched us forward.

Melchizedek's revelation, thousands of years later, picked up the thread, reminding humanity of the one true God and preparing the world for the fourth epochal revelation: the life and teachings of Jesus of Nazareth. And now, today, we stand at the precipice of an even greater understanding with the fifth epochal revelation, *The Urantia Book*.

The truths revealed in *The Urantia Book* go beyond anything we've seen before. They don't just touch on the practical or the spiritual—they stretch all the way back to the beginnings of time and space, back to the I AM and the Seven Absolutes of Infinity (UB 105:0.1). Can you imagine that? The Truth of Reality is so vast, so staggering, that it's hard to even wrap your head around it. But that's what this revelation does: it connects us not just to our planet or our little part of the universe, but to the grand, infinite panorama of existence.

This revelation is the culmination of everything that's come before. It's like every piece of the puzzle finally falling into place, showing us the full picture. The Caligastia 100, Adam and Eve, Melchizedek, Jesus—each of them added a piece to the puzzle, bringing us closer to the truth of reality. And now, with *The Urantia Book*, we have a prodigious tome that pulls it all together, expanding our understanding of truth from the dawn of time to the far reaches of eternity.

Endnotes

1. "The Planetary Prince of Urantia," *The Urantia Book* Paper 66, Section 5.

2. In the context of *The Urantia Book*, the term "detach" refers to the temporary separation of a Thought Adjuster (a divine fragment of God) from a human or celestial personality. While the Caligastia 100 were not Adjuster-fused—meaning they had not yet achieved the final and eternal union with their Thought Adjusters—they were nonetheless possessed of Adjusters prior to their mission. These Adjusters were not permanently united with them but served as inner guides, enhancing their spiritual perception and moral discernment. (These were previous humans who had transitioned to the morontia mansion worlds after human death; they retain their Thought Adjusters until fusion or personality annihilation). To participate in the Caligastia 100 mission on Urantia, these volunteers were required to "detach" (or be temporarily detached of) their Adjusters. This means their Adjusters withdrew from active indwelling, leaving them without this divine inner guidance during their mission. This detachment did not negate the fact that they were advanced and spiritually aware beings; rather, it placed them in a state where they were reliant on their inherent wisdom, training, and loyalty to divine principles without the direct influence of an Adjuster. Understanding this distinction is critical, as it highlights how, despite their advanced status, they became vulnerable to the moral and spiritual confusion that followed the Lucifer rebellion.

Chapter 7
The Edenic Teachings—the History of Adam and Eve

Let me tell you, friends, there's a cosmic story hidden in the dusty trails of ancient legends that goes deeper than you might think. It starts with Adam and Eve, but not the ones you've heard about in Sunday School, as discussed. They were a Material Son and Daughter—like cosmic engineers—whose job was to give humanity a much-needed upgrade. They were tall folks, around eight feet high, with a striking violet hue to their skin. Their mission? To improve the human race, help civilization grow, and push humanity toward its spiritual destiny. As it turns out, things didn't go quite according to plan.

The Cosmic Blueprint

First, let's lay out some basics. Adam and Eve were sent here to work on what we call "biologic uplifting." Now, that's just a fancy term for giving humanity a bit of a nudge in the right direction—genetically speaking. *The Urantia Book* tells us that every inhabited planet gets its own Adam and Eve when the time is right, but Earth was a special case. The two were beings of high origin who are physical and even sex-creature-like Urantia mortals. They could see and comprehend the invisible Planetary Prince. In normal circumstances, on those planets that have not experienced rebellion, the A&E pair interpret him to the mortal creatures of the realm, for the Material Sons and Daughters are able to see all of the lower orders of spirit beings; they visualize the Planetary Prince and his entire staff, visible and invisible.

Before Adam and Eve arrived, the planet had been through a bit of a mess, thanks to the aforementioned rebellion. So, when Adam and Eve touched down, they weren't coming into a world ready for progress—they were walking straight into chaos.

When word of Eve's mistake spread throughout the first Garden, it was like lightning striking dry grass. Chaos erupted. Up until that point, things in Eden had been running smoothly, or at least as smoothly as you could expect on a planet that had already seen rebellion and failure. However, Eve's desire to accelerate their mission led her to be deceived by Serapatatia, a Nodite leader, into an ill-advised union with Cano—the most brilliant mind and active leader of the nearby friendly Nodite colony—causing all the careful planning and hopes for an unhurried, peaceful uplift to begin unraveling.

The Garden, which had been a place of beauty and order, quickly became a scene of confusion and fear. The people, who had once revered Adam and Eve, became divided. Some were in outright shock, unable to comprehend how their beloved leaders could falter. Others were scared—fearful that this failure meant the end of Eden itself. Caligastia, the rebellious former Planetary Prince, was more than happy to stir the pot, feeding on the unrest and using it to further undermine Adam and Eve's authority. It wasn't long before the situation in Eden became untenable. Adam, realizing the magnitude of what had happened, knew they could no longer stay. To protect their followers and themselves, they had to leave.

THE EDENIC TEACHINGS—THE HISTORY OF ADAM AND EVE | 151

It wasn't just a matter of packing up and moving down the road, though. The departure from Eden was a heartbreaking moment. They had invested so much in the Garden, and it had been meant to be their home base for generations. But now, in the face of mounting hostility and the risk of violence from confused tribes, there was no choice. Adam and Eve, along with their closest supporters, began a long journey to find a safe haven far to the east, in the fertile lands between the Tigris and Euphrates rivers—what we now call modern-day Iraq.

This area, where they would establish the Second Garden, was much less ideal than Eden. The first Garden had been a paradise, a ready-made sanctuary for their mission. In contrast, the land between the rivers required hard work and a fresh start from the ground up. As they settled in this new location, Adam and Eve were forced to grapple with the full consequences of their actions. The beauty of Eden was now a distant memory, replaced by the need to build homes and plant crops in a land that was far less forgiving. Here, they would lay the foundation for a new chapter, but the world would never be the same.

When Adam and Eve arrived, they quickly realized that their mission wasn't going to be easy. They were supposed to bring about cultural and biological evolution, but the folks on Earth weren't ready. The races were divided, the languages were a jumble, and people's minds were clouded by confusion and rebellion. Adam often remarked to Eve, "I thought this was going to be a quick fix, but it looks like we're in for the long haul."

Let's dive into how Adam and Eve fit into the big, cosmic picture. As members of the Material Sons and Daughters, they're a whole lot more than just a couple who got caught up in eating the wrong fruit.

Who are the Material Sons and Daughters? These beings, taller than most of us and built for durability, were made to act as intermediaries between the divine realms and the evolving worlds. Adam and Eve came in as cosmic "parents" meant to give the human race a boost, but they weren't your typical parents. You see, they stood over eight feet tall and were designed to live for a very long time, all while carrying within them the genetic power to improve the human species.

Material Sons and Daughters are custom built for their missions. They're designed on the system capital worlds like Jerusem, where they live and work until they're called to descend to their respective planets. And here's where it gets fascinating—they always work in pairs. Adam and Eve weren't just thrown together; they were created as a perfect balance of male and female, embodying the best qualities of each. Their connection goes deep—spiritually and biologically—and they work in sync to carry out their cosmic tasks.

These beings don't just spring into existence randomly. Their creation happens under the direction of local universe rulers, with each Material Son and Daughter crafted specifically for their role in the worlds they'll eventually be sent to. They're not only physically powerful but also incredibly intelligent, prepared for ages to tackle the challenges of advancing a planet's evolution.

Elevating humanity was not just about making sure everyone gets taller or stronger (though there was some of that too); it's about evolution. Their very presence was meant to jump-start the slow grind of biological advancement. Think of it like a booster shot for the gene pool. The human races

THE EDENIC TEACHINGS—THE HISTORY OF ADAM AND EVE | 153

on Earth were diverse but stagnant, and Adam and Eve came with the genetic material, or "life plasm," to improve the overall mental and physical capabilities of the species.

They didn't just descend from the sky and get started right away. There's a lot of preparation before a Material Son and Daughter can take up their role. On Jerusem, they worked as directors in experimental laboratories, tweaking and refining living forms. They were experts long before they ever set foot on Urantia. That's how they were so well-prepared to help out here. They knew how to deal with energy, biology, and the complexities of life. Before being chosen for their mission, they had over fifteen thousand years of experience under their belts!

When the time comes for a Material Son and Daughter to descend to an inhabited world, it's a bit of an adventure. First, there's a long process of examination. When Adam and Eve were selected for Earth, they went through rigorous assessments to make sure they were up for the task. Once they were cleared, they packed up, so to speak, and left their family behind in Jerusem. Adam and Eve had a whole bunch of children before leaving Jerusem—fifty sons and fifty daughters, all faithfully serving the universe's needs in other capacities.

When they arrive on a planet, they don't just walk off the spaceship and get to work. In Adam and Eve's case, they arrived via seraphic transport—cosmic transport ships, if you will—accompanied by a full crew from Jerusem to assist in the process. And when they land, they don't exactly look human at first. Their bodies had to be rematerialized in a process that took about ten days. After that, they were ready for their mission. The pair arrived in Eden, where they were welcomed as the planet's new rulers and leaders.

154 | EXPLORING THE URANTIA REVELATION

But here's where things take a turn. They quickly realized that Earth wasn't ready for their grand plan. Rebellion had left the planet in shambles, with the previous Planetary Prince Caligastia having caused all kinds of trouble. Adam and Eve were stepping into a world that was, in many ways, broken. Communication circuits to the universe were down, leaving them isolated. But, as beings of great patience and resolve, Adam and Eve rolled up their sleeves and started on their mission.

Mission Not Just of Body, but of Mind and Spirit

The role of the Material Sons and Daughters isn't just about tweaking genes and planting gardens, though those things are certainly part of the job. Their purpose goes deeper—to inspire spiritual progress and help civilizations rise to a higher level of awareness. Adam and Eve came prepared to teach the people of Earth how to live in harmony, to worship the Universal Father, and to work toward a better, more enlightened future.

But they weren't just teaching in the traditional sense. One of their most important jobs was to model what a civilization could be. In the Garden of Eden, they set up a prototype society, where there was balance between work and leisure, where education was valued, and where the worship of the Father was central to life. They believed in raising up both men and women equally, an idea that was radical for its time. Eve stood by Adam's side as an equal partner in every way, showing the people that progress wasn't just about physical strength but about wisdom, compassion, and spiritual insight.

THE EDENIC TEACHINGS—THE HISTORY OF ADAM AND EVE | 155

Through their influence, Adam and Eve were supposed to spark a new age of civilization. On most planets, the arrival of a Material Son and Daughter signals the beginning of a great scientific and cultural age. In normal circumstances, this is when invention and intellectual progress take off. The human races would have intermarried with the offspring of Adam and Eve, strengthening their genetic stock and boosting their intellectual capacity. However, as we know, things didn't quite go according to plan.

The Challenges They Faced

Besides the previously discussed resistance and challenges related to the rebellion, even within the Garden, some folks just couldn't grasp the mission. Some of them started to worship Adam and Eve, thinking they were gods themselves, not realizing that Adam and Eve were just cosmic helpers here to show them a better way.

But Adam and Eve pressed on. They tried to establish new trade centers, new governments, and a better way of life. They built primitive manufacturing plants, set up trade routes, and did everything they could to bring order to a chaotic world. Yet, as history shows, the road ahead was rocky.

Truth of Reality: Science and Religion Collide

Now, here's where things get really interesting. Adam and Eve's story is cosmic and not just a religious tale. When you look at it from this perspective, Adam wasn't just the first man, as the old stories go. He was the first of a special kind of man, one who carried within him the genetic material to lift humanity to new heights. This is what I call the Truth of Reality. It's a truth that cuts through the divide between science and religion, showing us that both are just different ways of understanding the same cosmic plan. This truth is crucial because it helps us understand why Adam and Eve's mission was so important.

Plan B: Adam's Plasm and the Backup Plan

After some one hundred years, things weren't moving fast enough. The world was still a mess, and the pressures of their mission weighed heavily on them. They decided to take matters into their own hands.

Adam and Eve's Plan B wasn't the ideal solution, but it was necessary. The idea was that Adam's life plasm—his superior genetic material—would be passed on to a select group of women from the surrounding tribes. Adam personally impregnated 1,682 women, and these children, known as the Andites, became the carriers of his genetic legacy. This wasn't just about biology, though—it was about upgrading humanity's mental power. The Andites had sharper minds, quicker reflexes, and a greater capacity for civilization. This was the seed of what would later bloom into the advanced cultures of the ancient world.

Emergence of the Andites

Now, here's the part that's going to make history buffs perk up. The Andites didn't just carry Adam's genes—they carried the seeds of civilization itself. Over the course of twenty thousand years, the Andites spread across the world, mingling with the

THE EDENIC TEACHINGS—THE HISTORY OF ADAM AND EVE | 157

local populations and passing on their superior mental abilities. This wasn't an overnight transformation, mind you. It took millennia, but slowly came the rise of advanced cultures.

The Sumerians, for example, were direct descendants of these Andites. When you look at ancient history, it often seems like civilization just showed up out of nowhere, but that's not the case. The rise of cities, writing, and organized religion wasn't random—it was the result of these Andites, with their upgraded minds, bringing order to the chaos of the ancient world.

But the Andites, in addition to being farmers and builders, were dreamers and thinkers. Their superior intellect allowed them to create the first cities, and their spiritual insight helped them develop some of the first organized religions. The connection between the cosmic mind and spiritual insight is essential to building civilization, and you can see this in the earliest human constructions—like the mysterious Göbekli Tepe.

A Glimpse of the Future

Let's talk about Göbekli Tepe briefly and recall what we discussed in chapter 3. This ancient site, buried beneath the sands of time for millennia, was one of the first hints that something special was happening in the human race. Built around 9,600 BC, long before the Sumerians, Göbekli Tepe is a stunning example of what happens when the cosmic mind starts to blossom. The people's minds had been touched by the cosmic truth that Adam and Eve came to bring. Göbekli Tepe is a reminder that the development of civilization didn't happen overnight, but it also didn't happen by accident. It was part of the grand design, the plan that began with Adam's arrival.

158 | EXPLORING THE URANTIA REVELATION

The Cosmic Mind

The story of Cain and Abel, after Adam and Eve settled in the second garden, runs deeper than sibling rivalry. It's about identity, belonging, and how the choices we make can either bring us closer to or further away from the divine. Cain, as the son of Eve and the Nodite Cano, was different from his younger brother Abel, who was born after Adam and Eve's move to the Second Garden. From the beginning, Cain struggled with feeling like an outsider. He wasn't of pure violet race like his brother, and deep down, he knew it. His bloodline carried the mark of Eve's misstep, and that weighed heavily on him.

As the boys grew, their differences became more pronounced. Cain became a farmer, working the soil, while Abel was a herder, tending to the flocks. In those days, it was customary to offer sacrifices to the priests—Cain would bring the fruits of his labor, and Abel would bring offerings from his flock. But here's where the trouble started. Cain's offerings were less favored than Abel's, and his frustration only grew as he watched his younger brother gain the approval he so desperately sought. Abel, perhaps unknowingly, rubbed salt in the wound, reminding Cain that Adam was his father and Cain was of mixed descent. The resentment simmered until it finally boiled over.

One fateful day, after a heated argument, Cain's anger got the better of him. In a fit of rage, he killed Abel. That shocked Adam and Eve, and it filled Cain with immediate regret. He knew he had done something terrible, and in his grief and fear, Cain sought refuge from the only one he thought might still accept him—his mother. Despite the weight of his actions, Eve embraced her son and urged him to seek divine help. It

THE EDENIC TEACHINGS—THE HISTORY OF ADAM AND EVE | 159

was in this moment of sincere remorse that something miraculous happened. Cain, for the first time in his life, reached out to God with an open heart, genuinely seeking forgiveness and guidance.

And it was then that Cain received a Thought Adjuster. This divine gift, a fragment of God himself, indwells mortals who sincerely seek to align their will with the Father's will. Cain's plea for help wasn't just a cry for relief—it was a sincere decision to change, to seek connection with the divine. That's the key: sincere decisions, even after a life of mistakes, can open the door to cosmic connection. Once Cain made the decision to seek God, his entire inner world began to shift. His life, once marked by resentment and rage, began to be shaped by a new awareness of the Father's presence.

But Cain's journey didn't end there. Fearing retaliation from his fellow men, Cain fled to the land of Nod, the homeland of the Nodites—his father's people. Cain's exile wasn't a punishment, but rather a necessary step in his path toward redemption. He married a woman from the Nodite tribes, and together they began a new lineage. Over time, Cain grew into a leader among the Nodites, promoting peace between his people and the descendants of Adam. In fact, despite his earlier actions, Cain's later years were marked by efforts to bring harmony between the two races, fulfilling, in a way, the hopes Adam and Eve had for unity between the evolutionary peoples and their own descendants.

Cain's story is a powerful example of how our decisions—even in the wake of our worst mistakes—can bring us back into alignment with God's will. When Cain chose to seek divine guidance, the cosmos responded, and he was given the means to start anew. This idea ties into a central truth that runs through the teachings of Adam and Eve: no matter how far one strays, sincere decisions toward goodness, truth, and beauty can realign a person with the Father's will. In the grand scheme of things, it's not about where you come from, or even the mistakes you've made—it's about the sincerity of your choices moving forward.

And that's where my story comes into play. Like Cain, I found myself on a quest for truth, grappling with my own uncertainties and struggles. My sincere search for reality led me to the discovery of *The Urantia Book*, just as Cain's remorse led him to his Thought Adjuster. Both stories remind us that when we earnestly seek truth, the universe responds. There is always a chance for redemption, a path forward that brings us closer to the divine plan, no matter where we've been or what we've done.

Cain's journey to the land of Nod, where he became a peacemaker and leader, mirrors the journey many of us take when we make amends for our past mistakes. It's a reminder that sincerity of heart, even in our darkest moments, has the power to transform not only our own lives but also the world around us. This connection to God's will, this alignment with the cosmic truth, is the very foundation of spiritual progress. Cain's story—and my search—both show us that when we turn toward the light, the universe will guide us toward our highest potential.

My search for the truth of reality is also a mirror of Adam's mission. Just like Adam came to Earth to bring higher knowledge and spiritual insight, I have been on a quest to understand how science and religion intersect. I've been digging through the layers of history, sifting through the sands of time to find the same cosmic truth that Adam and Eve carried with them when they first set foot on Urantia.

THE EDENIC TEACHINGS—THE HISTORY OF ADAM AND EVE | 161

The story of Adam and Eve is more than just a legend—it's a cosmic blueprint for how science and religion can work together to elevate humanity. It's a reminder that we are all part of a bigger plan that stretches across the universe and beyond. And as we continue to explore this intersection, we move closer to the truth of our own place in the cosmos.

Chapter 8
Melchizedek of Salem

Do you ever feel like you're wandering through life, just trying to figure out where you fit in the grand scheme of things? I sure felt that way, and if you're like me, you probably have too. Just like I had my moment when I found *The Urantia Book*, Abraham had his when he encountered Melchizedek. But more on that later.

Way back, long before the Bible stories happened, folks on Earth were spiritually lost. The first two major attempts by celestial beings to bring some order to the planet hadn't panned out. Humanity was smart, learning all sorts of things about survival, but they were losing touch with the big questions—the spiritual ones. You know the ones I'm talking about: Who are we? Why are we here? Who made all this? 93:1.1 (1014.3). The whole idea of God was fading, and the universe couldn't let that happen.

The revelators don't pick people based on status, wealth, or anything else we tend to think is important. They ensure impartiality to every individual, and that's part of the beauty of these revelations.

Imagine individuals in the celestial realms having a council meeting, and one of them, a Melchizedek, says, "I'll go." He volunteers to come down to Earth to remind people about the Universal Father. So, Melchizedek shows up near a little town called Salem, later known as Jerusalem, and starts his mission to bring light back to humanity. 93:1.2 (1014.4)

The first guy Melchizedek meets is Amdon, a shepherd in the fields. Picture it: stars twinkling above, the quiet of the countryside. Melchizedek says to him, "El Elyon, the Most High, made all of this—the stars, the earth, everything—and he's the one and only God." 93:2.3 (1015.3) That was the start of something big, but it wasn't just talk. Melchizedek didn't complicate things with rituals or long prayers. Nope, he kept it simple.

In fact, if you wanted to follow Melchizedek's teachings, you just had to sign your name—or make your mark—on a clay tablet. In doing so, you agreed to three things: You believe in one God, the Most High; you accept that God's favor comes through faith, not sacrifices; and you promise to tell others the good news. 93:4.2 (1017.4) No fancy ceremonies—just bread and wine to celebrate, like a simple picnic. That was it. You were in.

But let me tell you, not everyone could wrap their heads around it. People were used to sacrificing animals and paying priests to get on God's good side. This whole faith thing? It seemed too good to be true. So, Melchizedek, being the wise teacher he was, set up schools. His students became disciples, and they spread his message far and wide. 93:2.4 (1015.4)

Initially, it looked like Terah, Abram's father, was going to be the primary one Melchizedek was going to work through to hopefully salvage the idea of monotheism. Terah was already interested in this new idea of one God, but his sudden death changed things. Melchizedek adjusted. He shifted gears and found Abram, who would go on to be a major figure in spiritual history. That's how it works. You might think someone

164 | EXPLORING THE URANTIA REVELATION

else is better suited, more qualified, or just readier, but the revelators know what they're doing. It's not about who seems most important in the eyes of the world—it's about who is open, who will listen and act.

Now, here comes Abraham—Abram back then—who would become a central figure in this whole story. His father, Terah, was already interested in what Melchizedek was teaching, but when Terah died on the way to Salem, Melchizedek turned his attention to Abram. He sent a message to Abram: "Come to Salem, and I'll teach you about the one true God." Abram, eager to learn, made the journey with his nephew Lot. 93:5.3 (1018.8)

Although Melchizedek first encountered Amdon, it was Abram who ultimately became the central figure in spreading the strongest message of monotheism—one that would resonate far beyond the Hebrews. Initially, Melchizedek focused on establishing schools in Salem, laying a foundation for his teachings on monotheism. It was nearly a decade later that Abram emerged as Melchizedek's primary focus. Meeting Amdon beneath the vast canopy of stars, Melchizedek delivered a simple, direct revelation: "El Elyon, the Most High, is the divine creator of the stars of the firmament and even of this very earth on which we live, and he is also the supreme God of heaven."[1] It was this same message that was taught in his schools and ultimately influenced Abram. No elaborate ceremonies, no complex doctrines—just clear, unadorned truth. The message was perfectly suited to the time and place, just as *The Urantia Book* speaks to the needs of our modern era.

Abram was a natural leader and a strong one at that. He wanted to bring the whole region under the rule of Melchizedek's God. He even started a war, gathering allies,

MELCHIZEDEK OF SALEM | 165

defeating tribes, and expanding his influence. But Melchizedek wasn't too thrilled about Abram's military ambitions. He tried to steer Abram back to spiritual matters. 93:5.12 (1020.1)

And then came a special moment. One night, Melchizedek took Abram outside, pointed up at the stars, and said, "Look at all those stars. Someday, your descendants will be as numerous as them." 93:6.3 (1020.6) This wasn't just a feel-good message. It was a covenant, a promise that God would always be there for Abram's people, as long as they had faith. 93:6.4 (1020.7)

It wasn't all smooth sailing, though. Abram, who had been so fired up about expanding his territory, started to calm down. He had a son, Isaac, and realized that maybe there was more to life than conquest. 93:6.7 (1021.3)

Melchizedek was methodical. He set up a school in Salem to teach the basics of this new faith, and the best students became disciples who spread the message far and wide. 93:2.4 That's exactly what I see happening today. After I committed to the revelation of *The Urantia Book*, I started running into people everywhere who were already studying it, spreading its messages, and trying to live by its truths. More than just casual readers, they were organizing study groups, attending conferences, and dedicating themselves to expanding the gospel of Jesus in a contemporary way.

It's funny how things come full circle. Back then, Melchizedek's students fanned out to teach others about the one true God, and here we are today, in the middle of another epochal revelation, doing the same thing in our own way. Whether it's through study groups, online forums, or international conferences, the effort to spread the truth goes on. People just like me are drawn to the revelation not because

166 | EXPLORING THE URANTIA REVELATION

it's flashy or promises material success, but because it resonates with something deep within us—a thirst for the Truth of Reality.

Abram, after learning from Melchizedek, felt a drive to take that truth to the world around him, sometimes in ways that were a little too forceful for Melchizedek's liking. But Abram's enthusiasm wasn't unlike what I've seen in people today. Meanwhile, Melchizedek's teachings were spreading, even reaching Egypt and faraway places like China and Japan. But it wasn't easy, and not everyone took to the new ideas. Once you get a taste of that truth, once you know there's something real and profound behind the noise of the world, you want to share it. Abram did that, even organizing his people to bring other tribes under the rule of this one God (UB 93:5.9), and today we're doing something similar, though hopefully in a more peaceful way!

Melchizedek knew he couldn't do it alone, and that's why he trained others to carry on his mission. The same is true today. This isn't a one-man show. It's a collective effort, a community of people who've encountered the same truth I did and feel compelled to share it.

Eventually, Melchizedek knew his time on Earth was coming to an end. People were starting to treat him like a god, and that wasn't the point. He didn't want to overshadow the message of the one true God, so one night, he just vanished. (UB 93:8.1) It hit Abraham hard, but the mission had been accomplished. People now knew about the Universal Father, and they were expecting the arrival of a messiah, though it would be a while before that happened. (UB 93:9.1)

And that's the story of Melchizedek, a simple man with a big mission. His teachings were like a bridge between the old ways and what was to come. Just like my experience with the *Urantia Book*, Melchizedek offered a revelation that resonated with the people of his time, pointing them toward the truth of reality.

Endnote

1. *The Urantia Book*, 93:2.3 (1015.3).

Chapter 9
Jesus of Nazareth

Introduction

Let me shout this to the highest treetops: the life and teachings of Jesus, as recorded in part 4 of *The Urantia Book*, run deeper than anything you've heard before. It's the story of the Creator Son, Michael, of the local universe Nebadon, becoming one of us. More than just a religious figure or a moral teacher, Jesus is the very Creator of our local universe, Nebadon, who took on human flesh to show us the personal character of God. His life here on Earth was a mission of love, truth, and the revelation of the Father to a world that had long been lost in confusion and rebellion.

The following four segments briefly summarize the sequential narratives of Michael's final bestowal (bestowal #7) in logical segments. You can read just this abstract, the expanded description following, or a summary on Bob Debold's website.[1] But nothing truly substitutes for an entire reading of the 77 Papers in *The Urantia Book* itself.

1. Paradise Guidance, Social Context, and Jesus's Infancy (Papers 120–122.7)

This segment provides the overarching divine counsel and guidance Michael receives in preparation for his incarnation on Earth. It highlights his choice to experience human life

168

fully as Jesus of Nazareth. The focus is on the prebestowal insights he gathers to manifest God's will through a mortal life, embodying the nature of God while retaining the limitations and growth processes of humanity. This phase involves receiving the guidance to balance divinity with human vulnerability, laying the foundation for his earthly mission to reveal God's personality in a way that humanity can understand and emulate.

The time of Jesus's birth was one of significant social, political, religious, and spiritual tension and transformation. The Roman Empire held political dominance, bringing both the stability of rule and the oppression of many. The Jewish people, living under Roman occupation, maintained their hope for a prophesied Messiah who would deliver them from subjugation and restore their nation's glory. Religiously, Judaism was marked by rigid traditions and priestly hierarchies, leaving the common people with a legalistic and often inaccessible path to spiritual fulfillment. Spiritually, however, humanity was yearning for a deeper connection with the divine, as multiple world religions—from the pagan practices of the Roman pantheon to the philosophical and ethical teachings of Eastern religions—sought to answer profound questions about life, destiny, and God. The time was ripe for a transformative spiritual revelation that could unify and uplift humanity, setting the stage for Jesus to embody and reveal God's will and personality to a searching world.

Leading up to this unprecedented bestowal, announcements and preparatory events were set in motion on both a celestial and earthly level. The vast administrative bodies of the local universe, from Paradise to the constellation headquarters, prepared for this one-of-a-kind event. Various orders

170 | EXPLORING THE URANTIA REVELATION

of celestial beings were mobilized to support and witness this bestowal mission. The angelic hosts were briefed, and spiritual agencies were aligned to assist in implementing the divine plan. Even on Earth, prophecies and expectations in certain traditions hinted at the coming of a world savior, resonating with the universe-wide anticipation of Michael's incarnation. This cosmic coordination and alignment emphasized the magnitude of Jesus's bestowal as a pivotal moment for all beings within the local universe, one that would forever change the spiritual trajectory of humanity and reveal God's character in a profound and personal way.

2. Mortal Beginnings (Papers 122.8–134.8)

"Mortal Beginnings" covers Jesus's birth, the early years of soul growth, and his development into adulthood. This period includes key formative experiences that cultivate his personal connection with his inner Thought Adjuster.

In the earliest phase of Jesus's life, from birth to his first recognition of an inner divine presence, the circumstances surrounding his entry into the world were both humble and profound. Born into a modest family in Nazareth, Jesus brought hope and wonder to his parents, while his lineage and arrival fulfilled long-standing prophecies cherished by the Jewish people. This phase is characterized by his initial exposure to the social, cultural, and religious environment that would shape his earthly experience. His early interactions with his family and the community introduced him to the realities of human life, grounding him in the experiences that would later enable him to fully empathize with the common struggles of humanity. These years laid the foundation for his character, instilling in him a deep respect for human dignity, personal responsibility, and the profound value of family and community life.

As Jesus grew from childhood into adolescence, his spiritual and intellectual journey evolved into a profound period of soul growth. During these formative years, he began to question, explore, and internalize the nature of God, morality, and his own place within the world. These years marked his first conscious awareness of an inner divine presence, which subtly guided his decisions and fostered his burgeoning understanding of spiritual truths. He developed a remarkable sense of empathy and insight, engaging with people from all walks of life and exploring various beliefs and philosophies. This growth process led Jesus to refine his understanding of righteousness, kindness, and justice, laying a solid spiritual foundation and building a character aligned with divine values that would later become central to his teachings. This phase was essential for developing the empathy and wisdom that defined his later ministry.

The third period in Jesus's early life focused on his preparation, mastery, and commitment to service as he reached adulthood. Having deeply explored the intricacies of human experience, Jesus undertook various responsibilities, including work and study, which further prepared him for his life's mission. He became a master of his own mind, body, and emotions, achieving a remarkable level of self-discipline, understanding, and spiritual maturity. Through his daily interactions and work, he learned the art of humility and service, fully embracing his role in the lives of those around him. This stage of his life solidified his connection with both the divine and human aspects of his identity, marking a transition

172 | EXPLORING THE URANTIA REVELATION

from self-discovery to purposeful action. His life became a living testament to service and love, paving the way for the ministry that would follow and exemplifying the divine pattern of selfless dedication to others.

These stages underscore Jesus's assimilation into the human experience while gradually preparing for the public phase of his mission, all while keeping his higher purpose hidden.

3. Public Work (Papers 134.9–187)

This phase involves Jesus's active ministry, where he manifests God's will through teachings, healings, and interactions with the people of his time.

The transition into Jesus's public work began with his baptism, a pivotal moment that signaled the start of his open mission to reveal God to humanity. This event, held at the Jordan River, marked his formal acceptance of his divine mission and affirmed his unity with God. Witnessed by John the Baptist and others, his baptism symbolized a personal commitment to the work ahead and demonstrated to those around him the sacred purpose of his life. This profound moment also served as a spiritual awakening for many, who sensed the presence of divinity in Jesus. His baptism bridged his years of preparation with his public mission, setting him on a course that would change the lives of countless individuals and establish him as a spiritual leader in a society yearning for truth and guidance.

Following his baptism, Jesus gathered a group of twelve apostles, each selected to help carry out and eventually continue his mission. The training of the twelve was intensive; Jesus imparted core principles of love, faith, humility, and service. These men came from diverse backgrounds, reflecting the universal scope of Jesus's message. Through parables, teachings, and personal mentorship, he guided them in understanding the nature of God and the reality of the spiritual kingdom. Jesus emphasized the importance of spreading the gospel of love and spiritual brotherhood, preparing his apostles to serve as bearers of his message after his departure. This phase was essential for establishing a foundation of discipleship, rooted in a profound understanding of God's love and purpose.

In the early stages of his public work, Jesus reached out to communities across the region, sharing his teachings and performing acts of compassion that showcased the nature of God's love. Through healing, comforting, and inspiring the people, he attracted both followers and skeptics. Jesus's teachings on the kingdom of God and the Fatherhood of God resonated deeply with those searching for spiritual truth, while his compassionate acts demonstrated his commitment to addressing human suffering. This period marked a time of growing influence, as individuals from all walks of life began to see him not only as a teacher but as a genuine embodiment of divine love and understanding. His early public work laid the foundation for a ministry that would expand and transform hearts and minds.

As Jesus's ministry progressed, he faced significant opposition and challenges that tested his resolve and commitment to his mission. Known as the crisis period, this phase was marked by confrontations with religious authorities and growing tensions among those resistant to his teachings. Despite the pressures, Jesus remained steadfast, using each challenge as an opportunity to deepen his message of love, forgiveness, and faith. *The transfiguration*, a spiritually momentous event during this period, reaffirmed his divine mission and provided

174 | EXPLORING THE URANTIA REVELATION

his closest apostles with an undeniable witness to his connection with God. This powerful experience bolstered the faith of his followers and symbolized the fusion of his human and divine natures, preparing him for the ultimate sacrifices ahead.

In the course of what the midwayers (celestial beings who narrated Jesus's life in *The Urantia Book*) call his Third Preaching Tour, Jesus not only proclaimed a revolutionary spiritual message but also broke new ground in the realm of social transformation. In Paper 150 of *The Urantia Book*, the establishment of the Women's Evangelistic Corps is presented as a pivotal moment in his ministry—a deliberate move to redress deep-seated cultural inequities. Here, Jesus set apart ten dedicated women for gospel teaching and ministry. Their commission was nothing short of transformative: "The charge which Jesus gave these ten women as he set them apart for gospel teaching and ministry was the emancipation proclamation which set free all women and for all time; no more was man to look upon woman as his spiritual inferior."[2]

This statement encapsulates the heart of the initiative. By empowering these women, Jesus not only advanced his mission of salvation but also declared that spiritual leadership is not confined by gender. This act was both an immediate call to action and a timeless mandate, inviting all believers to embrace a vision of equality and mutual respect. It was a forward-thinking proclamation that paved the way for a more inclusive ministry—one that continues to inspire the pursuit of social justice and spiritual liberation.

In the later stages of his ministry, Jesus intensified his teachings, focusing on preparing his followers for the coming changes and sharing his final messages of love and unity. His later ministry included some of his most profound teachings, where he delved into themes of forgiveness, the nature of true worship, and the promise of eternal life. His final teachings, delivered in intimate settings and larger gatherings, were designed to inspire his followers to live according to divine principles, regardless of his physical presence. This period was marked by a sense of urgency and depth, as Jesus sought to leave a lasting impact that would guide his followers through his impending departure. His later ministry solidified the spiritual foundation of his teachings, ensuring that his message would continue to resonate and guide humanity long after his time on Earth.

This segment reveals Jesus as the Son of Man, bridging divine insight with human experience, seeking to guide humanity into a deeper understanding of God.

4. Postmortal Events (Papers 188–195)

This final segment in the midwayers' narration of the life and teachings of Jesus addresses the culmination of Jesus's bestowal mission through his betrayal, death, resurrection, and postresurrection appearances.

In the final days of his earthly life, Jesus faced betrayal and death with profound courage and forgiveness. Despite knowing the suffering he would endure, he remained steadfast in his commitment to embody God's love and mercy. The betrayal by one of his closest followers and the subsequent events leading to his crucifixion revealed the extent of his compassion, as he forgave those who condemned him. His death on the cross became a symbol of ultimate sacrifice and selfless love, demonstrating to his followers and to future generations the depth of divine forgiveness. Jesus's response to betrayal and his

176 | EXPLORING THE URANTIA REVELATION

willingness to face death with grace reflected his unwavering dedication to the revelation of God's loving character, leaving an indelible impact on the hearts and minds of his followers.

The resurrection of Jesus marked a victorious affirmation of life beyond death, offering humanity a glimpse into the eternal nature of the soul. Rising from the tomb, he demonstrated the reality of spiritual triumph over physical demise, fulfilling his promise of life after death. This event not only comforted his grieving followers but also transformed their understanding of God's power and the promise of immortality. The resurrection became a foundational pillar of Jesus's message, solidifying the belief that the soul persists beyond mortal life and energizing his followers' mission to share his teachings.

Following his resurrection, Jesus appeared to his followers in a morontia form, bridging the physical and spiritual realms in ways they could comprehend. His morontia appearances provided a unique opportunity for his followers to experience his continued presence and guidance, affirming their faith and preparing them for his final departure. These encounters deepened their understanding of spiritual realities and reinforced the teachings he had shared throughout his ministry. By engaging with his followers in this new form, Jesus offered them an enduring connection to the divine, nurturing their spiritual growth and equipping them to carry forward his message of love, service, and eternal life.

In the period following Jesus's ascension, his followers were gifted with the Spirit of Truth, which would continue to guide, inspire, and strengthen them in his absence. This divine presence was an enduring reminder of Jesus's teachings and a source of wisdom and courage for his apostles and disciples. The Spirit of Truth became a unifying force among his followers, empowering them to spread his message of love and brotherhood to all humanity. Jesus's final departure and the subsequent arrival of the Spirit marked the beginning of a new era in his followers' lives, ensuring that his mission would endure and expand beyond his earthly life, touching lives across generations and cultures. This postmortal phase established the foundation for a spiritual calling rooted in the love and wisdom he had shared.

The postmortal events encapsulate the fulfillment of Michael's mission to reveal God's nature fully, providing a pathway for humanity to comprehend the divine personality and aspire to spiritual union with God.

Each segment demonstrates how Michael's mission through Jesus embodied the will and personality of God, offering humanity a direct and personal understanding of divine love, wisdom, and eternal life.

Expanded Narration of Part 4

The following narration expands significantly upon the aforesaid summary accounts of the four logical breakdowns of Jesus's life as depicted by the midwayer commission in part 4 of *The Urantia Book*.

Paradise Guidance, Social Context, and Spiritual Preparation (Papers 120–122.7)

Let's dig into the richly woven fabric of the "Paradise Guidance" section, where the journey of Michael—who would become Jesus of Nazareth—begins long before he ever walked the dusty roads of Palestine. The journey is the cosmic tale of a

178 | EXPLORING THE URANTIA REVELATION

Creator Son's purpose, a divine mission that echoes across the universe and ultimately finds its way to a humble birth in a stable in Bethlehem.

A Creator Son Takes Human Form

In the vastness of the universe, Michael, a Creator Son, was already a being of replete power and authority, having shaped and ruled over his own local universe, Nebadon. Yet there was something essential to the full understanding and experience of divine love and sovereignty that required Michael to walk among his own creation as one of them. For reasons even the revelators admit to not fully understanding, it was necessary for a Creator Son to become part of the world he shaped. By doing so, Michael would bring his universe into a more complete unity with Paradise—the spiritual center of all creation—and reveal God's personality in a way that would touch the hearts of beings everywhere.

So, Michael embarks on a journey that's both extraordinary and, in its final chapter, incredibly intimate. His goal to reveal God's nature and love through a mortal life involved limitations, temptations, and struggles like those of any human being. He chose Earth as the setting for his ultimate bestowal mission, a world particularly troubled by rebellion and spiritual confusion. But to carry out this mission, he was afforded guidance.

Immanuel's Counsel: Wisdom from Paradise

Enter Immanuel, Michael's Paradise brother and counselor, who lays out the road map for this earthly mission with remarkable clarity and insight. Immanuel's guidance is specific and deeply thoughtful, given the complexity of taking on a finite form and living among creatures who often misunderstand and fear what they cannot see. Immanuel counsels Michael on the necessity of self-limitation. Michael must refrain from using his divine powers, focusing instead on revealing God's love and character through his actions, teachings, and interactions. This mission is about manifesting God's personality rather than displaying divine might.

Immanuel clarifies that Michael's bestowal will require him to experience life with the vulnerability and limitations of a human. No calling upon cosmic knowledge, no summoning angels at will. Instead, he's to grow up learning and discovering things step by step, from toddler to adult. This means facing challenges, doubts, and difficulties—not to mention the misunderstandings and opposition he would encounter from those around him.

Michael's mission is also framed within the context of love. It's a mission limited by the human experience of love and growth, bound to the ways of a family, community, and culture. As Immanuel points out, it's Michael's personal connection to the people he meets and his embrace of their condition that will most clearly reveal God's love and bring light to a world shadowed by confusion and doubt.

But Michael's mission was also about setting things right. The rebellion was unadjudicated on Urantia. As noted, the rebellion threw the system of Satania (of which Earth is a part) into chaos, and much of the suffering and confusion we experience in this world can be traced back to that rebellion.

As Michael, Jesus could have easily terminated Lucifer's rebellion by his own authority as the Creator Son of the local

180 | EXPLORING THE URANTIA REVELATION

universe of Nebadon. Immanuel reminded him that part of his mission on Earth was to *technically terminate* the Lucifer rebellion. Jesus was tasked with ending this cosmic rebellion through faith and submission to the Father's will, showing that even in weakness, great power comes from aligning with divine purpose.

This approach was a game changer. It showed that the way to overcome evil and rebellion isn't through force or domination but through love, faith, and the alignment of one's will with God's will. And through his life as Jesus, Michael achieved exactly what he set out to do. He ended the rebellion not with his Creator prerogatives, but by steadfast dedication through love and faithfulness to the Father.

The World Jesus Was Born Into

By the time Jesus entered the world, society was at a pivotal point. In the ancient Levant and the Roman Empire, religious and spiritual currents were strong, but they weren't always pure or beneficial. On one hand, the Jewish people clung to a messianic hope, fervently awaiting a deliverer who would restore Israel's sovereignty and bring them closer to God. Yet, despite their deep spiritual heritage, their religious leaders often became entangled in legalism, emphasizing ritual over faith and making God seem distant and difficult to reach. Still, the Jewish people held on to an intense monotheism and a moral code rooted in centuries-old teachings, providing fertile ground for new spiritual insights.

Beyond Judaism, Roman philosophy and religion had its influence, shaping the culture Jesus was born into. The secular mindset in Rome promoted a focus on the material and practical, emphasizing power, prosperity, and earthly achievement. Roman gods were more archetypal figures representing virtues and vices than true spiritual guides, leaving many Romans yearning for a more profound understanding of existence. As a result, mystery religions, cults, and philosophical schools emerged, attempting to answer deeper questions about life, death, and the divine. From stoicism, which taught resilience and rationality, to the worship of Eastern gods, there was a broad, eclectic search for meaning that left many unsatisfied, primed for a message of love, hope, and eternal life.

Sources and Religious Context

The midwayer revelators mention that in crafting the narrative of Jesus's life, they relied on existing written records, which included not only the Hebrew scriptures but also historical accounts and philosophical texts of the time. These records helped frame the context of Jesus's mission in a way that would resonate with readers familiar with historical figures and prevailing thoughts of the era. Using these resources allowed the revelators to accurately depict the sociopolitical and spiritual landscape into which Jesus was born, adding authenticity and accessibility to his story.

The midwayers provide fascinating insights into the sources and limitations of the canonical gospels, offering an understanding of the narratives and motives behind each account. This information adds depth to how we read the gospels and enhances our appreciation for the careful work done to preserve Jesus's story amid the limitations and contexts of early Christianity.

The world Jesus was born into wasn't only shaped by

182 | EXPLORING THE URANTIA REVELATION

politics, religion, and culture but also by the remarkable individuals who would be closest to him, especially his parents, Joseph and Mary, and his cousin John the Baptist. Each of them brought unique qualities and strengths that helped prepare and support Jesus in his life and mission.

Joseph: Man of Faith, Simplicity, and Strength

Joseph, Jesus's father, was a humble yet deeply spiritual man who combined quiet strength with a profound devotion to God. A skilled carpenter by trade, Joseph wasn't wealthy, nor was he someone who sought out positions of authority. But he had a reputation in Nazareth for being honest, kind, and generous. Joseph approached life with a practical wisdom that came from years of hard work, yet he held a deep-seated belief in God's presence and purpose. His faith wasn't ostentatious or legalistic but grounded in a genuine desire to follow God's will in his daily life. This steadfastness would become a strong influence on young Jesus, who would observe in his father the embodiment of humility, responsibility, and spiritual integrity.

Joseph's character was essential in shaping Jesus's early sense of identity. Although Joseph was initially surprised and even uncertain about Mary's miraculous pregnancy, he accepted it with the conviction that he was part of a divine plan. His support of Mary and his acceptance of his role in Jesus's life demonstrated a remarkable level of trust in God. Joseph would go on to teach Jesus the value of honest work, humility, and the importance of serving one's community, all of which played a role in preparing Jesus for his later life of service. As a father, Joseph provided a stabilizing, nurturing

JESUS OF NAZARETH | 183

presence in Jesus's formative years, modeling an earthly reflection of the divine patience and love that Jesus would later reveal to the world.

Mary: Heart Full of Love and Deep Spiritual Insight

Mary, Jesus's mother, was known in Nazareth for her purity of heart, gentle spirit, and unwavering faith. She came from a long line of devout believers and was well versed in the Hebrew Scriptures. While still young when she received the announcement from the Bright and Morning Star, chief executive of Nebadon, Gabriel of Salvington, Mary's wisdom and maturity far surpassed her years. The biblical account records that when Gabriel appeared to her with the message that she would give birth to a son who would be called the "Son of the Most High," she responded with humility and grace, saying, "Let it be to me according to your word."[3] The midwayer account cleans up the fact that Gabriel merely told Mary that her son would be a "child of destiny." Her acceptance of this unique role wasn't out of blind obedience but rather a deep, spiritual understanding that her life was part of a larger purpose. Mary's spiritual insight and loving nature were instrumental in guiding Jesus through his early years, helping him grow in wisdom, compassion, and self-understanding.

The Truth of Reality, the revelators suggest, is always relative to an individual's cosmic knowledge and maturity within the bounds of what is acceptable in his or her era. As emphasized in *The Urantia Book*, "Divine truth is a spirit-discerned and living reality. Truth exists only on high spiritual levels of the realization of divinity and the consciousness of communion with God. You can know the truth, and you can live the truth; you can experience the growth of truth in the soul and enjoy the liberty of its enlightenment in the mind, but you cannot imprison truth in formulas, codes, creeds, or intellectual patterns of human conduct."[4] This understanding reveals that truth is dynamic and experiential, transcending static formulations or intellectual systems.

The difference between the biblical and *Urantia Book* accounts of Mary's encounter with Gabriel highlights this dynamic nature of truth. Whereas the biblical narrative emphasizes her humility and grace in accepting her role as the mother of Jesus, *The Urantia Book* provides a cosmic context, clarifying that Gabriel described Jesus as a "child of destiny." Yet, these differing accounts do not conflict, for the truth remains the same—Mary's spiritual insight and her acceptance of this role arose from a living realization that her life was part of a larger purpose. In this way, both narratives work together to portray truth as a living, spirit-discerned reality that grows with one's soul experience.

Throughout Jesus's life, Mary remained a pillar of support, navigating the challenges and mysteries of raising a child marked by such a profound mission. She showed him tenderness, wisdom, and an unbreakable bond of motherly love, even when she didn't fully understand the divine nature of his calling. Her relationship with Jesus was filled with moments of quiet devotion and shared wonder at God's unfolding plan. As Jesus grew, Mary continually fostered his connection with God, teaching him prayers, sharing stories from the scriptures, and providing a safe and nurturing environment for his spiritual and emotional development. Mary's love and devotion would be a source of comfort and strength for Jesus, grounding him in the human experiences of family and faith.

John the Baptist: Cousin Destined to Prepare the Way

Jesus's cousin, John the Baptist, played a uniquely complementary role in the unfolding of Jesus's mission. While the midwayers describe Jesus as bringing the light of divine love, John was the herald, preparing the way and calling people to repentance. John's mother, Elizabeth, was also visited by Gabriel, who revealed to her that her son would have a special role in preparing people's hearts for the arrival of the Messiah. More than a comforting assurance, the message was a directive that Elizabeth and her husband, Zechariah, took to heart. They knew their son's life would be marked by a fervent spiritual mission, turning the hearts of many toward God in anticipation of the One who would follow.

As John grew, his parents instilled in him a strong sense of purpose and devotion. He was raised with the knowledge that his life would be dedicated to preparing people for Jesus's teachings. John's upbringing was more austere and marked by a fiery zeal, setting him apart from others and shaping him into the formidable preacher he would later become. His message wasn't gentle; it was a call to action, a summons to repentance, and an invitation to turn toward a higher path. John's distinctive voice, boldness, and unswerving conviction would shake the religious establishment and attract followers from all over, laying the groundwork for Jesus to later bring them the message of God's love and the spiritual kingdom.

In John and Jesus, we see two parts of a divinely orchestrated plan: one, a bold and impassioned prophet calling for repentance, and the other, a teacher of love, mercy, and spiritual rebirth. Their paths would converge later in life, each fulfilling their part in the revelation of God's purpose, setting

EXPLORING THE URANTIA REVELATION

the stage for a movement that would transform lives across generations.

Matthew's Gospel: Jewish Emphasis and Fulfillment of Prophecy

The Gospel of Matthew is described as having been written with a distinctly Jewish audience in mind, with its author keen on framing Jesus as the long-awaited Messiah fulfilling Jewish prophecy. This gospel frequently references the Old Testament to underscore that Jesus's life and mission are in alignment with Jewish messianic expectations. For Matthew, proving Jesus's legitimacy to a Jewish audience meant linking his actions and teachings to the Hebrew scriptures. As a result, Matthew's gospel emphasizes Jesus's lineage, his fulfillment of specific prophecies, and his role as a new Moses or Davidic king, leading readers to see Jesus as the culmination of Jewish religious hopes. However, the midwayers point out that this focus sometimes limits the gospel's universality, as it tends to filter Jesus's teachings through the lens of Jewish tradition rather than the broader, inclusive nature of his message.

Mark's Gospel: Simplest and Earliest Account

Mark's gospel, the midwayers explain, is the earliest and likely the most straightforward account, often regarded as a primary source that other gospel writers drew upon. Mark's narrative is vivid and action-oriented, portraying Jesus as a man of powerful deeds and compassion. Written for a broader, primarily Gentile audience, Mark's account focuses on the immediacy and humanity of Jesus's mission, presenting him as a servant of God and healer who moves swiftly through his ministry. The midwayers indicate that Mark's gospel lacks some of the theological embellishments present in later writings, offering a raw and heartfelt portrayal of Jesus's life and challenges. Its simplicity makes it highly accessible, though it omits certain details that other gospels later expanded upon, such as the detailed teachings and events surrounding Jesus's birth and early life.

Luke's Gospel: Gentile Perspective with Historical Richness

Luke, writing with a more educated and Hellenistic audience in mind, crafted a gospel that emphasizes Jesus's compassion, inclusivity, and universal message. The midwayers note Luke's dedication to historical detail, as he interviewed numerous eyewitnesses and investigated various sources to compile his account. Luke's gospel presents Jesus as a friend to all—including Gentiles, women, and marginalized individuals—reflecting Luke's broader worldview. By emphasizing parables, acts of kindness, and interactions with society's outcasts, Luke paints Jesus as a compassionate figure whose mission extended beyond Jewish boundaries. The midwayers acknowledge Luke's gospel as more polished and historically conscious, aiming to build a cohesive and harmonious narrative while highlighting Jesus's humanity and deep empathy for diverse people.

John's Gospel: Spiritual and Theological Portrait

The Gospel of John is distinct from the synoptics (Matthew, Mark, and Luke), offering a deeply theological portrayal of

Jesus as the incarnate Word of God. John's gospel emphasizes Jesus's divinity and the spiritual implications of his life, often using symbolic language and profound theological statements. The midwayers note that John, having had the advantage of reflecting on Jesus's life over many decades, provides a mystical and philosophical view that resonates with a more mature spiritual audience. John's focus is less on chronology and more on conveying the essence of Jesus's spiritual identity and his relationship with God, especially emphasizing the theme of light and life. However, John's gospel can be challenging to those unfamiliar with its symbolic depth and philosophical language, as it requires the reader to approach Jesus's teachings as profound spiritual revelations rather than simple historical events.

Limitations and Inspiration of Gospel Accounts

The midwayers acknowledge that each gospel has its limitations and reflects the perspectives and motivations of its authors. In their time, written records were not as precise as today, with oral traditions forming the backbone of religious storytelling. As a result, the authors faced the challenge of conveying profound spiritual truths through stories shaped by cultural biases, memory gaps, and differing theological aims. The midwayers highlight that these early Christian writers were inspired, though not infallible, in their efforts. They sought to faithfully capture Jesus's message, but they did so in ways they believed would be compelling and relevant to their respective audiences. In this way, each gospel provides a unique glimpse of Jesus's life and teachings, contributing to a fuller, if imperfect, understanding of his mission.

In recognizing these diverse perspectives, the midwayers compiled their own account to present a cohesive, clarified portrait of Jesus, free from the theological and cultural filters applied by the gospel writers. This doesn't undermine the gospels but rather honors the efforts of early Christian authors, providing readers with an enriched appreciation of the complexities involved in preserving the story of Jesus. The midwayers' account aims to offer a more universal perspective, illuminating aspects of Jesus's life that transcend any one culture, era, or theological interpretation, while respecting the deep love and dedication that drove the early gospel authors to preserve his story in the first place.

Principals in Jesus's Life

From his birth, the people closest to Jesus were chosen for their unique roles in supporting and shaping his earthly experience. His parents, Joseph and Mary, were carefully selected for their faith, humility, and openness to divine guidance. Joseph, though a humble carpenter, held a deep respect for God's ways and was well-equipped to provide Jesus with a grounding in Jewish traditions. Mary, known for her spiritual insight and steadfast love, would become a nurturing force, guiding Jesus in his early years with wisdom and gentleness.

The apostles who would later join Jesus as his closest followers came from a variety of backgrounds, each bringing unique perspectives and skills. Some, like Peter, James, and John, would become pillars of the early Christian movement, deeply internalizing Jesus's message and spreading it far and wide. Their selection was no accident; these men were chosen

190 | EXPLORING THE URANTIA REVELATION

for qualities that would make them effective bearers of Jesus's teachings, despite their imperfections. They had hearts open to truth and minds willing to be challenged, embodying the diversity and dynamism that would characterize the early faith community.

Even those who opposed Jesus, from Pharisees to Roman authorities, played vital roles in his life, presenting the challenges and conflicts that would sharpen and reveal the clarity of his mission. Figures like Pontius Pilate and Herod each had their roles in the unfolding story, contributing to the dramatic climax of Jesus's life and underscoring the contrast between worldly power and spiritual truth.

Through this cosmic yet intimately personal journey, Michael's bestowal as Jesus becomes a story not only of God's love but also of divine patience, humility, and empathy. It's a journey that mirrors humanity's own struggles for understanding, growth, and love, offering insights as relevant today as they were two millennia ago. Jesus, born into a complex world of cultural, religious, and political forces, showed through his life that God's love transcends every boundary, binding all people in a family united by faith and service to one another.

Mortal Beginnings (Papers 122.8–134.8)

Truth About Wise Men and Herod's Interest in Jesus

The story of the wise men who visited Jesus shortly after his birth is one of those cherished narratives that spark mystery and wonder. However, the midwayers clarify that these men weren't kings but wise individuals, Chaldean priests from Mesopotamia. They tell us,

> These wise men saw no star to guide them to Bethlehem. The beautiful legend of the star of Bethlehem originated in this way: Jesus was born August 21 at noon, 7 BC. On May 29, 7 BC, there occurred an extraordinary conjunction of Jupiter and Saturn in the constellation of Pisces. And it is a remarkable astronomic fact that similar conjunctions occurred on September 29 and December 5 of the same year. Upon the basis of these extraordinary but wholly natural events the well-meaning zealots of the succeeding generation constructed the appealing legend of the star of Bethlehem and the adoring Magi led thereby to the manger, where they beheld and worshiped the newborn babe. Oriental and near-Oriental minds delight in fairy stories, and they are continually spinning such beautiful myths about the lives of their religious leaders and political heroes. In the absence of printing, when most human knowledge was passed by word of mouth from one generation to another, it was very easy for myths to become traditions and for traditions eventually to become accepted as facts.[5]

When they arrived in Jerusalem and sought information about a rumored child-king, it triggered a wave of interest and suspicion, particularly in Herod. This is where things get interesting. Herod, as ruler of Judea, was wary of threats to his throne, and the news of a prophesied leader deeply troubled him. Given that Jesus was indeed the firstborn in his family,

192 | EXPLORING THE URANTIA REVELATION

this detail could have added weight to Herod's concerns. Herod summoned the wise men, and upon learning of the timing and significance of their sighting, he feigned interest in worshipping the child himself. In reality, he wanted to locate Jesus to eliminate him as a potential threat. Yet, the wise men were truly wise not to return to Herod, and they departed another way, leaving Herod's schemes thwarted. Mary and Joseph, warned of the danger, fled to Egypt, taking Jesus to safety. Herod's search ultimately turned fruitless.

Growing Up in Nazareth: A Rich Social and Cultural Environment

After returning from Egypt, Jesus's family settled in Nazareth, a bustling village where different cultures and influences converged. This small town provided Jesus with a unique exposure to varied social and cultural influences. Nazareth, positioned near trade routes, often saw traders, travelers, and settlers from different regions, bringing with them a mix of languages, beliefs, and customs. This environment was instrumental in expanding Jesus's understanding of humanity and giving him a taste of the diversity that he would later address in his teachings.

Within his own family, Jesus found love, discipline, and a grounding in Jewish traditions. His parents instilled in him respect for the scriptures, family values, and a strong work ethic. Joseph involved Jesus in his carpentry work as soon as he was old enough, teaching him patience, craftsmanship, and the dignity of labor. Through these early years, Jesus began to understand the simple joys and struggles of the people around him, which would later enable him to connect with people from all walks of life.

Soul Growth and the Arrival of Jesus's Thought Adjuster

As Jesus grew from a child into adolescence, his spiritual journey deepened. Like any other normal human, he received the arrival of his Thought Adjuster (indwelling spirit), that divine fragment of God that guides individuals toward their spiritual destiny. This moment marked a significant point in Jesus's growth. The arrival of the Adjuster signaled the beginning of a deeper spiritual awakening, a subtle but profound awareness that would shape his developing sense of mission. The Adjuster's presence fostered in Jesus a heightened intuition and an inner guidance system that, while typical in all humans, played a special role in the life of someone destined for such a unique mission.

In his soul growth, Jesus wasn't exempt from the normal struggles and questions of adolescence. He, too, experienced moments of doubt, curiosity, and wonder about the world around him. His growing understanding of God, combined with the gentle promptings of the Adjuster, allowed him to develop a strong moral compass, aligning his inner convictions with divine love and purpose. By embracing these spiritual insights, Jesus's soul became finely attuned to the needs of others, deepening his empathy and compassion—qualities that would become central to his later teachings.

Temple Visit at Age Thirteen: Young Jesus in the Spotlight

When Jesus turned thirteen, he reached an age of maturity in Jewish tradition, and his family took him to Jerusalem for the Passover, marking his coming of age. After the festival, Mary and Joseph joined the caravan back to Nazareth, assuming

194 | EXPLORING THE URANTIA REVELATION

Jesus was somewhere in the group of friends and family. But as they went along, they realized they hadn't seen him all day. Panicked, they retraced their steps and headed back to Jerusalem, searching high and low for their son.

Three days later, they finally found him, not lost or frightened but calmly sitting among the teachers in the temple. He was right there, seated with the rabbis, holding his own in conversation, asking questions, and offering insights that left these learned men scratching their heads in amazement. Here was a young boy, barely a teenager, whose knowledge and wisdom went far beyond his years. When his parents anxiously asked why he'd stayed behind, Jesus, with an innocent curiosity, replied, "Did you not know that I must be in my Father's house?" He was aware, even at this young age, of a connection with God that ran deep, though he wasn't quite ready to reveal the full depth of that relationship.

This episode is one of the few detailed glimpses we get of Jesus's early life in the Bible. At Luke 2:41–52, the story of Jesus being found in the temple by his parents is one of the few stories from Jesus's youth that offers a glimpse into his spiritual awareness and engagement with Jewish religious teachings. There is a gap in the biblical narrative from this story until the beginning of Jesus's public ministry. Luke notes generally that Jesus "grew in wisdom and stature, and in favor with God and man" (Luke 2:52), summarizing his growth without detailing specific events. This verse implies a period of normal growth and development but does not provide further anecdotes from his youth or young adulthood. The Bible then resumes the narrative with Jesus's baptism by John and the start of his public ministry around the age of thirty. It shows us a young boy already tuned in to a calling that went beyond his earthly family—a calling to live out a love and wisdom that would one day reshape the lives of people around the world.

But *The Urantia Book* does not leave us with a few glimpses and a gap in the story of Jesus's early life. Instead, it offers a profoundly detailed and humanizing narrative of his childhood, adolescence, and young adulthood—years filled with the joys, struggles, and learning experiences that define every human journey. We see Jesus not just as a divine figure but as a young boy who helps his family, learns a trade, navigates friendships, and experiences loss. We watch as he wrestles with profound questions of faith, justice, and purpose, developing insights that will one day form the foundation of his world-changing ministry. Yet even in the midst of this relatable human journey, we are reminded of an astonishing truth: this young boy from Nazareth is also the Creator Son, the architect of an entire local universe destined to contain ten million inhabited worlds. His growth is not just a human story—it is the unfolding of divine love and wisdom in human form, a model of spiritual development accessible to all of us.

The "Two Crucial Years" of Soul-Searching

Fast-forward to Jesus's fourteenth and fifteenth years, a period often called the "two crucial years" because they were filled with soul-searching and self-discovery. During this time, Jesus began realizing the full weight of his life's purpose and making some big decisions about his future. He lost his father, Joseph, during this time and suddenly found himself the head of the family, responsible for his mother, Mary, and his seven younger siblings: James, Miriam, Joseph, Simon, Martha,

196 | EXPLORING THE URANTIA REVELATION

Jude, and Ruth. It was a lot for a young man to take on, but he embraced these responsibilities, stepping into the role of provider and guide.

This experience grounded him. Supporting his family, managing a household, and working as a carpenter gave him a deep empathy for the struggles of everyday people. He learned about the hard choices, the worries, and the little triumphs that come with family life. In these years, Jesus was learning not just about God but also about people, which would later become one of the hallmarks of his ministry.

Young Man with a Calling — And a Heart That Stood Strong

Life wasn't all work for young Jesus. In his late teens, he continued to study and observe, building a deep well of knowledge about God and people. He had the respect of folks around Nazareth who saw him as wise beyond his years. But he was also becoming more aware of the limitations and narrowness in many of the religious teachings of the time. He felt a powerful desire to reveal a different kind of understanding of God based on love and mercy rather than rules and rituals. He didn't announce this to everyone but held these thoughts close to his heart, waiting for the right time to share this vision of a spiritual kingdom built on those qualities.

During these adolescent years, Jesus faced an emotional test in the form of a young woman named Rebecca. She was drawn to Jesus, not only for his gentle nature and wisdom but also for the way he made her feel deeply seen and understood. Rebecca's admiration grew, and she began dreaming of a future with him. But Jesus knew that his mission required complete dedication, and there were certain rules he couldn't break. One of these was the mandate from Sonarington[6]—a bestowal Son, like Jesus, couldn't leave human offspring behind. This was part of the "incarnation mandates." So, with a heavy heart, Jesus gently let Rebecca know that his path would be different, choosing devotion to his spiritual calling over the bond of romance. This episode was a defining moment, as it underscored his commitment to his divine mission and the love he would offer the world.

Alongside His Brothers and Sisters

Being the oldest sibling, Jesus was a father figure to his seven younger siblings (with one to be yet born—Ruth): James, the responsible one who looked up to Jesus; Miriam, the tender-hearted sister; Joseph, who took on his father's name and later stepped into the family business; Simon, energetic and sometimes impulsive; Martha, gentle and patient; Jude, unstable in temperament; and Amos, still an infant.[7] Each sibling had their unique qualities, and Jesus made it his business to know them well and guide them in ways that best suited their individual needs. He wasn't just a brother; he was their mentor, protector, and friend.

These years were a period of quiet yet profound growth for Jesus. He lived a seemingly ordinary life, but through every responsibility he took on, every family meal, every moment of teaching and learning, he was becoming the person who would one day touch countless lives. The years between thirteen and twenty shaped him in ways that prepared him to connect with people from all walks of life. He learned humility, patience, resilience, and the priceless value of family, all of which would serve him well in his future as a teacher and healer. By the time he was ready to step into the public eye, Jesus had grown not only in wisdom but in heart, deeply attuned to the needs, hopes, and struggles of the people he would come to serve.

Years Twenty-One to Twenty-Six: Laying the Groundwork

Between the ages of twenty-one and twenty-six, Jesus lived in and around Nazareth, gaining deep insight into the lives of those around him and taking on responsibilities within his family. Following his father Joseph's death, Jesus shouldered the responsibility of supporting his mother and siblings, becoming not just the head of the household but also a stabilizing force for his family. He continued his work as a carpenter, providing for his family and leading a quiet, diligent life. During this period, he grew increasingly aware of his unique mission, but he held back from prematurely revealing it, instead focusing on fully understanding human relationships and struggles.

One key episode from this period is often referred to as the "Damascus episode." Jesus was invited to travel to Damascus to work as an interpreter and assistant to a wealthy merchant. This opportunity provided him with invaluable experience outside of his familiar community and introduced him to the broader cultural and philosophical ideas of the world. In Damascus, he encountered a wide variety of people and views, enriching his understanding of humanity's diverse spiritual, intellectual, and cultural landscapes. This experience confirmed his calling to reach out not only to his own people but to all humanity, a realization that would become central to his later teachings.

Jesus's Twenty-Seventh Year

By his twenty-seventh year, Jesus had developed a profound spiritual understanding and inner stability, balancing his growing awareness of his divine mission with a genuine empathy for humanity. This year was marked by a sense of patience and restraint, as Jesus knew he would ultimately reveal himself but felt the importance of timing. His soul continued to mature as he remained rooted in his responsibilities, balancing his inner life with his outward duties. Through his interactions with community members, he honed his skills of understanding and helping others, becoming a quiet yet powerful presence in Nazareth.

Jesus's Twenty-Eighth Year: A Year of Preparation and Spiritual Insight

In his twenty-eighth year, Jesus's sense of purpose became more crystallized, as he readyied himself for the mission ahead. He often withdrew to meditate and pray, seeking alignment with God's will and preparing mentally, emotionally, and spiritually. His wisdom was evident to those around him, yet he maintained a humility that made him accessible to all. He grappled with the significance of his future mission and the immense responsibility it carried. His relationships with others continued to grow richer, as he genuinely engaged with people from all walks of life, becoming a source of comfort, wisdom, and understanding in his community.

Jesus's Twenty-Ninth Year: The Mediterranean Tour and the Roman Experience

In his twenty-ninth year, Jesus embarked on an extensive tour of the Mediterranean, traveling with an Indian merchant, Gonod, and his son, Ganid. This journey was monumental for Jesus, as it exposed him to a wide array of cultures, philosophies, and religions, each bringing fresh insights and expanding his perspective. His travels took him to Egypt, Greece, and Asia Minor, where he interacted with philosophers, spiritual leaders, and everyday people from diverse backgrounds. These experiences provided him with a rich tapestry of human experiences and further solidified his understanding of humanity's hopes, struggles, and spiritual aspirations.

Rome, however, held a special place in this journey, as it was the epicenter of cultural, intellectual, and political life. In Rome, Jesus immersed himself in the city's intellectual circles, observing and learning from its philosophers, teachers, and religious leaders. He spent time in public forums and meeting places, engaging with people from all walks of life, from slaves to scholars. Though he didn't reveal his true identity or mission, he became a quiet but profound influence on those he encountered, imparting wisdom and offering insights that touched the lives of many.

One of the unique aspects of Jesus's time in Rome was his relationship with Ganid, Gonod's young son. Ganid was deeply inquisitive, often asking Jesus questions about life, morality, and spirituality. Jesus took this opportunity to teach Ganid about God's love and compassion and about the concept of a spiritual kingdom that transcends earthly boundaries. His relationship with Ganid became one of mentorship and friendship, and he planted seeds of spiritual understanding that would shape Ganid's worldview long after their journey ended.

In addition to his discussions with Ganid, Jesus offered practical guidance to people he met across the city. In one instance, he counseled a young Roman senator struggling with the ethical challenges of political life. In another, he comforted a slave who felt trapped and devalued, teaching him that, despite his physical bondage, his soul remained free and loved by God. These moments of connection were profound for those who encountered him, as Jesus quietly sowed seeds of compassion, understanding, and spiritual insight that would have a ripple effect in their lives.

Jesus's Earthly and Cosmic Teachings

During his travels, Jesus shared profound insights on a variety of earthly and cosmic topics, engaging listeners with teachings that expanded their perspectives. In his Discourse on Jonah,[8] for example, Jesus used the story of Jonah as a springboard to discuss the difference between the literal and symbolic interpretations of religious texts. He explained that the true message of Jonah's story lay not in the miraculous survival inside a fish but in the profound call to spiritual awakening, repentance, and God's enduring mercy. By reframing traditional tales, Jesus encouraged his listeners to seek the deeper moral and spiritual truths rather than getting caught up in literal interpretations.

In the Discourse on Reality, Jesus tackled the nature of existence itself, addressing questions about what is truly real and enduring versus what is temporary and illusionary. He emphasized that although earthly life is meaningful, it is part of a larger, eternal framework where spiritual values transcend material realities. Jesus taught that love, truth, and beauty were the foundation of true reality and that aligning oneself with these values was the path to experiencing a fuller and more connected life. He pointed out that even though human perceptions might be limited, individuals could still connect with this higher reality through faith, love, and service.

The Discourse on Time and Space was particularly illuminating, as Jesus explained these concepts in ways that merged spiritual insight with human understanding. He described time as a sequential journey for mortals, a process through which they experience growth, change, and progression. Space, in Jesus's teachings, was portrayed as part of a vast cosmic theater where countless worlds and beings exist, all interconnected within God's plan. Jesus encouraged his listeners to look beyond the limitations of their immediate physical reality and to recognize their place within a grand, unfolding cosmic adventure, in which time was a gift for growth and learning and space a canvas for discovery.

Lessons on Inner Readjustment: The Encounter with Fortune

Jesus's encounter with a Roman named Fortune offered a powerful lesson on inner transformation and spiritual rebirth. Fortune was a troubled man, weighed down by dissatisfaction and feelings of futility. Jesus, in his compassionate way, explained that the key to peace and fulfillment lies not in changing external circumstances but in readjusting life within oneself. He taught Fortune that by seeking alignment with his own inner values and purpose, he would find that the universe itself seemed to align with him.

This passage explains this so well, it deserves special emphasis:

Jesus learned much about men while in Rome, but the most valuable of all the manifold experiences of his six months' sojourn in that city was his contact with, and influence upon, the religious leaders of the empire's capital. Before the end of the first week in Rome Jesus had sought out, and had made the *acquaintance of, the worth-while leaders of the Cynics, the Stoics, and the mystery cults, in particular the Mithraic group. Whether or not it was apparent to Jesus that the Jews were going to reject his mission, he most certainly foresaw that his messengers were presently coming to Rome to proclaim the kingdom of heaven; and he therefore set about, in the most amazing manner, to prepare the way for the better and more certain reception of their message. He selected five of the leading Stoics, eleven of the Cynics, and sixteen of the mystery-cult leaders and spent much of his spare time for almost six months in intimate association with these religious teachers. And this was his method of instruction: Never once did he attack their errors or even mention the flaws in their teachings. In each case he would select the truth in what they taught and then proceed so to embellish and illuminate this truth in their minds that in a very short time this enhancement of the truth effectively crowded out the associated error; and thus were these Jesus-taught men and women prepared for the subsequent recognition of additional and similar*

truths in the teachings of the early Christian missionar-
ies. It was this early acceptance of the teachings of the
gospel preachers which gave that powerful impetus to
the rapid spread of Christianity in Rome and from there
throughout the empire. 132:0.4 (1455.4)

Jesus explained that this inner transformation is like a rebirth that realigns an individual's perception with a broader, spiritual perspective. "When readjusted to life within yourself," Jesus said, "you become likewise readjusted to the universe." This concept of being "born of the spirit" was foundational to Jesus's teachings, emphasizing that once one makes this internal shift, life becomes an expression of "victorious accomplishment." Fortune's encounter with Jesus marked a turning point for him, which left him with a newfound sense of hope and purpose.

Jesus's Time in Rome: Engaging Religious Leaders and Philosophers

While in Rome, Jesus engaged with people from many different backgrounds, including religious leaders, philosophers, and thinkers. One of the most notable groups Jesus encountered were the Cynics, a philosophical school that valued simplicity and virtue while rejecting societal norms and materialism. The Cynics were intrigued by Jesus, whose lifestyle and teachings resonated with some of their core values. However, Jesus's approach differed from that of the Cynics in one crucial way: he emphasized a compassionate, service-oriented life rather than merely a renunciation of material comforts.

With the Cynics, Jesus shared insights on the importance

of self-discipline and authenticity but also encouraged them to channel their ascetic lifestyle toward the service of others. He acknowledged their rejection of societal conventions and pointed out that true freedom wasn't about rejecting society but about finding meaning and purpose within it. Jesus challenged them to live not only for personal virtue but also for the betterment of humanity, encouraging them to see their lives as opportunities to inspire others and serve as examples of love and kindness.

Jesus also engaged with leaders from various other philosophical and religious sects, including the Stoics and followers of Mithraism, each bringing a unique viewpoint. In all his encounters, Jesus displayed a deep understanding of their beliefs and values, using their perspectives as a basis for expanding on spiritual truths. His time in Rome allowed him to plant seeds of new understanding across these diverse groups, subtly influencing the spiritual landscape in ways that would echo for generations. His respectful, insightful approach won him admirers and allies among many of these thinkers, setting the stage for the spread of his teachings in the Roman world.

Jesus's Mediterranean journey, particularly his time in Rome, was a culmination of years of growth, preparation, and insight. By the time he returned home, he was ready to begin the next phase of his mission. His soul had matured fully, enriched by the countless lives he had touched and the diverse perspectives he had encountered. Jesus returned from this journey with a complete understanding of the world he was about to serve, prepared to reveal the love and wisdom of God to humanity.

Responsibilities, Work, and Study

As he matured, Jesus took on increasing responsibilities, both within his family and in the broader community. After his father's passing, Jesus became the primary breadwinner for his family, taking over Joseph's carpentry business and shouldering the responsibility of caring for his younger siblings. Through hard work and commitment, he learned to balance personal ambition with the needs of those around him. This experience fostered humility, resilience, and self-discipline, helping him develop the qualities necessary for a leader.

Jesus didn't limit his education to carpentry; he was an eager student of human nature drawn to the interactions and stories of the people he met. He engaged in discussions with travelers, religious teachers, and community members, absorbing diverse perspectives. His interests spanned beyond Judaism, as he became familiar with Greek and Roman thought, as well as the ideas of other religious sects and philosophies. This openness gave him a nuanced understanding of various worldviews, enriching his teachings with a universal appeal that transcended religious and cultural boundaries.

From Self-Discovery to Purposeful Action

As Jesus transitioned from adolescence into young adulthood, his sense of mission became more defined. He understood that his life held a purpose beyond his own desires or ambitions, yet he didn't rush this awareness. Instead, he approached it with patience, choosing to grow into his mission rather than forcing it. This period was marked by thoughtful reflection and a growing commitment to service. He wasn't seeking followers or fame; rather, he was motivated by a genuine desire to help others and share the love and wisdom he was cultivating within himself.

This journey from self-discovery to purposeful action is a profound part of Jesus's story, illustrating the gradual unfolding of his divine mission. As he became more attuned to the world's suffering and people's search for meaning, his compassion grew deeper, and his desire to serve became stronger. By the time he was ready to embark on his public ministry, he had developed a rich and full understanding of human life, prepared to speak to the heart of each person he encountered.

In these early years, Jesus laid the groundwork for a ministry that would change the world, all while living an ordinary life in an ordinary village. Through the experiences, struggles, and quiet victories of his "mortal beginnings," he was becoming the man who would later reveal God's love to humanity in a way that was deeply personal, accessible, and universal.

A Great Decision

Here's something you may not have considered. Jesus could have ended his mission much sooner than he did. When he was baptized in the Jordan River and the Father spoke to him from Paradise, Jesus had completed the perfection of his communication with his Thought Adjuster.. At that moment, the Father let Jesus know that he could end his mission right there. He had achieved everything required of him in terms of perfecting his relationship with the Father.

Let's unpack that for a moment because it has both individual and civilizational impacts. Just how did Jesus perfect his relationship with the Father?

208 | EXPLORING THE URANTIA REVELATION

Jesus's perfection of communication with his Thought Adjuster and his communion with the Father were the result of a gradual, deliberate process rooted in spiritual practice. The revelation teaches that Jesus's journey required conscious alignment of his human will with divine guidance, achieved through regular periods of active reflective thinking, or worshipful meditation. Jesus had to consciously align his human consciousness with the divine guidance of his Adjuster. It was a cooperative effort, where his material mind consistently assented to the spiritualizing influence of the Adjuster. The midwayers refer to this effort as "compared to the act of tuning in the soul to catch the universe broadcasts of the infinite spirit of the Universal Father."[9] Over time, Jesus achieved complete harmony between his human will and the divine will, which resulted from persistent dedication to understanding and carrying out the Father's will.

We find that Jesus's approach to worship integrated the intellectual, morontial, spiritual, and personal dimensions of reality portrayed in *The Urantia Book*, demonstrating how these aspects converge to foster a dynamic relationship with the Father. Jesus exemplified the process of worship as described in *The Urantia Book* at 5:3.8 (66.4), where worship is portrayed as the "material mind's assent to the Adjuster's attempt to communicate with the Father." By embracing his role as a "faith son," Jesus fully trusted in the Father's guidance and goodness, the essence of divine sonship. Here's the passage in full:

> *The worship experience consists in the sublime attempt of the betrothed Adjuster to communicate to the divine Father the inexpressible longings and the unutterable aspirations of*

the human soul—the conjoint creation of the God-seeking mortal mind and the God-revealing immortal Adjuster. Worship is, therefore, the act of the material mind's assenting to the attempt of its spiritualizing self, under the guidance of the associated spirit, to communicate with God as a faith son of the Universal Father. The mortal mind consents to worship; the immortal soul craves and initiates worship; the divine Adjuster presence conducts such worship in behalf of the mortal mind and the evolving immortal soul. True worship, in the last analysis, becomes an experience realized on four cosmic levels: the intellectual, the morontial, the spiritual, and the personal—the consciousness of mind, soul, and spirit, and their unification in personality.

This intentional practice aligns closely with the framework of not only the worship experience but also true worship as described in the passage. Jesus's actions demonstrated how the material mind, under the guidance of the Adjuster, facilitates deeper spiritual connection and *communion* with God. His faith and trust in the Father—and concomitantly ours—is central to this process, illustrating how intellectual assent, emotional longing, and spiritual aspiration unite to achieve true worship. These insights reveal that Jesus's perfected communication with the Adjuster was not instantaneous but a deliberate journey of aligning his mind, soul, and spirit in harmony with the Father's will, ultimately serving as the supreme example of faith sonship and divine communion.

Although we may not achieve perfection of communication, our consenting to worship consistently builds upon our growth; I believe it progresses exponentially as we make this a consistent habit. I concur with what the late Peter Holley said, that this is truly "Jesus-style meditation."[10] It captures the essence of this practice. Unlike contemporary understandings of meditation, which often emphasize detachment or mindfulness, Jesus's approach was deeply relational and intentional. It involved actively engaging his mind, soul, and spirit in dialogue with the Adjuster and the Father. Through this process, Jesus not only sought divine insight but also harmonized his human experience with spiritual purpose. This Jesus-style meditation was not merely an exercise in self-awareness but also a dynamic act of worship. It exemplifies the description in *The Urantia Book* that true worship involves the material mind assenting to the Adjuster's spiritualizing influence to communicate with God as a faith son of the Universal Father.

True worship, as described in *The Urantia Book*, has the potential to profoundly impact both individual spiritual growth and the collective progress of civilization, especially as societies confront significant challenges. While often seen as a personal act, worship's influence can ripple outward to shape broader social dynamics in transformative ways. At its core, true worship fosters alignment with higher spiritual values such as truth, beauty, and goodness. Individuals who engage in sincere worship naturally reflect these values in their actions, and when they come together, their shared spiritual alignment can inspire collective ethical frameworks that prioritize altruism, justice, and compassion. This elevation of values can lead societies to address global challenges like poverty, inequality, and environmental degradation through cooperative, value-driven approaches.

Worship also transcends cultural, racial, and ideological barriers by focusing on the universal sonship under the Universal Father, fostering unity amid diversity. Such a unifying force could help civilizations move beyond divisiveness, encouraging collaboration in addressing crises like pandemics or climate change. Furthermore, true worship shapes leaders who are grounded in humility, vision, and purpose aligned with divine will. Such spiritually refined leaders could guide society with wisdom and prioritize long-term progress and planetary well-being over personal gain. Worship also enhances inner resilience by anchoring individuals in faith and divine purpose, and when this resilience is collective, it equips communities to face existential threats with hope and solidarity.

When all is said and done, true worship is an experience that inspires the pursuit of truth and expands creativity, fueling breakthroughs in science, philosophy, and the arts. A worshipful society may channel these creative energies toward solving humanity's greatest challenges, such as developing sustainable technologies or exploring space, harmonizing material progress with spiritual advancement, all with an ethical-moral substrate conditioning innovation. Over time, true worship lays the foundation for a civilization that balances spiritual, material, and intellectual development, creating a harmonious, equitable, and sustainable culture. This redefinition of progress—focused on human potential, planetary stewardship, and spiritual enlightenment—positions worship as a transformative force capable of addressing the complexities of modern civilization while guiding it toward a more enlightened future.

Six More Great Decisions

Jesus apparently had unfinished business. He made six great decisions to stay on Earth and continue his mission, even though he could have returned to his position in the universe.

212 | EXPLORING THE URANTIA REVELATION

Why? Because he wanted to finish what he had started. He wanted to reveal the Father's character fully and to experience every aspect of human life, including death. It wasn't enough for Jesus to live a perfect life; he wanted to face everything that humanity faces, right down to the final moments of mortal existence.

During Jesus's forty days of seclusion after his baptism, he faced six monumental decisions that would shape the course of his life and his mission on Earth; they involved how he would carry out his public ministry and the larger spiritual implications for the universe he created. Each decision reflected his unwavering commitment to doing the will of the Father, and through them, he revealed profound truths about the nature of power, faith, and divine purpose.

These decisions should be understood in the context that before baptism Jesus was a Son of Man and lived his life as if in the presence of God by living faith. After baptism he now had the *power* to conduct himself as the Son of Man or the Son of God.

The First Great Decision: Power and Divine Intervention
The first decision Jesus faced was whether to use his vast powers as the Creator Son to aid in his earthly mission. While in the wilderness, Jesus was confronted with the reality that he had at his disposal legions of celestial beings and superhuman assistance. The entire universe of Nebadon was at his command, ready to help him in any way he desired. But Jesus knew that using such power would not align with the Father's will. He realized that his mission was not to demonstrate divine might, but to show how, through faith and submission to God, one could accomplish great things even in human form.

So, Jesus made the decision to set aside the help of these celestial beings, except in cases where the Father willed it. This was a significant choice because it meant that throughout his ministry, he would live and work as an ordinary man. He chose to live as one of us, to face the trials of life as we do, without calling on divine powers to make things easier. This decision set the tone for his entire ministry—one of humility, faith, and complete trust in the Father's will.

The Second Great Decision: Self-Preservation and Miraculous Provision

The second decision Jesus faced was about self-preservation and the use of his powers to meet his own needs. After several days in the wilderness, Jesus began to feel the pangs of hunger. He knew that he had the power to turn stones into bread, to provide for his own physical needs through miraculous means. But again, he chose to submit to the Father's will. Rather than using his divine powers to satisfy his hunger, Jesus chose to rely on the natural processes of the body and the environment to meet his needs.

This decision dealt with the principle of self-preservation. Jesus decided that throughout his ministry, he would not use his powers to protect or provide for himself. This decision demonstrated Jesus's deep commitment to living a life of faith and reliance on God, rather than using his divine powers for personal gain.

The Third Great Decision: Protection from Harm

The third decision Jesus faced was about his personal safety. As he wandered through the wilderness, he encountered situations where he could have called on divine protection to shield himself from harm. For example, he could have thrown himself off a cliff and relied on angels to catch him, demonstrating his divine status and protecting himself from injury. But Jesus knew that such actions would not be in line with the Father's will.

He decided that he would not use his divine powers to protect himself from harm. Instead, he would rely on the natural laws of the universe and take reasonable precautions to ensure his safety. That demonstrated his commitment to living in accordance with the Father's will, even when it meant facing potential harm.

The Fourth Great Decision: Performing Miracles for Popularity

The fourth decision Jesus faced was about whether to use his powers to perform miracles to gain popularity and attract followers. The Jews of his time were expecting a Messiah who would perform great miracles and wonders, demonstrating his divine authority through supernatural acts. Jesus certainly had the power to do this—he could have performed dazzling miracles that would have drawn crowds and won him immediate recognition as the Messiah.

But Jesus knew that performing miracles for the sake of popularity would not fulfill the Father's will. He decided that he would not use his powers to win followers through spectacle. Instead, he would focus on teaching people about the kingdom of heaven and leading them to the Father through faith, not through signs and wonders. This decision demonstrated Jesus's commitment to the spiritual nature of his mission and his refusal to use divine powers for selfish or superficial reasons.

The Fifth Great Decision: Establishing the Kingdom Through Force

The fifth decision Jesus faced was about how he would establish the kingdom of God on Earth. Many of his followers expected him to lead a political revolution, overthrowing Roman rule and establishing a new kingdom of Israel. Jesus could have easily done this—he had the power to rally the people and lead them to victory. But he knew that this was not the Father's will.

Instead of using force to establish the kingdom, Jesus chose to build it in the hearts of men and women. He knew that the true kingdom of God was not a political entity, but a spiritual reality. His decision to reject the use of force and violence to achieve his goals was a profound demonstration of his commitment to love, peace, and the higher spiritual values of the Father's kingdom.

The Sixth Great Decision: Complete Submission to the Father's Will

The sixth and final decision Jesus made during his time in the wilderness was a complete and total commitment to the Father's will. After considering all the challenges he would face during his ministry, Jesus pledged to remain completely obedient to the Father in all things. He knew that his path would be difficult, that he would face rejection, suffering, and ultimately death. But he chose to walk that path willingly, trusting that the Father's will was the best and only way.

In making this final decision, Jesus demonstrated the ultimate act of faith and submission. He committed to living his life as a man, facing the trials and tribulations of mortal existence, and relying on the Father's guidance every step of the

216 | EXPLORING THE URANTIA REVELATION

way. This decision was the culmination of all the others, as it represented Jesus's complete alignment with the will of God.

These six great decisions shaped the rest of Jesus's life and ministry. They reflected his unwavering commitment to living as a man among men, without relying on his divine powers to make his path easier. Through these decisions, Jesus showed us what it means to live a life of faith, humility, and complete submission to the will of the Father. And in doing so, he revealed the true nature of God as a loving, caring Father who desires a personal relationship with each of his children.

They were moments of profound choice, where Jesus consciously decided to continue his journey as the Son of Man, even though the Son of God could have returned to glory at any time. Jesus's commitment to completing his mission, even in the face of suffering and death, showed his deep love for humanity and his desire to reveal the fullness of God's character.

Jesus's Public Ministry (Papers 134:9–181)

It's downright astonishing to realize that by the time Jesus had reached the point where the Father expressed his overwhelming satisfaction with him, he hadn't even chosen his apostles or begun what the New Testament refers to as his "public ministry." By this point, Jesus had spent his life quietly preparing, growing in wisdom, and aligning himself perfectly with the Father's will. His baptism marked the potential end of his purely human life, and at that moment, the Father publicly expressed his approval, proclaiming, "This is my beloved Son in whom I am well pleased." And yet, what's mind-blowing is that the events we think of as central to Jesus's life—his teachings, miracles, and the selection of the apostles—hadn't even started yet!

This approval from the Father was based on the perfection of Jesus's relationship with his Thought Adjuster and his unbroken communion with God, not on public achievements. It shows us that the Father's pleasure is not in outward success but in the alignment of the heart and mind with His will. At this point, Jesus had lived as a man among men, facing all the challenges and struggles that come with human life, and yet he had done so in perfect harmony with the Father's plan. The Father's satisfaction with Jesus, even before the beginning of his public ministry, is a testament to the personal nature of God. It tells us that what matters most is the internal relationship between the soul and God, not external accomplishments.

A particularly salient theme throughout the *Urantia Papers* is the idea that "Christianity exhibits a history of having originated out of the unintended transformation of the religion *of* Jesus into a religion *about* Jesus."[11] After Pentecost, when the Apostles went out to preach the gospel, the path of least resistance—with the Gentiles for sure, and even others like accepting Jews and Gnostics—was to preach *about* Jesus and forgo the main tagline Jesus constantly preached *of* the gospel combining the Fatherhood of God with the brotherhood of man. In fact, "Nathaniel [a disciple of Jesus] differed increasingly with Peter regarding preaching *about* Jesus in the place of proclaiming the former gospel *of* the kingdom" (emphasis added). 193:6.4 (2058.3).

About Jesus or Of Jesus

Upon consideration, the reason why the message *about* Jesus crowded out the gospel *of* Jesus is obvious: hero worship! Let me get a little technical and evangelistic here. First, one has to understand the spiritual depth of the Lucifer rebellion. Although Urantian humans were totally unaware (maybe that's not exactly true, since the Bible does mention Lucifer) of the spiritual war going on, the outcome from the loss of our spiritual helpers was significant. *The Urantia Book* is the only source Urantian humanity has that tells us of not only what is in Lucifer's manifesto but also the outcome for us earthlings of Caligastia casting his lot with his rebellion.

Two significant thinkers have discussed this at length but with differing views. Joseph Campbell, in *The Hero with a Thousand Faces* (1949), explores the hero's journey as a universal motif across myths, which continues to influence modern culture's conception of heroes. Although Campbell does not explicitly discuss hero worship's societal impact, he rates the importance of heroic figures for inspiring individual transformation. Sigmund Freud, on the other hand, in *Group Psychology and the Analysis of the Ego* (1921), discusses how individuals project their desires and ideals onto leaders, often leading to idolization. Different from Campbell, Freud is critical of this, suggesting that this idolization can hinder personal development by creating dependencies and reducing personal autonomy.

My perspective, regarding the outcomes of the rebellion as depicted in *The Urantia Book*, aligns with Freud. Contemporary researchers in psychology and sociology also examine celebrity and hero worship, often questioning its effects on self-identity, self-worth, and societal values. For example, studies in parasocial relationships find that idolization can offer psychological benefits (for example, motivation or a sense of belonging) but also risks promoting unrealistic ideals and hindering personal agency.

A fair number of our great thinkers on this idea, like Campbell and Freud, portray the concept of hero worship as a global phenomenon. According to many if not most who examine this aspect of humanness, this worldwide psychological mechanism has been around since at least the Sumerians. The revelation informs us it has been around much, much longer.

The point I am making here (if you haven't figured it out so far) is that the success of the early church fathers, like Paul, was to take advantage of this drive, which had been embedded since the rebellion. Abner[12] took the high road and failed. The other point I want to make is that this book, my approach to Jesus's public ministry, does not fall into that trap. So far, we have attempted to balance the narrative about Michael's bestowal as Jesus with information *about* his beginnings along with his spiritual growth *of* living in the presence of his Father. *The Urantia Book* midwayer account in part 4 of *The Urantia Book* does spend a fair amount of time on Jesus's progressive growth in learning about his creation. We can't avoid that. So, now we'll spend the bulk of our discussion on Jesus's public ministry and how the true Jesus gospel is expanded exponentially from the Bible.

Quantifying Some Differences

The portrayal of Jesus's public ministry in *The Urantia Book* offers a remarkably comprehensive narrative, far exceeding the brevity of the Gospel of Mark. Mark's sixteen concise chapters provide a fast-paced, action-packed account *about* Jesus's life, highlighting key events like his baptism, miracles, parables, and ultimate journey to Jerusalem, culminating in the Passion. *The Urantia Book*, on the other hand, dedicates nearly six hundred pages across fifty papers to Jesus's public life, presenting a detailed, day-by-day chronicle that often expands on or introduces aspects *of* his epochal teaching ministry.

The expanded coverage in *The Urantia Book*, with detailed dialogues and extended lessons, captures the philosophical and spiritual nuances of Jesus's ideas. It also provides rich backstories, delving into the personalities, motivations, and reactions of those Jesus encountered, bringing a fuller, more relatable dimension to the narrative.

Beyond simply elaborating on the events described in the New Testament, *The Urantia Book* introduces additional miracles, encounters, and counsel. For instance, it includes numerous healing stories that aren't found in the Bible, illustrating Jesus's profound compassion and the lasting impacts of these healings on those who experienced them. Furthermore, the book adds unique parables and teachings that reflect Jesus's style but explore a broader range of themes, offering a cosmic and philosophical perspective on his earthly mission.

A particularly rich feature of *The Urantia Book* is its portrayal of Jesus's relationships. It vividly describes his personal connections, including intimate conversations with his apostles, mentorship of women followers, and meaningful interactions with marginalized individuals. Women like Rebecca, Susanna, and Mary of Magdala are presented as active participants in his ministry, adding an inclusive dimension often absent in traditional gospel accounts.

The Urantia Book also addresses the so-called missing years of Jesus's life, offering insights into his travels, philosophical discussions, and encounters with religious leaders across the Mediterranean. This fills gaps in the New Testament narrative, providing a continuous story that connects his youth, preministry years, and eventual public mission.

Finally, the resurrection appearances, briefly described in the New Testament, are given greater detail in *The Urantia Book*. These encounters are presented with profound emotional depth, illustrating their impact on those who witnessed them and expanding on the spiritual significance of the resurrection.

Overall, *The Urantia Book* weaves an intricate tapestry of Jesus's life, offering a deeply layered and enriched portrayal that complements and transcends the traditional gospel accounts. It provides not just a record of events but a profound exploration of his teachings, relationships, and the cosmic implications of his mission.

Overlaps and Enhanced Context

Although *The Urantia Book* recounts many of the same events found in Mark, such as the baptism, calling of the apostles, the feeding of the five thousand, the Sermon on the Mount, and the Transfiguration, it provides significantly expanded context. For example, *The Urantia Book* often describes the settings, explains the reactions of Jesus's audience, and delves into Jesus's inner thoughts and motivations. It offers explanations of misunderstandings, opposition, and the dynamics among religious leaders, disciples, and ordinary people.

What follows are three notable examples where the midwayers present an immersive view, showing the unity between Jesus's message, personality, and divine purpose. First, though, this is what is meant by the "living Jesus":

Christianity is seriously confronted with the doom embodied in one of its own slogans: "A house divided against itself cannot stand." The non-Christian world will hardly capitulate to a sect-divided Christendom. **The living Jesus** *is the only hope of a possible unification of Christianity. The true church—the Jesus brotherhood—is invisible, spiritual, and . . . characterized by unity, not necessarily by uniformity. Uniformity is the earmark of the physical world of mechanistic nature. Spiritual unity is the fruit of faith union with the living Jesus. The visible church should refuse longer to handicap the progress of the invisible and spiritual brotherhood of the kingdom of God. And this brotherhood is destined to become a living organism in contrast to an institutionalized social organization. It may well utilize such social organizations, but it must not be supplanted by them. 195:10.11 (2085.3)*

Ordination of the Twelve (Paper 140)

This chapter details Jesus's profound training and commissioning of the apostles, going beyond a simple list of names or brief recounting of their duties. Here, the midwayers carefully describe how Jesus imparted the essence of his gospel message, which focused on the love of God and the love of humankind. His teachings on humility, sincerity, and the courage to live faith-filled lives receive a depth and specificity that creates a vivid scene. The midwayers' portrayal shows Jesus's care in preparing his apostles to represent his mission, revealing not only his teachings but also his tender, instructional demeanor—balancing authority with gentleness. The scene conveys how Jesus's message was intrinsically linked to his relationship with each of his apostles, uniting his teachings with his compassion.

Sermon on the Kingdom (Paper 170)

In this sweeping discourse, Jesus presents a broad and clarifying vision of the kingdom of God, refining and expanding the concept beyond the expectations of his followers. The midwayers describe Jesus's speech with detailed attention to his gestures, pauses, and varying tones he used to reach different listeners. He carefully redefines the *kingdom* as an inner, spiritual reality—something beyond any political or nationalistic aspiration. The portrayal here fills in the theological gaps and brings readers closer to Jesus's vision of a universal and inclusive kingdom based on spiritual love and moral responsibility. The midwayer authors show how Jesus engaged with the crowd, countering their limited understandings with warmth, intelligence, and a deep desire to guide them toward higher ideals.

Final Appearance and Ascension (Paper 193)

This episode unfolds as a majestic conclusion to Jesus's earthly life and mission. Unlike the brief descriptions in the New Testament, this account richly details Jesus's final interactions with his followers and his profound messages of peace and encouragement, portraying him as both a divine figure and a deeply connected friend. The midwayers describe his parting words with cinematic detail, showing Jesus in a moment of transcendence that encompasses both his divinity and humanity. His final blessings and promises are given with such attention that readers can feel his comforting presence, sensing the completeness of his mission and the fulfillment of his promises. The scene shows the enduring nature of his teachings and the hope he inspires, leaving readers with a deep sense of Jesus's unwavering love and purpose.

224 | EXPLORING THE URANTIA REVELATION

Final Teachings, Death, Resurrection, and Eternal Impact (Papers 182–196)

Beginning with Paper 182, *The Urantia Book* offers an in-depth narrative of the final hours of Jesus's earthly life, his morontia resurrection, and the profound messages he left in his postresurrection appearances.

Betrayal and Arrest

Jesus's final hours of free movement on Earth begin with his time in the Garden of Gethsemane, where he spends a contemplative evening in prayer, fully aware of the events to come. He grapples with the weight of his mission and chooses to remain steadfast, ultimately surrendering his human fears to divine will. Judas arrives with soldiers and, in an act of betrayal, identifies Jesus with a kiss. Jesus surrenders calmly, choosing to prevent his apostles from resisting. This moment reflects both the strength of his character and his commitment to fulfilling his bestowal purpose nonviolently.

Examination and Trial

Following his arrest, Jesus is brought before multiple authorities, including the high priest, Caiaphas, and the Roman governor, Pilate. These examinations reveal the biases and inner conflicts of those who judge him. Pilate, who finds no fault in Jesus, is pressured by the crowd and religious leaders to authorize his crucifixion. The midwayers describe each interrogation with detail, portraying Jesus as calm, dignified, and largely silent, refusing to defend himself against false accusations. The back-and-forth nature of his trials underscores the political and social tensions surrounding him, illustrating how his spiritual message clashed with the established powers.

Crucifixion

Jesus is condemned and subjected to crucifixion, an agonizing process that he endures with grace. His words from the cross reflect forgiveness and compassion—toward his mother, his followers, and even those responsible for his suffering. His death is portrayed as a powerful culmination of his earthly ministry, the ultimate demonstration of love and forgiveness. This act cements his legacy as a spiritual leader willing to sacrifice himself rather than abandon his mission of revealing God's love.

Morontia Resurrection

The narrative shifts to Jesus's resurrection, which *The Urantia Book* describes as occurring not in his physical body but in a new morontia form—a higher, transitional state between the material and spiritual. This morontia resurrection marks a significant revelation, emphasizing that Jesus's spiritual essence transcends physical death. The morontia body represents a new kind of existence, designed to communicate spiritual truths beyond the limitations of material reality. His appearances after the resurrection thus reflect not a return to physical life but a step toward greater cosmic truths.

Morontia Appearances

In his morontia form, Jesus appears to Mary Magdalene, the apostles, and other followers, conveying messages of hope, offering new spiritual insights, and instructing them to continue spreading his teachings. Each appearance is filled with peace and love, showing that Jesus has transcended physical boundaries and now embodies a universal presence. His message is clear: the kingdom of God is real, enduring, and accessible to all through faith and love.

Final Messages and Ascension

Before his final ascension, Jesus offers instructions to his apostles, encouraging them to spread his teachings of love, forgiveness, and unity. His messages reflect a shift from local ministry to a global spiritual mission, emphasizing that his followers should live and spread his gospel as ambassadors of a divine truth that transcends earthly institutions. His ascension marks the completion of his earthly mission and opens the path for his teachings to reach beyond geographical and cultural boundaries.

In these closing papers, *The Urantia Book* offers a comprehensive portrayal of Jesus's final acts and spiritual legacy. The midwayer authors emphasize that Jesus's resurrection was not bound to the material but was a step into a morontia state, highlighting his role as a bridge between the material world and the divine. His postresurrection messages encourage believers to see beyond physical existence and embrace a broader vision of spiritual growth, reflecting his profound love and universal mission.

Endnotes

1. Debold, "COSAR Concept."
2. The Urantia Book. 150:1.3 (1679.2).
3. Luke 1:38 (New Revised Standard Version), www.biblegateway.com /passage/?search=Luke+1%3A38&version=NRSV.
4. *The Urantia Book*, 180:5.2 (1949.4).
5. *The Urantia Book*, 122:8.7 (1352.3).
6. Sonarington is one of the sacred seven sacred spheres of the Father, which orbit around the Isle of Paradise in the cosmology of *The Urantia Book*. Specifically, Sonarington is the "sacred world of the Father and the Son," dedicated to the administration and fellowship of all orders of descending and ascending Sonship. It is a realm of profound mystery, accessible only to those divine beings who are of the order of Sons of God, including the Eternal Son, the Creator Sons (like Michael of Nebadon), and the various orders of Paradise Sons. For ascending mortal beings, Sonarington is a place they may one day visit as perfected and ascended sons of God, but its innermost secrets are known only to the Sons who serve and administer throughout the universes. The Urantia Book describes it as a world of profound spiritual fellowship, where the divine nature of Sonship is both revealed and experienced in its purest form.
7. Amos died at age four when Jesus was eighteen. Ruth was only two at the time.
8. *The Urantia Book*. "At Joppa—Discourse on Jonah." Paper 130, Section 1. Chicago: Urantia Foundation, 1955. https://www.urantia .org/urantia-book-standardized/paper-130-jerusalem.
9. *The Urantia Book*, 144:4.8 (1620.15).
10. Peter Holley, "Meditation in *The Urantia Book* (Jesus-Style Meditation)," Preston Thomas (website), accessed December 12, 2024, https://www .prestonthomas.org/jesus-style-meditation/.
11. *The Urantia Book*, 195:4.4 (2075.2).
12. In *The Urantia Book*, Abner is portrayed as a significant yet often overlooked figure in early Christian history. A lifelong Nazarite and former chief of John the Baptist's apostles, Abner embraced Jesus's teachings and became the leader of the seventy evangelists appointed

228 | EXPLORING THE URANTIA REVELATION

by Jesus to spread the gospel. He played a pivotal role in organizing and leading the mission in Perea, which was the final phase of Jesus's public ministry. After Jesus's death and resurrection, Abner established and led the Philadelphia church, maintaining its independence from the Jerusalem church led by James, Jesus's brother. This separation contributed to Abner's relative obscurity in traditional biblical accounts. Beyond *The Urantia Book*, the name Abner appears in the Hebrew Bible as the cousin of King Saul and commander of his army. This biblical Abner is a distinct historical figure and is not associated with the Abner described in *The Urantia Book*.

Chapter 10
Urantia Papers *and* The Urantia Book, *1955*

The Urantia Book has this fascinating way of explaining how the religion of Jesus gradually morphed into the religion about Jesus. There's quite a difference between the two. The religion of Jesus is all about this simple yet powerful idea—God as our loving Father and all of us as spiritual brothers and sisters. But somewhere along the way, Christianity got tangled up in rituals, doctrines, and the glorification of Jesus himself. Don't get me wrong, honoring Jesus is all well and good, maybe even divine, but it's like we've built a beautiful house and then forgot to live in it. The focus shifted from practicing the universal brotherhood and living the gospel to defining Jesus's divinity over and over again.

The Urantia Book tells us this shift into a religion about Jesus has kept Christianity stuck in what it calls "low spiritual gear." It's like driving in first gear—not fully engaging with the deeper truths that could really rev up the spiritual life. Instead of moving forward into a full experience of spiritual reality, much of Christianity has been busy polishing the same parts of the car. Meanwhile, the real power—Jesus's message of the Fatherhood of God and the brotherhood of man—has been idling under the hood, waiting to take folks on a much greater journey.

230 | EXPLORING THE URANTIA REVELATION

Just like when Christianity became about Jesus rather than his gospel, there's a danger of making the same mistake when talking about the book. You see, if someone sets out to write about *The Urantia Book*, it's mighty easy to get caught up in explaining the book instead of really engaging with what the book reveals. That's a bit like giving someone a treasure map but never showing the person where the treasure is buried.

So, how do you thread the needle? The real trick is to show how what the book offers applies to life, how it can deepen our understanding of the universe and our relationship with God. The beauty lies in its ability to deliver spiritual truths that resonate in the deepest parts of our being, truths that push us forward, not just intellectually but spiritually. When you approach *The Urantia Book* with an open heart and mind, it's like you shift into high gear, and suddenly, the road opens up before you, filled with new understanding, cosmic perspective, and, ultimately, a richer connection to the divine.

I've narrated my story here, specifically how *The Urantia Book* has delivered spiritual truths that resonate in the deepest parts of my being. The road truly opened into a wide vista, one that extends millions of light years beyond the Milky Way and presents a genesis that begins with the infinitude of the I AM. So now, let me tell you about a close friend; we'll call him Bob.

Wisdom in Revelational Delay

Bob is a baby boomer like myself; we both negotiated the exponential path of an exploding post–World War II US economy, at the same time the decade of the 1960s saw so much turmoil and breakaway from conventional society. All the while, we were worried that the world could turn into a nuclear winter in a fraction of an hour. In this backdrop, Bob attended both Catholic high school and college. He told me of a moment he had sophomore year in high school world history class. They were discussing the Great Schism, which formally occurred in 1054 AD; it was a major split between the Eastern Orthodox Church and the Roman Catholic Church. There were a variety of underlying issues, but the schism was essentially the result of cultural, political, and theological differences that had been brewing for centuries.

The Roman Empire, as it developed, split into two regions—the Western Roman Empire and the Eastern Roman Empire (or Byzantine Empire). The Western side spoke Latin, while the Eastern side primarily spoke Greek. Over time, this language barrier led to misunderstandings and different ways of practicing and thinking about Christianity. It was like having two branches of the same family grow up in different towns, each developing its own ways of doing things.

The East and West were also politically divided. The Western Church was centered in Rome, where the pope wielded significant power. In the East, the Byzantine Empire had its capital in Constantinople (modern-day Turkey), and the patriarch of Constantinople led the church there. The pope in Rome believed he had authority over all Christians, but the Eastern patriarchs didn't see it that way. They felt their church should operate independently, and they didn't appreciate the pope telling them what to do. This was a classic power struggle, with both sides wanting to call the shots.

There were theological differences too. One big one was the *filioque* controversy. The Western Church added a phrase to the Nicene Creed (the statement of Christian faith) saying

232 | EXPLORING THE URANTIA REVELATION

that the Holy Spirit proceeds from both the Father and the Son (*filioque* means "and the Son" in Latin). The Eastern Church didn't agree with this addition, arguing that it changed the original meaning of the creed and hadn't been agreed upon by the whole church. For the Easterners, this was a big deal because they believed in sticking to the original text as determined by the early church councils.

There were also differences in how each side practiced Christianity. For example, the Western Church used unleavened bread in communion, while the Eastern Church used leavened. They also disagreed on things like clerical celibacy (in the West, priests couldn't marry, while in the East, they could), and how the church calendar should be structured. These might seem like small details, but they represented deeper philosophical divides.

The immediate cause of the split came in 1054, when Pope Leo IX sent a delegation to Constantinople to try to resolve some of these issues. It didn't go well. The papal envoys ended up excommunicating the Patriarch of Constantinople, Michael Cerularius, who responded by excommunicating the pope's representatives in return. This mutual excommunication marked the formal break between the two churches. It sounds like the classic phrase "the straw that broke the camel's back."

The split created the Roman Catholic Church in the West and the Eastern Orthodox Church in the East, each developing its own distinct theology, liturgy, and church governance—apparently while worshipping the same God, mind you. While efforts have been made over the centuries to heal the rift, the two branches remain separate to this day. In short, the Great Schism happened because of cultural, political, and theological differences that finally came to a head, the culmination of centuries of growing apart. The resulting split has defined much of Christian history ever since.

One of the major underlying issues in the Great Schism was the dispute over papal authority, specifically the claim of each side—Rome and Constantinople—to be the true custodian of apostolic succession, particularly as it related to Peter, whom both regarded as the leading apostle.

Bob tells me that the main theme he took away from the lesson that day was that the Roman Catholic Church has long held that the pope in Rome is the direct successor of the Apostle Peter. According to Catholic tradition, Jesus gave Peter a top role of leadership in the early church, symbolized by the famous passage in Matthew 16:18–19 where Jesus says, "You are Peter, and on this rock, I will build my church." The Roman Church interpreted this as meaning that Peter had authority over all Christians, and since Peter is believed to have been the first bishop of Rome, all future bishops of Rome (popes) inherited this supreme authority.

However, the Eastern Orthodox Church did not agree that the pope had this kind of universal authority over all Christians. Instead, it viewed Peter as a figurehead among equals, the "first among equals" (*primus inter pares*) of the apostles. They acknowledged that Peter had a special place in early Christianity but did not believe this meant the bishop of Rome had jurisdiction over all the churches. The Eastern Church argued that the leadership of the universal church should be shared among all the bishops, especially the major patriarchates like Constantinople, Alexandria, Antioch, and Jerusalem, with no one bishop ruling supreme over the others. To this day, the disagreement over papal succession and authority is one of the

234 | EXPLORING THE URANTIA REVELATION

lasting differences between the Roman Catholic Church and the Eastern Orthodox Church. During the schism, both sides believed they were the rightful heirs of apostolic succession. Mind you, this is just Western or Occidental society. "World" history apparently didn't include the orient.

Interestingly, Bob tells me he was not particularly interested in history; he wound up a math major in college. But as he was sitting there as a naive sixteen-year-old, all of a sudden something seemed to enhance his field of vision, and a huge gestalt-like thought went over his self: *It's all bull-hockey!* Bob said this wasn't a voice he heard; it was more like a feeling that somehow translated into a huge connected thought. The connections subsumed in the "all" Bob describes as the entire thousand years beginning with Jesus's statement to Peter, which the Bible recalls as unconditional. Elements of his catechism classes were in a part of this overall singularly integrated impress. Some of the Benedictine priests who administered and taught in the school would have been aghast at Bob's thinking if they were privy to this. Bob offers a heartfelt thanks to those who drove home the idea that keeping an open mind was more divine than unequivocal obedience. Very Jesus-like, I'd say!

Bob has difficulty describing the whole event, but to this day, he still remembers the instructor, Mr. Schiller the football coach; where he was sitting in the room; and the color of the walls, to mention a few facets of that event more than sixty years ago. Bob tells me that now that he understands the cosmology of *The Urantia Book* better these days, he can now liken the event to being in the intersection of fact and truth, the nexus between experience and feeling, the channel between rationalization and emotion. Is this how religious revelation works? Is this an example of how some people say they hear God speaking? He mentioned to me that the pithy statement by the Melchizedek in Paper 101, section 5, "Religion Expanded by Revelation" challenged his thinking but allowed Bob a sliver of an idea that the truth of the reality of his experience in that high school class was in fact not a figment of his imagination. The Melchizedek writes:

> *Scientists assemble facts, philosophers co-ordinate ideas, while prophets exalt ideals. Feeling and emotion are invariable concomitants of religion, but they are not religion. Religion may be the feeling of experience, but it is hardly the experience of feeling. Neither logic (rationalization) nor emotion (feeling) is essentially a part of religious experience, although both may variously be associated with the exercise of faith in the furtherance of spiritual insight into reality, all according to the status and temperamental tendency of the individual mind. 101:5.9 (1110.12)*

This aha! moment didn't really affect Bob substantially in any way for at least a decade. And it didn't disrupt his faith; he continued to attend church services and maintain most of the required rituals essential by the theology, like abstaining from eating meat on Fridays. Bob recalls that the flash from high school history class recurred when one Sunday he and his first wife were looking for a local church to attend in a new area they just moved to. About forty minutes into the service, they came to the realization that they were in a Greek Orthodox church! It had the same God, nearly the same approach to worship. Still, the high school revelation didn't come to the front of consciousness.

236 | EXPLORING THE URANTIA REVELATION

But even that epiphany in attending the "wrong" church truly didn't shake Bob's faith. Deep down he knew there was truth in all of it; the trappings were in need of some reflection, however. He "knew" there was a bigger picture somewhere that may be just over some unknown vista beyond a hill blocking the view—maybe in a book? Maybe in another church? Another religion?

For a few more years Bob took a deep dive into science fiction, transcendental ideas that were coming into the United States from India, and literature that heralded scientific and social discoveries. Just before Bob left the teaching profession for a leap into corporate America (IT industry), a colleague who shared a homeroom with him said one morning, "Hey, Bob, I know you to be a deep thinker, always looking for interesting ideas. I just came upon a book that changed my buddy's life—totally. You see, this friend was on a train to Turkey to sell a cache of drugs when he came upon this big blue book that got him to turn around and forget the transaction forever."

As always, Bob was interested. So, he responded, "Okay, what is this book?"

His coworker said, "*The Urantia Book*."

Bob then said something like, "So . . . what's the big deal?"

And his homeroom partner said, "Well, among other things, it tells us Adam and Eve were eight feet tall and purple."

The rest is history, as the saying goes. And fifty years later, Bob is still gaining insights from the revelations in this tome.

Another Prescient Revelation

I went into some detail with this story to point out that revelation—the Truth of Reality—can sometimes take a relatively long time, but if one maintains open-mindedness, the truth will most certainly set one free. Cosmic mind will most definitely respond.

Let's look at some of those cosmic insights that *The Urantia Book* delivers within its pages to hopefully pique your interest.

The book delivers scientific, spiritual, philosophical, social and ethical, historical and cultural, and psychological revelations. Many of these revelations are only scaffolding however. For example, *The Urantia Book* presents a theory about the structure of the universe that directly contradicts the current, widely accepted model of an expanding universe. It maintains that the universe is actually static and that the redshift-distance relation, a cornerstone of the expanding universe theory, is incorrect. Here's what a Perfector of Wisdom[1] says quite authoritatively about this:

Although your spectroscopic estimations of astronomic velocities are fairly reliable when applied to the starry realms belonging to your superuniverse and its associate superuniverses, such reckonings with reference to the realms of outer space are wholly unreliable. Spectral lines are displaced from the normal towards the violet by an approaching star; likewise, these lines are displaced towards the red by a receding star. Many influences interpose to make it appear that the recessional velocity of the external universes increases at the rate of more than one hundred miles a second for every million light-years increase in distance. By this method of reckoning, subsequent to the perfection of more powerful telescopes, it will appear that these far-distant systems are in flight from this part of the universe at the unbelievable rate of more than thirty thousand miles a second. But this apparent speed of recession is not real; it results from numerous factors of error embracing angles of observation and other time-space distortions. 12:4.14 (134.3)

Current evidence from the James Webb Space Telescope is now supporting the static model *The Urantia Book* reveals, including the observation of galaxies that are too large, too bright, and too old to be explained by the expanding-universe model. The detailed description of the universe based on *The Urantia Book*, which includes concentric space levels arranged around a central Isle of Paradise, is now supported by astronomical evidence that appears to uphold the existence of these space levels, using data from various sources, such as the Sloan Digital Sky Survey (SDSS) and the 2-degree Field Galactic Redshift Survey (2dFGRS). This evidence has been discovered within a year of this writing—a good example of COSAR.

When science and religion, or the spiritual, are united, human progress leaps forward in both knowledge and value. The integration can fuse into wisdom. Progress is slow, but inevitable. We didn't go into the detail of the COSAR in chapter 7; we'll do so here.

Science and Religion: Complements of Each Other

Chapter 7 contrasts the skepticism of modern readers with the growing scientific evidence that, in the author's view, aligns with the revelations in *The Urantia Book*—specifically in areas like genetics and archaeology. For instance, the discovery of the microcephalin gene, which regulates brain development and dates to around the time Adam and Eve were said to arrive, is seen as supporting evidence of their influence on human evolution.

The discovery of the microcephalin gene by Dr. Bruce Lahn stirred up quite a bit of excitement—and controversy—back in the early 2000s. So, let's break it down in simple terms and show how this scientific discovery relates to the religious story of Adam and Eve.

Dr. Lahn and his research team at the University of Chicago were looking into how certain genes might affect the growth of the human brain, specifically the size of it. They found a variant of a gene called microcephalin, which plays a critical role in brain development. According to their research, this gene variant first appeared about 37,000 years ago (the same date Ol' Blue disclosed in 1955!), and it's now found in about 70 percent of humans worldwide. Now, that's already interesting, but here's where it gets really intriguing: this variant seemed to spread quickly through the human population, as if there was some evolutionary advantage to having it.

The timing of this gene's emergence lined up with some important milestones in human history. Around 37,000 years ago, humans started doing things like making more sophisticated tools, creating art, and developing early forms of culture. The idea was that maybe this gene variant gave humans a boost in brainpower right when our ancestors were starting to become more civilized.

Dr. Lahn's research suggested that this genetic change might have given some populations an intellectual leg up, which, as you can imagine, didn't sit well with everyone.

240 | EXPLORING THE URANTIA REVELATION

People got nervous because the idea of linking brain size, intelligence, and specific gene variants to different human populations can be a really touchy subject. Some critics were worried that this kind of research could fuel arguments about racial superiority or lead to discrimination, even though Lahn himself wasn't making those kinds of claims.

But let's keep it simple here: Lahn was just trying to figure out how human brains evolved and whether certain genetic tweaks helped speed up that process. He wasn't saying that one group of people was inherently smarter than another. In fact, he was fascinated by how genes can spread and change across populations over time.

But the backlash led to some awkward moments in the scientific community, with Lahn eventually stepping away from this line of research. The controversy wasn't really about the science itself, but more about how that science might be interpreted or misused by others.

In the end, the discovery of the microcephalin gene showed that human evolution is an ongoing process, and that our brains are still changing in ways we don't fully understand. It also highlighted how tricky it can be to discuss genetics and evolution, especially when it touches on subjects that people have strong feelings about. But Dr. Lahn's work remains a significant milestone in our understanding of how humans got to be the way we are today, even if it ruffled some feathers along the way. Sometimes the Truth of Reality is uncomfortable.

Practical Outcomes

Our second look at the revelation is in the area of development of civilization. *The Urantia Book* provides a fascinating explanation of how civilization evolved from its primitive beginnings to the modern age, emphasizing how religion, science, and politics are deeply intertwined in this development. This scaffolding of insights can be used to explore current global challenges—especially cultural evolution, the tension between materialism and spirituality, and the journey toward a more unified world. Let's break down these ideas and see how they might be applied to today's issues.

Cultural Evolution

The Urantia Book describes cultural evolution as a long, gradual process, influenced by both biological evolution and spiritual progress. Early human societies were shaped by basic survival needs, but as humans developed physically and mentally, new cultural layers emerged—art, religion, philosophy, and science began to shape the way people lived and thought. Religion, in particular, played a crucial role in guiding early civilizations toward a more moral and ethical life, giving meaning to their existence and helping them form community bonds.

Cultural evolution is still happening today, but the forces driving it have shifted. Technology and globalization have accelerated the exchange of ideas and the blending of cultures. However, this rapid cultural change brings challenges, such as the loss of traditional values and the clash between different belief systems.

Example of using the insightful scaffolding—*The Urantia Book* suggests that cultural evolution thrives when guided by spiritual values that transcend time and place. This insight could serve as a foundation for addressing today's cultural tensions. For instance, in a globalized world, where cultures are constantly interacting, the idea of universal brotherhood and the Fatherhood of God—key principles Jesus developed and reiterated in *The Urantia Book*—could offer a common spiritual framework that respects diversity while promoting unity. By focusing on these higher truths, societies can find ways to harmonize differing cultural perspectives rather than allowing them to become sources of division.

Clash Between Materialism and Spirituality

The Urantia Book warns of the dangers of excessive materialism, which can lead to spiritual stagnation. It recognizes the importance of material progress—science and technology have improved our quality of life—but it also stresses that without spiritual growth, material achievements are ultimately hollow. The clash between materialism and spirituality is a recurring theme throughout human history, but in today's world, this clash is more visible than ever. As people chase wealth, power, and technological advancement, there's often a growing sense of spiritual emptiness.

The Urantia Book teaches that true progress involves balancing material and spiritual needs. In today's world, this balance could be addressed by integrating spiritual education and values into everyday life, business, and governance. For instance, companies could move beyond profit-driven motives and embrace more ethical practices that honor the welfare of their workers and the environment, incorporating spiritual values like compassion and service into the corporate world, thereby creating a sense of spirituality in the workplace. Likewise, educational systems could incorporate teachings that emphasize the development of the whole person—body, mind, and spirit—ensuring that students grow up with an understanding of both material success and spiritual fulfillment.

The Path to a More Unified World

The Urantia Book envisions a future where humanity moves toward global unity, guided by the realization of the universal brotherhood of all people—the understanding is not just a political or social but also a spiritual. True unity will come when people recognize their shared spiritual origin and destiny, transcending the divisions of race, nationality, and class.

Example of using the insightful scaffolding—in today's fractured world, with conflicts between nations, political ideologies, and economic systems, the insights from *The Urantia Book* can offer a road map toward unity. One practical application could be in international diplomacy. If global leaders embraced the idea of a common spiritual purpose for humanity, they might be more inclined to seek peaceful solutions to conflicts, prioritizing long-term global welfare over short-term nationalistic gains. In terms of social movements, grassroots initiatives that focus on global citizenship and the promotion of universal values—such as equality, justice, and the stewardship of the planet—could help bridge divides between different cultural and national groups, laying the groundwork for global cooperation and peace.

Addressing Global Challenges with Spiritual Insights

The insights from the *Urantia Book* provide a philosophical framework for understanding how religion, science, and politics can work together to shape civilization. By applying its revelations to today's global challenges—cultural evolution, the clash between materialism and spirituality, and the pursuit of global unity—humanity can take practical steps toward addressing these issues in a balanced and spiritually grounded way. The key message is that true progress requires us to look beyond material success and embrace the deeper spiritual truths that unite us all. This is the foundation upon which a better, more unified world can be built.

God Grows Along with Us

This brief look into the practical aspects of the revelational COSAR now leads me to the connected spiritual revelation called the seven psychic circles of spiritual growth. *The Urantia Book* describes seven levels of spiritual progress, known as the psychic circles, through which humans can grow in their understanding of God and reality. They represent milestones in moral and spiritual attainment, potentially offering a spiritual psychology framework for personal growth.

The circles are stages through which a person advances in spiritual, moral, and cosmic awareness. More than personal development, they signify the deepening partnership between an individual and the prepersonal fragment of God, often referred to as the Thought Adjuster. What makes these circles particularly interesting is that they unfold right here on Urantia, our planet, meaning this growth is part of our earthly journey.

Thought Adjuster and Indwelling Spirit Partnership

At the core of the growth process is the relationship between the individual and one's Thought Adjuster. The Adjuster, our indwelling spirit, is gifted to each of us to guide us spiritually, help us make moral decisions, and steer us toward our eventual union with God. As we progress through the psychic circles, this partnership strengthens, and both parties—us and the Adjuster—participate actively in this journey. The Adjuster brings divine wisdom and insights, but our personal decisions, especially those reflecting moral courage and faith, are key to this process.

This partnership is reciprocal, but not in a strict ratio sense. The reciprocity lies in the decision-making and spiritual experience. As we choose to align more with spiritual values, the Adjuster is able to influence us more directly, providing insights that go beyond our material minds. It's not a simple give-and-take equation; it's about an evolving relationship where each choice we make draws us closer to God and each step opens us to greater spiritual insights from the Adjuster.

Cosmic-Circle Attainment and Spiritual Experience

The progression through the psychic circles concerns intellectual or moral growth, but it is fundamentally tied to spiritual religious experience. As a person advances through the circles, their experience of God becomes more personal and profound. This is where the idea of reciprocity comes in: the more we give ourselves over to spiritual truth, the more the Adjuster can work within us to reveal deeper cosmic realities.

The reciprocity becomes especially significant from the third circle onward. At this stage, the adjutant mind spirits (which influence human thinking) progressively diminish in their control over the individual, and the influence of the Adjuster becomes much stronger. In simpler terms, as we grow spiritually, we become less driven by basic survival or intellectual drives and more by higher spiritual values. The reciprocity here is not a one-to-one exchange but an increasing partnership between our decisions and the Adjuster's guidance. The Adjuster becomes more active as we willingly choose the higher path.

This dynamic shows the unbroken nature of truth, from the infinite to the finite. Our spiritual progression on Earth is connected to the wider cosmic framework of God's universe, and the partnership with our Adjuster reflects this eternal truth.

Jesus's Example of Perfecting Adjuster Communication

Jesus is the perfect example of this partnership in action. Throughout his life, he developed an unparalleled connection with his Thought Adjuster. By the time of his baptism, this connection had become so complete that his Adjuster actually became a personalized being—a unique event. His spiritual decisions, his ability to live out God's will fully, and his perfect communion with the divine fragment of God, set the highest example of what it means to reach the peak of psychic-circle attainment. For Jesus, the reciprocity was complete, as every decision he made reflected the Father's will.

Now, imagine this: You're on a journey, trying to figure out the big questions in life, like what's the meaning of it all and how you can live your best self. God's already got a little piece of Himself riding shotgun with you on this trip—the Thought Adjuster. As you make good decisions, ones that really reflect kindness, truth, and love, the Adjuster gives you clearer directions on where to go next. It's like having a wise friend whispering in your ear, but you've got to listen to the friend more and more to hear the message clearly.

Now, by the time you reach those higher psychic circles, it's less about you just getting through the day and more about the big picture—your soul's journey. You and the Adjuster are working more like a team, partners who share the same goal. You're both contributing to making this journey toward God as rich as possible. And the more you trust, the more you grow, and the clearer everything becomes.

So, realize that we don't do this alone. God's in this with us, from the very start, helping us every step of the way—if we let Him. It's not about being perfect but about trusting the process, keeping the faith, and knowing that, ultimately, we're heading toward something infinitely beautiful.

The Thought Adjuster knows exactly what's best for us and is always guiding us to make good choices. The Adjuster doesn't coerce anybody to do anything, but it's always there, whispering the best way to go. If we listen closely and follow those good, loving thoughts, our helper gets even more excited to help us out.

In a passage from *The Urantia Book* (110:7.10), the Thought Adjuster says something like this about someone: "You're amazing! You're on this great adventure to figure out life and get closer to God. I'm here with you every step of the way, helping you find the right path. Even though you might not see or hear me clearly all the time, I know you're trying your best. Every sincere choice you make—whether it's being kind to someone, learning something new, or standing up for what's right—brings you and I closer together. I'm proud of how you're growing and can't wait to see where your journey takes you—or better yet, us!"

One More Significant Revelation

The concept of family holds universal significance in *The Urantia Book*, emphasizing not only its importance for human development but also its integral role throughout the vast reaches of God's universe. Family life, rooted in marriage and parenthood, is portrayed as essential to spiritual growth, societal stability, and even cosmic harmony. At its core, the family represents a divine structure mirrored in the relationships of the Paradise Trinity, the universe Sons, and the creatures of time and space. This section will explore these divine parallels and highlight the revelations about the universal importance of family in God's grand design.

In fact, the midwayers relate that the family occupied the very center of Jesus's philosophy of life—here and hereafter. He based his teachings about God on the family, while he sought to correct the Jewish tendency to overhonor ancestors. He exalted family life as the highest human duty but made it plain that family relationships must not interfere with religious obligations. 140:8.14 (1581.1)

Universal Father and Family of God

In *The Urantia Book*, God is consistently referred to as the Universal Father, which underscores His relationship to all beings as a loving parent, albeit an infinite one. This concept elevates family life beyond mere human experience, framing it as a reflection of the divine order. Just as a child learns to relate to its parents, so do humans learn to relate to God by understanding the parent-child dynamic. The relationship between the Universal Father and His children is the foundation for the brotherhood of man, a divine family that includes every will[2] creature in the universe.

The revelation further teaches that God's fatherhood is not abstract or distant but rooted in personal relationships, much like those found within human families. The Father's love glorifies each child of God, affirming his or her uniqueness and intrinsic value, just as parents treasure the individuality of their children. This familial model is a blueprint for human families, where love, patience, and service are essential in fostering growth and harmony. Through the experience of family, humans are given the opportunity to grasp the broader cosmic relationships that govern the universe.

Marriage and the Foundation of Home

Marriage, according to *The Urantia Book*, is much more than a social contract or a biological necessity. It is the bedrock upon which family life is built, and it plays a critical role in the evolution of society. The home, which springs from marriage, is described as civilization's most enduring institution. Within the home, individuals first learn the lessons of cooperation, sacrifice, and love that will prepare them for broader societal interactions.

Marriage is not merely a human institution but also one that reflects higher cosmic patterns. Even in the governance of the universe, the cooperative relationship between divine beings such as the Creator Son and the Divine Mother Spirit mirrors the partnership found in human marriage. This partnership is marked by mutual respect, shared responsibilities, and a dedication to the welfare of the universe family. The proclamation of equality between Michael of Nebadon (Jesus) and his Spirit companion is a transcendent pattern for the family organization across all domains of existence.

The Cosmic Role of Parenthood

Parenthood, another cornerstone of family life, is presented in *The Urantia Book* as a direct reflection of God's creative and sustaining love. The responsibility of caring for offspring mirrors God's ongoing care for His creatures. Through parenthood, individuals are invited to participate in the creative process, not just biologically, but also in shaping the character and spiritual potential of the next generation.

The parental role is seen as one of the highest privileges and responsibilities granted to mortals. Through the act of parenting, humans begin to understand God's patience, nurturing, and unconditional love. In guiding their children, parents experience a small reflection of the divine ministry exercised by higher beings throughout the universe. Thus, parenting serves as both a practical and spiritual training ground, preparing mortals for their eternal careers in the universe.

In fact, parenting is so important in the individual's spiritual growth that a Melchizedek teaches that all mortal survivors who have not experienced parenthood on the evolutionary worlds must obtain this necessary training while sojourning in the homes of the Jerusem Material Sons and as parental associates of these superb fathers and mothers. This is true except insofar as such mortals have been able to compensate for their deficiencies on the system nursery located on the first transitional-culture world of Jerusem. 45:6.6 (516.4)

Family as a Stabilizer of Civilization

One of the most profound teachings about family life in *The Urantia Book* is its role as the stabilizer of civilization. Families are the channels through which culture, knowledge, and values are passed from one generation to the next. They serve as the fundamental units of society, with each family contributing to the greater stability and progression of the whole.

The home is where children learn the basic social skills necessary for life in the broader community. In the family setting, young minds are first introduced to the concepts of cooperation, responsibility, and the greater good, which prepare individuals to participate in society, fostering the development of communities, nations, and, eventually, a more unified world.

The strength of human civilizations, such as the Chinese and Jewish cultures, is attributed to the centrality of the family unit. As are the families of a society, so is the society itself. If the family is strong and virtuous, the society will be stable and progressive. Conversely, the breakdown of family life is one of the greatest threats to the survival and advancement of civilization.

Universal Family Ideal

The concept of the family extends beyond the human experience and is mirrored in the higher orders of universe beings.

From the dual-phase personalities of male and female to the complementary roles found in seraphic and cherubic orders, the idea of family and partnership permeates all levels of universe life. This duality and cooperation are essential for overcoming the limitations inherent in isolated existence.

In the broader spiritual sense, the family represents the interconnectedness of all universe creatures. The divine love that animates family life on Earth is the same love that sustains the brotherhood of all beings. While universal, the brotherhood discloses the reality of the whole, emphasizing the all relationship over the each relationship. As each child of God finds a place within the family of the Father, the child also finds a role within the greater family of the universe.

Family as Pathway to God

The revelations of *The Urantia Book* present family life as a microcosm of divine reality. Through marriage, parenthood, and nurturing children, humans participate in the ongoing creative work of God. Family life offers mortals a glimpse into the deeper realities of the universe, teaching them about love, cooperation, and the eternal relationship between the Creator and His creatures.

Therefore, the family is not just a human institution but a reflection of the very structure of God's universe. By embracing the ideals of family life, individuals are prepared for their eventual roles in the greater cosmic family. The experiences of love, sacrifice, and service within the family unit are the tools needed for spiritual growth and the realization of the brotherhood of all beings. Family, in all its forms, remains the foundation of both human society and the universal order.

Final Thoughts

As we wrap up this chapter, it's clear that life is far more than what meets the eye. *The Urantia Book* has given us a fresh way to think about everything—about where we come from, where we're headed, and how everything is connected by a divine thread. From Adam and Eve's mission to lift humanity up to the unfolding story of civilization itself, this revelation is a living framework that challenges us to open our hearts and minds to higher truths.

If there's one thing we should take away from all this, it's that we're not alone on this journey. God has gifted each of us a personal guide—the Thought Adjuster—always there to nudge us toward better decisions, deeper understanding, and, ultimately, toward God Himself.

And let's not forget that, just like in the evolution of civilization, our cosmic and spiritual growth is a process. It happens in stages, with each step bringing us closer to that full partnership with the divine, and ultimately attaining God the Father. It's not about rushing or getting it perfect; it's about trusting the process and taking those small, everyday steps in the right direction. The universe is vast, but we've all got our part to play in its grand unfolding.

The Truth of Reality stretches from the infinite to the finite, and each of us is woven into that cosmic tapestry. Keep your heart open and your mind sharp, and trust that the divine path is always before you, waiting to be discovered.

Endnotes

1. A **Perfector of Wisdom** is a high-ranking divine personality belonging to the order of Trinity-origin beings in the cosmology of *The*

254 | EXPLORING THE URANTIA REVELATION

Urantia Book. Specifically, Perfectors of Wisdom are created by the Paradise Trinity—the union of the Universal Father, the Eternal Son, and the Infinite Spirit—and they serve as the supreme embodiments of wisdom in the superuniverse administrations. Each of the seven superuniverses is governed by a corps of Perfectors of Wisdom who, along with other Trinity-origin beings such as Divine Counselors and Universal Censors, ensure that divine wisdom, counsel, and judgment are impartially administered across the vast realms of time and space. Their primary role is to provide flawless insight and unerring wisdom to the governing authorities of the superuniverses, making them indispensable as advisors to the Ancients of Days, the supreme administrators of these immense domains. They are neither ascended beings nor created beings of local universe origin but are direct expressions of the perfect knowledge and wisdom of the Paradise Trinity.

2. A **will creature** in *The Urantia Book* refers to any being endowed with personality and the ability to make free-will decisions. This term encompasses all beings who possess self-awareness, rational thought, and the capacity to choose in alignment with or in opposition to divine will. Will creatures range from the highest order of spiritual beings, such as Paradise Sons of God, down to mortal humans and other ascending beings of time and space. The defining characteristic of a will creature is their moral freedom—the ability to discern and choose between good and evil, truth and error. This capacity for personal choice is central to their spiritual growth and ultimate destiny, which may lead to eternal union with God. Human beings on Earth (Urantia) are considered will creatures because they possess the ability to make free-will moral decisions, a quality that differentiates them from purely instinctual or mechanistic life-forms.

Epilogue to Part II

Well, folks, we've come a long way in this part of the book, haven't we? We've talked about some grand cosmic plans, from the Dalamatian teachings to the story of Adam and Eve, and right through to the revelations of Jesus of Nazareth. But what does all of this mean for you and me, sitting in the here and now?

Back in the day, when Jesus put away his carpenter's apron and set out to spread the good news, he wasn't just walking off to preach a few sermons—no, sir! He was "about his Father's business." That's the call to action I want to leave you with. Those of us who have found the truth in *The Urantia Book*—we're done with the dishes, so to speak. We've read the words and soaked up the insights, and now it's time to take off our aprons and get out into the world. It's time to be about our Father's business, spreading the leavened gospel in the light of this expanded revelation.

Paper 195 talks about how Christianity has been stuck in "low gear" for centuries. And you know, that's exactly what it feels like—we've been idling without ever really revving up the engine. But this book, this incredible revelation we've been handed, is the high-octane fuel we need to get the gospel into high gear. The world needs it now more than ever. The material side of life—the science and progress—has been speeding along like an Indy race car, but the spiritual side? Well, that's been lagging behind like a Model T. Paper 195 makes it clear: Christianity has been focusing too much on rituals and not enough on the actual teachings of Jesus—the message of the Fatherhood of God and the brotherhood of man.

We've polished that car so much—arguing about doctrines, divinity, and what color the interior should be—that we forgot to drive it. But *The Urantia Book* hands us the keys and says, "Here's how you get this thing into high gear." It's about harmonizing the truth of material science with the deeper reality of spiritual faith—the truth that we're all children of God and that the universe is teeming with life, love, and purpose. It's also teeming with trillions of humans who all have the opportunity to attain the Father of all—to be perfect as He is.

These two passages (195:10.20 and 195:10.21) are essential to driving home the core message of the *Urantia Book*—that Christianity has become entangled with the materialistic values of Western society, but there remains a powerful hope for renewal in returning to the living gospel of Jesus:

> *Christianity suffers under a great handicap because it has become identified in the minds of all the world as a part of the social system, the industrial life, and the moral standards of Western civilization; and thus has Christianity unwittingly seemed to sponsor a society which staggers under the guilt of tolerating science without idealism, politics without principles, wealth without work, pleasure without restraint, knowledge without character, power without conscience, and industry without morality. 195:10.20 (2086.6)*
>
> *The hope of modern Christianity is that it should cease to sponsor the social systems and industrial policies of Western civilization while it humbly bows itself before*

the cross it so valiantly extols, there to learn anew from Jesus of Nazareth the greatest truths mortal man can ever hear—the living gospel of the fatherhood of God and the brotherhood of man. 195:10.21 (2086.7)

The Urantia Book doesn't pull any punches when it says that Christianity is laboring under a heavy burden, as described in the first passage. It's like we've been carrying around all this extra baggage until the real gospel has gotten buried.

But here's the good news: Christianity can drop that baggage. It's not too late. Paper 195 tells us that the hope of modern Christianity is in laying aside the trappings of Western civilization, humbling itself once again before the cross. It's there, at the feet of Jesus, that we can rediscover the greatest truths ever told—the Fatherhood of God and the brotherhood of man. If Christianity can do that, if we can do that, the whole game changes. We'll move out of low gear, break away from the systems that hold us back, and finally start running on the gospel that Jesus lived and died for.

And that, my friends, is what we've got in *The Urantia Book*. We have to get back to basics—living and sharing the real, living gospel. The world has had enough of hollow philosophies and religious forms that don't lead to deeper spiritual realities. We've got to bring Jesus's message to life in a way that harmonizes the best of science and religion, material progress and spiritual growth. It's like we've been given the clearest road map possible, but we've just been sitting in the car, still polishing the dashboard instead of starting the engine.

So, what are we waiting for? The hope is alive. The dishes are done. It's time for us, just like Jesus did when he took off his apron, to set aside the distractions and get to work.

The world is waiting for us to share the living truths of the Fatherhood of God and the brotherhood of man. We've got the revelation; we've got the road map in the form of a spiritual GPS and a Truth of Reality Guide (TOR guide all in the *Urantia Book*). Let's shift into high gear and bring our world to the next level.

So, here's the challenge: we can't just sit back and admire the shiny new paint job. We've got to drive this thing. It's time to step out in faith, just like Melchizedek did when he showed up in Salem, and like Jesus did when he walked those dusty roads of Galilee. The truth we've found here in the *Urantia Book* isn't meant to stay locked up in our libraries or just bounce around in study groups. It's meant to move, to go, to transform the world. And if we're going to help shift humanity into spiritual high gear, we've got to roll up our sleeves and get to work.

We're standing on the edge of a great moment in history, friends. The future is now, and we've got the tools—the spiritual insights and the cosmic perspective—to help steer this world toward unity, peace, and a deeper connection with the divine. It's like Paper 195 says: "the hope of immortality became a part of the assurance of a recognized religion." That hope, my friends, is alive and kicking today, and it's up to us to spread it far and wide.

So, let's take off our aprons, put away the dishes, and get moving. The world is waiting, and its high time we shift into gear and bring the truth, love, and light of this revelation to a world in desperate need of it.

PART III

Chapter 11
The Good, the Bad, and the Sad

I might have seemed a bit harsh in challenging atheistic scientists and middle-of-the-road agnostics in their bold position of outright denial and disbelief of the existence of God; those who take, at best, an escapist position that there is no *material* evidence that God exists; or, worse yet, those who say there is no other-than-material evidence that a personal God, a loving heavenly Father, exists. The dedicated scientists who have contributed to humanity deserve recognition for the many benefits the sciences have given to mankind. However, to drift outside their wheelhouse and adamantly insist there is no God is unacceptable. I laid out in part 1 independently credible evidence of *The Urantia Book*'s prescient scientific facts revealed in 1934–1935 and published in 1955, well before the scientific community actually discovered them. The authoritative credibility of the revelation cannot be denied.

What is also at issue is an impending slow death of global religion, Christianity in particular, from formalism, overorganization, intellectualism, and other nonspiritual trends. Christianity is in deep kimchi if it continues to ignore the telltale signs in one of its own slogans: "A house divided against itself cannot stand." The non-Christian world will hardly capitulate to a sect-divided Christendom. Paper 195 in *The Urantia Book*, designated "After Pentecost," speaks of this situation, yet it posits a potentially self-correcting cure exists, in authoritative, compelling, and empathetic terms. It traces the reasons for Christianity's near-universal appeal to Western peoples when it came out of the small cult that seeded it in the Levant, to contain the largest global population of adherents two thousand years later. That said, I believe Western civilization finds itself at a crossroads of good, bad, and sad circumstances regarding the relationship between science and religion.

The good is the pure, unadulterated transformative teachings of Jesus, which remain the most profound spiritual gift humanity has ever received. It alone has the power to rehabilitate society of its compulsive romance with secularism. The bad is the ongoing tug-of-war between science and religion, a divide that has stifled both the pursuit of knowledge and the spiritual enrichment of humanity. This situation discloses how the sacred and profane are often seen as distinct, with little belief they can influence and transform each other. And the sad is the evidence of the well-nigh total forsaking of the spiritual as a result of the acute secularization of Western society.

Ironically, the secularization includes the religious. The midwayers make this strong statement:

> *At the time of this revelation, the prevailing intellectual and philosophical climate of both European and American life is decidedly secular—humanistic. For three hundred years Western thinking has been progressively secularized. Religion has become more and more a nominal influence, largely a ritualistic exercise. The majority of professed Christians of Western civilization are unwittingly actual secularists. 195:8.3 (2081.3)*

THE GOOD, THE BAD, AND THE SAD | 263

Professed Christians may be "unwitting secularists" because they unconsciously absorb and embody the values of secular culture while maintaining a nominal allegiance to Christianity. This statement by the midwayers in *The Urantia Book* critiques the philosophical and intellectual trends in Western civilization, identifying a subtle but profound shift in the relationship between professed Christianity and the dominant cultural mindset of secularism. Over the past three hundred years, Western civilization has undergone a process of secularization, where science, philosophy, and intellectual inquiry have progressively distanced themselves from religious frameworks. This shift has emphasized rationalism, humanism, and materialism over service, love, and faith—true Jesusonian injunctions. For many professed Christians, these cultural values subtly shape their worldview, leading them to prioritize secular concerns, such as economic success, political power, or personal gratification.

The statement proclaims that religion has become "largely a ritualistic exercise," which suggests, for many, that faith is practiced through attendance at church services, adherence to traditions, or observance of rituals. But it lacks transformative personal engagement. Many identify as Christian culturally or socially but do not integrate spiritual principles into their daily lives or decision-making. Modern secular culture encourages people to separate their religious lives from other areas such as work, politics, and education. Many Christians may support secular policies or ideologies without considering their alignment with spiritual principles or base their decisions on pragmatic or utilitarian grounds rather than on faith or moral conviction.

The term *unwitting* underscores that many are unaware of their alignment with secularism because they assume their nominal Christian identity insulates them from secular influence. However, many, maybe most, lack the spiritual discernment to recognize how their priorities, choices, and ideologies reflect secular rather than spiritual principles. The midwayer critique calls for greater self-awareness and a return to authentic, spiritually centered living that transcends mere ritual or cultural affiliation.

I will explain more fully in my conclusion to this section why I am so adamant that science and religion needs to actually dialogue in Jesusonian style—with an open mind and suspension of disbelief—even if only Urantia students are at the table!

How a Spiritual Movement Took Root

Let's paint the picture here. We begin with the time just after the resurrection of Jesus. Even the Roman centurion administering Jesus's crucifixion exclaimed of him, "This was indeed a righteous man; truly he must have been a Son of God." And from that hour he began to believe in Jesus. His death set off a ripple that turned despair into something powerful—hope with a mission. His followers, once down in the dumps, got busy spreading a message that turned hearts and heads across the Roman Empire. They shared freedom—of the soul and from the weight of old traditions.

Back in those days, the Roman Empire was like a pot of stew boiling over. Folks were tired of the same old gods and rituals. The Greco-Roman world of Zeus, Thor, and Aphrodite, to mention a few, had its glory days, sure, but by now, people were searching for something real. Enter Christianity, with its mix of Jewish roots and Greek philosophy, seasoned just right for the cultural stew of the time.

The Roman Empire had this deep respect for its history—all the myths, conquests, and ideas that made Rome great. But as the empire aged, that golden past started to feel like a fading sunset. Along came Christianity, not as a wrecking ball, but as a bridge, saying, "Hey, all that good stuff you love? We're here to take it to the next level." Early Christian thinkers like Justin Martyr and Origen of Alexandria hitched Jesus to Greek ideas of reason and cosmic order, making the faith sound familiar yet fresh to Roman ears.

How Greek Ideas Shaped Christianity

Greek philosophy was like the seasoning that made Christianity's message palatable to the Roman appetite. Ideas from folks like Plato and the Stoics found their way into Christian teachings. For instance, John's Gospel borrowed the idea of the Logos—the divine reason holding everything together. This helped early Christians talk to their Greek-educated neighbors in a language they understood.

But don't think this was just a one-way street. Christianity gave those high-minded ideas a heart. Whereas Greek philosophy centered on order and reason, Christianity added a personal touch—love, grace, and a God who cared deeply for each person. It wasn't just about thinking the right thoughts; it was about living with hope and purpose. That's why Christianity didn't just sit in some dusty library. It walked into people's lives and changed them.

Adapting to the times wasn't all smooth sailing. Jesus's original teachings were simple and heartfelt: love your neighbor, care for the downtrodden, build a personal bond with God. But as Christianity took on a Greek flavor, it became more institutional and philosophical. Some might say it lost a bit of its homespun charm. Still, this blend of cultures helped Christianity appeal to both the common folk and the educated elite. It was a tough balancing act, but it worked.

The Roman Empire: Fertile Ground for a New Faith

Let's shift gears to Rome. This empire was a patchwork quilt of peoples and religions. The Romans were pragmatic about it—they let folks keep their gods as long as they didn't rock the boat. That's how Judaism managed to stay under the radar for so long, and Christianity, being seen as a Jewish offshoot, got a pass at first. But when Christians started stepping out with their own identity—especially by refusing to worship the emperor—the trouble began.

Here's the irony, though: the very structure of the Roman Empire helped Christianity spread like wildfire. It's easy to picture. Rome had roads, trade networks, and a shared language (well, two—Latin and Greek). These were like highways for ideas. Early Christians used this infrastructure to carry their message far and wide, from bustling cities to sleepy villages. For example, if you were wandering around the Roman Empire in the first century and stumbled onto the Appian Way, you'd know you'd hit the jackpot of roads. It was a marvel of engineering that connected Rome to the far reaches of its empire. Think of it as the granddaddy of all highways, a straight and solid path built for chariots, soldiers, and traders alike.

The Appian Way wasn't picky about who traveled it. Soldiers marched down it, hauling supplies to the next battlefield.

Merchants wheeled their carts, bringing spices, silks, and all sorts of goodies to market. Even everyday folks—farmers, pilgrims, and messengers—used this road to get where they needed to go. It wasn't just a road; it was a lifeline, threading together the empire's many cultures and communities.

Ideas zipped down that road just as fast. Christianity, for instance, hitched a ride on those stone-paved paths. Early believers walked the Way, carrying the gospel from city to city, town to town. Thanks to the Appian Way and roads like it, the message of Jesus spread far and wide, reaching hearts hungry for hope and meaning.

The Appian Way symbolized something bigger than bricks and mortar. It was Rome's gift to humanity, a physical link that made the world feel a little smaller and a lot more connected. It brought people together, made trade flourish, and even laid the groundwork for the spread of ideas that would shape history. If there was ever a road that carried more than its weight in cobblestones, it was the Appian Way. It wasn't just a route through the empire; it was a route into the future.

But all was not perfect in the Roman state. The Romans feared that the Christian community's growing cohesion and distinct identity could foster disloyalty or rebellion. *The Urantia Book* insightfully observes that the Romans fought the church only when they feared it as a competitor of the state. Fear intensified as Christian populations grew and their organizational structures became more formalized. In fact, early Christians were often misunderstood by their Roman neighbors. Secretive rituals like the Eucharist were misinterpreted as subversive or even treasonous. Combined with the Christians' refusal to participate in state festivals and sacrifices, these misunderstandings fueled distrust.

268 | EXPLORING THE URANTIA REVELATION

Despite Roman fears, Christianity did not inherently seek to challenge political authority. Jesus's teachings, as outlined in *The Urantia Book* and the Gospels, emphasized a separation between spiritual and temporal realms: "Render unto Caesar the things that are Caesar's, and unto God the things that are God's." Early Christians followed this principle, often practicing quiet submission to Roman law while maintaining their distinct spiritual practices. This apolitical stance initially helped Christianity coexist with Roman governance.

Despite some later opposition from Romans, Christianity's inherently nonpolitical nature and its capacity to adapt to Roman structures ultimately allowed it to thrive. The evolving Christian church mirrored and preserved the Roman Empire's organizational genius, ensuring that its legacy endured long after the fall of its political institutions. By embracing Christianity, the Roman Empire found a spiritual force capable of addressing the deep cultural and moral yearnings described in *The Urantia Book* and continuing its mission of unifying diverse peoples under a common framework. This synthesis of Roman civilization and Christian spirituality shaped the foundation of Western civilization for centuries to come.

Organizational Wisdom

The empire's love of order and law rubbed off on the church. Early Christians organized themselves in ways that mirrored Roman governance. Bishops acted like regional leaders, and councils were their board meetings. This structure made the church stable and able to grow, even as Rome itself started to falter.

Christianity didn't come in with a wrecking ball; it came in with open arms. Romans loved their ideals of law, order, and virtue, and Christianity wove those values into its teachings. Stoic ideas like self-control and brotherhood? Christianity embraced them but added something deeper—grace and a personal relationship with a loving God.

For the everyday Roman, Christianity offered something the old religions couldn't: a sense of equality and hope. It didn't matter if you were a slave or a senator; the message was the same: God loves you, and there's a place for you in his kingdom. That's a hard message to ignore when the world around you feels like it's falling apart.

Even the so-called barbarian tribes couldn't resist. As they came into contact with Rome, many saw Christianity as a way to connect with the empire's grandeur. For them, the church wasn't just about faith; it was about stability and continuity in a chaotic time.

The View from Thirty Thousand Feet

So, why did Christianity thrive in the Roman Empire? It wasn't just luck. The empire's infrastructure, its reverence for the past, and its yearning for moral renewal created the perfect storm. Christianity didn't come to tear down; it came to fulfill. It took the best of Jewish monotheism, Greek philosophy, and Roman order and wove them into something greater.

As historian Diarmaid MacCulloch puts it, Christianity succeeded by transforming Rome's legacy, not rejecting it. It became a bridge between the empire's glorious past and the spiritual hopes of its future. And in doing so, it laid the foundation for Western civilization as we know it today.

Alright, let's talk about how those ancient Greeks added their secret sauce to Christianity. Picture this: Christianity started as a down-to-earth movement, rooted in Jesus's teachings about love, forgiveness, and living in harmony with God. But as it spread into the Greco-Roman world, it bumped into the towering ideas of Greek philosophy—Plato, Aristotle, and those Stoics who were all about keeping calm and carrying on.

The Greeks had some big ideas, like the Logos, the cosmic force of reason, the glue holding the universe together. Early Christians gave the concept a spiritual twist, and said, "Hey, this Logos isn't just an abstract idea. It's Jesus, the living word of God." Talk about a mic-drop moment! That's how Christianity started speaking the same language as the educated folks of the time.

The Greeks also loved to think about the big stuff, like the soul, morality, and the nature of existence. Stoics preached about living virtuously and being part of a universal brotherhood. Christians said, "We see your virtue and brotherhood, and we'll raise you grace and eternal life." It was a winning combo. Christianity didn't just fit into Greek philosophy; it gave it heart and hope.

This blending was practical too. Greek ethical ideas, like caring for others and living in harmony with nature, meshed beautifully with Jesus's teachings. Christianity didn't come across as some wild, foreign idea. It felt like the next chapter in a story people already knew.

Adapting to the Times

Adapting to Greek culture wasn't all wine and roses. Jesus's message was personal and simple: love God, love your neighbor, and trust in the Father's care. As it got wrapped up in Greek philosophy, some of that straightforward charm got lost in translation. The focus shifted a bit, leaning more on theology and less on that warm, relational side of Jesus's gospel.

Still, the fusion worked. It gave Christianity a foothold in a world dominated by Greek ideas. By the time Constantine came along in the fourth century, Christianity had absorbed so much from the Greeks that it felt familiar to even the most die-hard philosophers. It was like an old favorite recipe, just with a surprising new ingredient.

Blending cultures is always a bit messy. Some of Jesus's original teachings—like spiritual equality and forgiveness—didn't sit so well with the Roman and Greek hierarchies. Christianity challenged old moral norms, saying, "Hey, everyone's got dignity. Slaves, women, the poor—they're all beloved by God." That was revolutionary in a world where power and status ruled the day.

This clash wasn't a bad thing, though. It pushed Christianity to evolve and create a moral framework that resonated with all kinds of people. Whether you were a Greek philosopher pondering the nature of the universe or a Roman soldier looking for meaning, Christianity had something for you.

So, what's the takeaway? The Greek influence didn't just shape Christianity; it helped launch it into the cultural stratosphere. By blending Greek thought with Jesus's teachings, Christianity became a faith that could speak to the hearts and minds of a diverse empire. It kept the best of what the Greeks had to offer and added a divine twist that changed the world.

The Spread of Christianity

Christianity's adaptability enabled it to thrive as it moved through different cultures. When barbarians started rolling in and shaking things up in the Roman Empire, they found Christianity waiting for them. For many of these tribes, adopting Christianity wasn't just about faith; it was also about connecting to the legacy of Rome. The church became a bridge between the old empire and the new world.

From Jewish roots to a Greco-Roman expression, Christianity became a universal religion. However, this expansion came with compromises, where the radical and egalitarian ideals of Jesus were often subdued by societal norms. The yearning for a great God and monotheism, noted in Paper 121, found its answer in this widespread embrace of Christianity.

There is an interesting statement by the midwayers, who edited that paper and part 4 of *The Urantia Book*. "But we have often conjectured what would have happened in Rome and in the world if it had been the gospel of the kingdom which had been accepted in the place of Greek Christianity." 195:3.11 (2074.6)

Effectively, the statement invites speculative reflection on how the world might have evolved if the **gospel of the kingdom**, as Jesus taught it, had been accepted in its pure form rather than the Hellenized, institutionalized, and paganized version of Christianity that emerged. (*Hellenization*, derived from *Hellas*, the ancient Greek name for Greece, describes the spread of Greek cultural elements into the Mediterranean and Near Eastern regions, including into early Christianity as it expanded within the Greco-Roman world.) This gospel emphasized personal spiritual experience, universal brotherhood, and a dynamic relationship with God. Its transformative potential lay in its ability to address the deepest spiritual needs of individuals and society without the constraints of hierarchical structures and dogmatic formulations.

Shoulda, Coulda, Woulda

Speculating on how the gospel of the kingdom could have fostered a better integration of science and religion requires imagining a historical trajectory where spirituality and intellectual inquiry were seen as complementary, rather than antagonistic. This alternative path would have minimized the divide that developed between science and religion, particularly in the post-Enlightenment era. It also raises questions about whether monasticism, with its strengths and limitations, would have taken such a dominant role during the Dark Ages.

The gospel of the kingdom emphasized a personal, experiential relationship with God and a dynamic pursuit of truth. If this ethos had taken root, the quest for scientific understanding would likely have been viewed as a natural extension of seeking divine knowledge. Instead of opposing empirical observation, religious leaders might have encouraged scientific exploration as a way of uncovering the laws of God in the material universe. Unlike institutional Christianity's tendency to codify doctrines, the gospel's emphasis on personal spiritual growth would have encouraged openness to new discoveries. That might have prevented clashes between scientific innovation and religious orthodoxy, such as the trials of Galileo and other early scientists.

The gospel's emphasis on the universal brotherhood of humanity would have naturally extended to the promotion of education for all, reducing the monopolization of learning by clergy. A more literate and informed populace would have fostered a flourishing of both scientific and spiritual knowledge. If the gospel of the kingdom had been the guiding spiritual framework, studying nature could have been framed as an act of reverence, understanding the mind of God through the workings of the universe. This integration might have accelerated developments in fields like astronomy, biology, and physics, with less fear of heresy or religious condemnation.

A civilization shaped by the gospel might have developed a more unified worldview where scientific findings illuminated the intricacies of God's creation, while spiritual insights provided the ethical and moral guidance for applying this knowledge. The institutionalization of Christianity often led to the separation of spiritual and material truths, with religion governing morality and meaning while science was relegated to describing the physical world. The gospel of the kingdom, which integrated the spiritual and material realms, could have prevented this division.

Monasticism, while retaining its value as a spiritual discipline, would likely have evolved into a more open and integrative model, contributing more directly to societal progress. The alignment of science, spirituality, and service could have ushered in a more enlightened and unified civilization, avoiding centuries of antagonism and intellectual stagnation.

The Role of Pagan Religions

The long, winding journey of Christianity from its humble Galilean roots is an amazing story.

But once the church became an institution, it started acting a lot like an earthly kingdom itself, with more about rules and control than spiritual freedom. There were dark times when the faith got bogged down in dogma and even squelched free thinking. Yet, it never died. Even when it seemed like it was in a deep winter of moral and spiritual decline, it kept its roots alive.

Fast-forward from its early ascetic days to the Renaissance, and you'll see it bouncing back, splitting into all kinds of branches: Protestants here, Catholics there, reformations and revivals. Each time it looked like the tree might topple, it found a way to grow again. No matter how far it strayed from its original path, something was alive at its core, something that kept drawing people back to its roots.

But here we are now, and the challenges aren't what they used to be. Christianity's staring down a world where science reigns and materialism runs rampant. People have microscopes and telescopes, and they're questioning everything, sometimes even whether there's room for God in all these discoveries. And let's be honest, it's a hard sell to talk about miracles and heaven when folks are busy with quantum physics and artificial intelligence.

But the religion *of* Jesus—not the institutional stuff or the centuries of baggage, but the pure, simple faith he taught—has a power that can outlast all of this. Why? Because it speaks to the soul. It's about love, meaning, and purpose, things that no microscope can find and no material gadget can satisfy.

So, as the story of Christianity marches on, the question isn't whether it'll survive. It's *how* it'll thrive. The religion about Jesus might struggle, but the religion *of* Jesus is the part that's destined to win this tug-of-war with materialism. In the end, the heart always hungers for what's eternal, and Jesus's gospel offers just that.

Secularism and Modernity

Jesus's approach to spiritual growth mirrors, in many ways, the scientific method, but with a vital difference. Whereas modern science employs **experimentation** to uncover the laws of the material universe, Jesus embraced the **method of experience** to discover and share the truths of the spiritual universe. Science relies on **observation and hypothesis** to approach physical reality, but Jesus demonstrated that the soul finds God through the **leadings of spiritual insight**, a kind of inner discovery rooted in faith and nurtured by living the values of truth, beauty, and goodness.

While science and materialism may focus on observable mechanisms and deterministic laws, *The Urantia Book* reminds us that these are not the whole story. Materialism is there, but it is not exclusive. The physical world certainly exists as a tangible reality, but it is interwoven with spiritual purpose and meaning. Materialism alone cannot explain the love, creativity, and moral striving that define human life. Mechanism exists, but it is not unqualified. While the universe operates under orderly laws, these mechanisms are not self-existent. They are upheld by a divine Creator who imbues them with purpose. Mechanism describes the how but cannot answer the why. And determinism occurs in the universe, but it is not alone. Although physical processes often appear deterministic, human experience reveals the reality of free will, creativity, and moral choice. The universe is not a closed system of cause and effect but an open arena where spiritual will and divine purpose interact with material reality.

Modern science and religion may seem to operate on different planes, but they share a common pursuit: the discovery of universal truths. Science explores the external world, while religion seeks the inner realities of spirit and meaning. Jesus taught that these two approaches are not inherently at odds but are complementary methods of engaging with the same unified reality.

Revelation Can Be a Bridge

Revelation, as described in *The Urantia Book*, is the mechanism by which the divine illuminates truths that lie beyond the reach of both science and unaided religion. It catalyzes the harmony of science and spirituality, revealing the interconnectedness of material and spiritual realities. As science deepens its understanding of the physical cosmos and religion evolves toward the pure teachings of Jesus, these domains will become more attuned to the greater truths of the universe. The spiritual values that Jesus lived—truth, beauty, goodness, and love—provide a framework for bridging the gaps between secular knowledge and divine insight.

Materialism, skepticism, and spiritual apathy may seem insurmountable, but the religion of Jesus holds the key to transcending these barriers. His gospel of experience calls humanity to a higher plane of living, one that integrates the best of science and spirituality into a harmonious whole.

Through the love of the beautiful, the pursuit of truth, loyalty to duty, and the worship of divine goodness, humanity will find its way to deeper spiritual insight. And through the transformative power of love, individuals and societies will come to realize their divine potential, ushering in an era where science and religion work together to illuminate the full scope of reality. The religion of Jesus, centered on the method of experience, is destined to triumph.

Jesus's Enduring Influence: The Religion of Jesus vs. Christianity

Let's walk through the story of how the world came to be the way it is today, a tale of ideas and revolutions, progress and mistakes. Materialism, mechanism, humanism, and secularism show why the gospel of Jesus is needed more than ever today.

Materialism dictates that only thing that matters is matter. It's the belief that what you can see, touch, and measure is all there is. The soul? It's just neurons firing. Love? A biological trick to keep the species alive. Materialism gave us the tools to build skyscrapers and invent antibiotics, but it also tends to leave the spirit out in the cold.

Mechanism is materialism's cousin. It looks at the world like a big machine. Everything follows a cause-and-effect chain, from the planets orbiting the sun to the cells dividing in your body. It's great for understanding how things work but can't explain why you feel awe looking at a sunset or why a selfless act of love brings tears to your eyes.

Humanism teaches that humans are amazing and their potential is unlimited. It's a celebration of what we can achieve when we use reason, empathy, and creativity. That's a fine sentiment, but humanism tends to forget where those gifts came from—it sometimes elevates humanity so high that it pushes God right out of the picture.

Ah, now we come to secularism, the loud rebel of the group. Secularism rose up against the tyranny of religious institutions, as if it could say, "We don't need priests telling us how to think or kings claiming divine right!" It sought freedom, and thank goodness for that. Secularism gave Western civilization many of its freedoms—freedom of thought, speech, and self-determination. We enjoy liberties today because secularism fought back against the suffocating grip of religious authorities who tried to control every aspect of life. But in throwing off the chains of ecclesiastical control, it sometimes went too far, throwing God out with the church.

Sometimes subtly, other times boldly, secularism declared that humanity could thrive without any divine guidance. Science, reason, and progress became the new trinity, and God was relegated to the margins—or worse, denied altogether. But by severing itself from the spiritual, secularism left society with a big, gaping hole in the middle.

Secularism has helped humanity make great strides—longer lifespans, better education, and a more just society in many respects. But what happens when you strip the spiritual out of the equation? You get progress without purpose. Secularism champions individual freedom, but without a moral compass grounded in spiritual truths, freedom can turn into selfishness, greed, and apathy toward others.

So, should we "de-secularize" society and how is that done? Let's be clear—nobody's saying we should go back to the days when religious authorities controlled governments or dictated scientific inquiry. What we are saying is the **partnership of church and state in mutual independence of church and state** is vital because it ensures freedom for all. But how do we bring spirituality back into society without undermining that separation, which we know as "separation of church and state"?

The change starts within individuals. People need to reconnect with the values Jesus taught: love, compassion, truth, and goodness. This isn't about enforcing religion; it's about encouraging everyone to explore the divine within themselves. Education can include the moral and ethical insights that come from spirituality without preaching religion. Schools can teach the importance of service, kindness, and a sense of purpose as universal human values. Celebrate the spiritual legacy that underpins secular achievements. The values that drive human rights, equality, and social progress didn't come out of thin air. They're deeply rooted in the teachings of Jesus and other spiritual traditions. Acknowledge this lineage openly. Promote initiatives where scientists, philosophers, and theologians work together to explore the universe's mysteries, blending empirical knowledge with spiritual insight. And create spaces where people of all beliefs—secular and spiritual—can come together to work toward common goals. Service projects, environmental stewardship, and social-justice initiatives can unite people around shared values, regardless of their religious affiliations.

So, let's not forget that even amid the rise of secularism, the teachings of Jesus of Nazareth have continued to work in unseen ways. His message of love, forgiveness, and service remains embedded in the very fabric of Western civilization, often unrecognized and unacknowledged. Every act of kindness, every pursuit of justice, and every effort to lift the downtrodden carries the echo of his gospel, whether people realize it or not.

A truly balanced society doesn't reject secularism outright; it builds upon its achievements while reconnecting with the spiritual truths that give life meaning. Materialism and mechanism help us understand how the world works. Humanism inspires us to reach for greatness. But it's spirituality anchored in love and guided by divine values that gives us the wisdom to use those tools for the highest good.

By de-emphasizing secularism—not through coercion but through inspiration—we can bring the best of all worlds together. Science and religion, freedom and responsibility, progress and purpose can coexist in a harmonious whole. And in that union, we can begin to glimpse the kingdom of God that Jesus envisioned, a world where material and spiritual realities unite to uplift humanity toward its divine destiny.

The Future of Religion

Let me tell you something about faith and how it's meant to live and breathe, not sit on a dusty shelf. The midwayers, those unseen watchers of human progress, hit the nail on the head when they said this: "The living faith of Jesus' gospel and the institutions of ecclesiasticism are like oil and water—they just don't mix." The moment faith becomes too entangled in rules, rituals, and traditions, it starts losing its spark, its vitality. That's the great challenge facing Christianity today.

You know how sometimes people hang on to old things just because they're comfortable? It's like keeping a cracked teacup around because Grandma used it, even though it leaks when you pour tea into it. Traditions are like that. They're precious because they remind us of where we came from, but if we cling too tightly, they can keep us from moving forward.

The Christian churches of the twentieth century, for all their good intentions, have become like mighty walls. They were built to protect the faith, but now they're blocking the path of the real gospel. Instead of letting faith grow and adapt to modern minds, these walls keep people confined to outgrown systems that no longer satisfy the spiritual hunger of today. It's not that traditions are bad; they're just not enough. The spirit of Jesus's teachings is like a stream of water, always moving, always finding new ways to nourish the soul. When we try to freeze that stream into one rigid shape, we lose its life-giving power.

The church, for all its contributions, has often been its own worst enemy. The midwayers don't mince words when they say that the institutions of Christianity have become obstacles to the very message they were meant to spread. How does that happen? Churches sometimes focus so much on preserving the old ways, the ancient thought systems, rituals, and doctrines, that it fails to see the needs of modern people. It's like trying to solve today's problems with yesterday's tools. People turn away, looking elsewhere for spiritual nourishment. New ideas and methods are often seen as threats rather than opportunities. But Jesus did not play it safe. He engaged in fresh thinking, bold action, and meeting people where they are, not where tradition says they should be. When faith becomes an institution, it can lose its personal, firsthand connection to God. People start going through the motions instead of experiencing the joy and transformation of living faith.

But the true gospel of Jesus is still alive, just waiting to be rediscovered. The midwayers remind us that this gospel has immense potential to uplift civilization, heal divisions, and inspire people to live better, fuller lives because it focuses on relationships.

The gospel *of* Jesus connects people. It finds unity in diversity, seeing everyone as a spiritual brother or sister, and building a spiritual community that transcends race, nationality, creed, or SOGIESC (sexual orientation, gender identity and expression, and sex characteristics). Modern people still long for the universal truths of the gospel, even if they don't realize it. The gospel calls us to innovate, to find fresh ways of sharing its message with a changing world. Whether it's through new technology, modern education, or creative community-building, the teachings of Jesus can and should adapt to meet people where they are. The midwayers remind us that civilization doesn't need more walls.

No Smuggling Allowed

At the heart of *the good* is the pure, transformative gospel of Jesus, which remains the most profound spiritual gift humanity has ever received. *The bad* reminds us of the ongoing conflict between science and religion, a divide that has stifled both the pursuit of knowledge and the spiritual enrichment of humanity.

A polymath atheist, Eric Weinstein has a novel view of this "bad" issue. Weinstein is a Harvard PhD mathematician and public intellectual of recent renown. I would classify his position as one of a "religious-skeptic mediator." He expresses nuanced views on the intersection of science and religion that I agree with; his view of how to reconcile the divide is novel and insightful. His argument that science and religion need to make room for both the "religious scientist" and the "religious absolutist" hinges on creating a space for dialogue while avoiding what he terms "Jesus smuggling" or analogous covert insertion of religious doctrines into scientific discourse.

On the flip side, Eric critiques the "atheist-absolutist," which can be understood as the opposite situation to Jesus smuggling. The problem with atheist-absolutists lies in their tendency to impose a strictly materialistic worldview as an exclusive framework, often dismissing or invalidating the metaphysical, ethical, or existential dimensions of human experience that religion traditionally addresses. This is designated as "materialism smuggling." This issue that materialism or naturalism is the only valid lens through which to view reality in many situations dismisses or ridicules religious or spiritual perspectives without acknowledging their contributions to meaning, morality, and community. This approach parallels Jesus smuggling in that it dismisses alternative perspectives, creating a dogmatic reliance on atheistic materialism. This type of smuggling uses science as a rhetorical weapon to ironically assert metaphysical claims that go beyond the scope of empirical inquiry.

Weinstein does not dismiss religion outright, nor does he advocate for a strictly materialist or atheistic worldview. He appears to be open to the value of religion as a source of wisdom, meaning, and moral guidance. In many cases the religious scientist follows the rules of science; in many situations the insight of religion—left open for perceptive hypothesizing—often injects wonderful lines of inquiry that progress and grow society usually significantly.

There are many examples of the religious scientist Alhazen (Ibn al-Haytham), to Isaac Newton, Gregor Mendel, Georges Lemaître, Michael Faraday, Arthur Eddington, and Francis Collins.

And now, *the sad*. Secularists, humanists, atheists, and agnostics often reject the spiritual altogether, treating their ideologies and disciplines as untouchable dogmas, requiring no correction, no amendment, no external guidance.

The good, the bad, and the sad are all part of the human story. By choosing love as the guiding principle, blending science and spirituality and nurturing the highest values in human life, we can transform these struggles into triumphs and build a civilization worthy of its divine destiny.

There is hope out of babes and four-year-olds! Picking my youngest grandson, Alexander, up from preschool, we headed to our favorite In-N-Out Burger. His great grandma on his mom's side had died recently. As we were walking to our ritual ice cream spot, Alexander suddenly looked up at me and asked "Grandpa, does God build us another body after we die?"

Now let's venture into why I want to give a select few a seat at the table.

Chapter 12
Cocreation: Where the Divine Meets Human Imagination

The Urantia Book reveals that the creative process is not merely the result of human ingenuity or intellectual effort—it is a divine partnership. Through the superconscious mind, where the indwelling Thought Adjuster resides, humans experience moments of inspiration beyond ordinary understanding. There, we bridge the gulf between the finite and the infinite, the seen and the unseen, becoming cocreators in the ongoing cosmic journey.

Creativity offers a natural bridge between science and religion. The greatest scientific breakthroughs often emerge not through linear reasoning but through sudden flashes of insight, where solutions seemingly arrive from an unseen source. Similarly, the transformative power of religious experience lies in moments of profound inspiration—when truth, beauty, and goodness converge in ways that elevate the human spirit. Both forms of creativity share a common origin: the superconscious connection to divine reality. When we open ourselves up to this connection, we become vessels for truths that transcend material knowledge and enter the realm of spiritual wisdom.

This partnership allows humanity to participate in the Coordination of Science and Religion (COSAR). Science provides us with the empirical tools to understand the material universe, while religion gives us the moral and spiritual framework to interpret life's ultimate purpose. Creativity and inspiration stand at the intersection, the means through which the divine enters our human mind, harmonizing reason with revelation. In the works of great composers, visionary scientists, and spiritual leaders, we see the fruits of this cocreative process, which is not limited to extraordinary individuals but is available to anyone willing to embrace it.

The songwriter who humbly admits, "It wasn't me—it came through me," captures the essence of this divine collaboration. Humanity's most profound achievements are coauthored by the divine, flowing through individuals receptive to something greater than themselves. Whether it is the unveiling of a new scientific principle or the writing of sacred scripture, the process of discovery and creation involves a synthesis of human effort and divine guidance.

In bridging the modern-day gulf between science and religion, creativity invites us to see the universe as a cohesive whole in which material progress and spiritual growth are not separate pursuits, but complementary aspects of the same cosmic journey. Creativity reminds us that we are not passive observers of this unfolding reality, but active participants in the ongoing work of creation. Through our openness to inspiration, we continue to contribute to the divine plan, bringing forth insights, innovations, and revelations that lead humanity ever closer to its ultimate destiny.

Many examples exhibit this phenomenon. Lionel Richie has shared insights into his creative process that suggest a sense of being, a conduit for inspiration. He has mentioned that traveling and observing the world around him play significant roles in his songwriting. He stated, "Traveling did a great deal to me. I found that when I travel and just sit in the corner and watch, a million ideas come to me."[1] This reflects the idea that inspiration flows through him as he absorbs his surroundings.

Additionally, Richie has expressed humility regarding his success in the music industry, acknowledging the limited musical framework within which he operates. He remarked, "There are only twelve notes and if you're blessed enough to find 30 years in the business writing songs on twelve notes—I'm the luckiest guy in the world." This sentiment aligns with the notion of being a vessel for creativity, recognizing that his contributions are part of a larger, shared musical tradition.

Although Richie may not have explicitly stated that he is merely a conduit for his music, his reflections on the sources of his inspiration and his modest perspective on his achievements suggest an understanding of creativity as something that flows through him, shaped by external experiences and a universal musical language.

But it's not just artists who experience this inspirational connection. Friedrich August Kekulé, the renowned nineteenth-century chemist who discovered the structure of the benzene molecule, had an extraordinary experience of creative insight that he attributed to something beyond ordinary reasoning—an example of being a conduit for scientific discovery. Kekulé was struggling to understand how the atoms in the benzene molecule were arranged, a problem that had confounded scientists for years due to the molecule's unusual stability and symmetry.

One evening, after working tirelessly on the problem, Kekulé dozed off in front of his fireplace. As he drifted into a half-dreaming state, he envisioned a remarkable image: a snake biting its own tail, forming a ring. He awoke with a start, realizing that the benzene molecule might be structured as a closed hexagonal ring, a radical departure from previous linear models. This insight proved correct and revolutionized organic chemistry, forming the basis of modern structural theory.

Kekulé later reflected on this experience and described it as a moment of inspiration that *came to him* rather than something he consciously constructed. He remarked, "Let us learn to dream, gentlemen, and then perhaps we shall learn the truth." His discovery is a classic example of how scientific creativity often involves nonlinear, intuitive processes that seem to originate from an external or higher source.

This experience of being a conduit highlights how scientific breakthroughs often arise from the integration of rational analysis and moments of what I call "religious inspiration"—an interplay between our conscious mind and what *The Urantia Book* would describe as the superconscious connection to cosmic insight. Kekulé's vision demonstrates how creativity bridges empirical reasoning and the deeper mysteries of the universe, making even scientific discovery a form of cocreation with the divine.

My own journey with *The Urantia Book* mirrors this transcendent process of cocreation, where moments of insight and discovery emerge not solely from intellectual effort but from an openness to divine inspiration. Just as Kekulé saw the structure of benzene in a dream and Lionel Richie described songwriting as something that flows through him, my own spiritual awakening unfolded through a series of revelations that felt guided by something greater. My initial encounter with the book was the beginning of a dialogue between human curiosity and cosmic truth. As I explored its teachings on science, religion, and creativity, I realized that my role was not to take credit for the insights but to be a conduit, sharing them in ways that could uplift and unify others. This journey merely illustrates how any and all humans, when receptive to inspiration, participate in the ongoing cocreation of knowledge, wisdom, and progress in alignment with the divine plan.

Chapter 13
Seat at the Table

*MAN possessed a religion of **natural origin** as a part of his evolutionary experience long before any systematic revelations were made on Urantia. But this religion of natural origin was, in itself, the product of man's **super-animal endowments**. Evolutionary religion arose slowly throughout the millenniums of mankind's experiential career through the ministry of the following influences operating within, and impinging upon, savage, barbarian, and civilized man: The adjutant of worship; The adjutant of wisdom; and The Holy Spirit. —A Melchizedek of Nebadon (emphasis added) 92:0.1 (1003.1)*

Invitation to Dialogue

Pull up a chair, folks, because it's time to talk about the big stuff, the kind of conversations where science and religion, faith and reason, have been talking past each other for far too long. For thousands of years, these two perspectives have been like ships passing in the night, each with their loyal crews, but rarely sharing the same course. It's high time for a meeting of the minds, and what better way to do that than with an open invitation to the boldest voices out there alongside the revelations of the *Urantia Book*? That's the idea behind "A Seat at the Table."

The concept starts with a simple challenge, drawn from

the pages of this book's epilogue to part 1. The cosmology of the *Urantia Book* that claims to illuminate the truth of reality through five epochal revelations, the fourth being Jesus's gospel of the Father's kingdom, has much to offer materially, and metaphysically, and spiritually. It's high time the world's sharpest progressive thinkers and conservative skeptics sat down to really test its ideas. This isn't about preaching or converting; it's about dialogue, plain and simple.

The Challenge

Imagine Neil deGrasse Tyson, Richard Dawkins, Michael Shermer, Stephen Meyer, or even Howard Stern taking a seat and tackling these revelations head-on. These folks are opinionated leaders in their fields, trusted voices for their audiences, and bold enough to challenge the status quo. They've spent years questioning traditional and sometimes emerging views. Now it's their turn to put those convictions to the test against what *The Urantia Book* has to say about God, the cosmos, and humanity's path forward.

The seat at the table goes beyond just about discussing God's existence or the cosmos; the dialogue would test its tripartite cosmology against the very truths they have advocated. With science uncovering hints of a transcendent designer, as intellectuals like Stephen Meyer rationalize, the stage is set for an honest exchange. Consider the view of those like Rupert Sheldrake, who theorize that morphogenetic fields are transcendent invisible, nonmaterial organizing principles that guide the development and behavior of living organisms. Are these ideas encroaching on the revelation of adjutant mind-spirits? If these individuals hold steadfast to their ideals of truth and reality, then they owe it to their audiences—and indeed to humanity—to explore and challenge what *The Urantia Book* claims to reveal about the deepest questions of existence.

To create a forum for this dialogue, I've reached out to prominent scholars, scientists, and religious thinkers—over a thousand individuals across many domains. Although the response has been sparse, the intent is unwavering: those who are courageous enough to sit down, debate, and examine these claims are invited to do so at any of the major conferences where ideas intersect and clash. This invitation is both friendly and serious, a call to engage, examine, and consider that there may be more to reality than either science or religion, alone, has revealed.

This isn't some casual invitation to chat over coffee. It's a serious call to nonattributional[1] debate—on stages, at conferences, and in forums where ideas collide, evolve, and sometimes go belly-up. The goal is to pit reason and belief against revelation, not to win but to illuminate, to provide rational and reasonable reflection ideas and ideals. If these thinkers are as committed to truth as they say, then it's only fair they meet *The Urantia Book* on its terms, exploring the cosmology and Truth of Reality claims laid out in its pages.

Just as Jesus offered the Sanhedrin one last chance to accept the truth of a loving Heavenly Father, this challenge is a friendly but pointed reminder that time waits for no one. If this invitation is declined, history will note the silence. But for those who accept, the conversation could be transformative, not just for those in the debate but also for anyone listening.

So, here's to the table, the chairs, and the brave souls willing to sit down and talk. The ball's in their court. Let's see who steps up.

The Format

To create a context for the challenge, I point to three polymath individuals: the late Christopher Hitchens, Dinesh D'Souza, and Eric Weinstein. I'll start with Christopher and Dinesh to present and explain two positions of religion and secularism or materialism that exhibit an extreme of human thought in the twenty-first century as well as why they exhibit that these ideas are circling around in a cul-de-sac of intellection. Although Hitchens passed away in 2011, he remains the beacon of atheism, or, as he referred to it, "anti-theist."[2]

Christopher Hitchens, known for his unrelenting critique of religion, viewed it as a fundamentally human construct that mirrored humanity's flaws, fears, and prejudices. He argued that religious doctrines, far from being divinely inspired, were the products of societies grappling with their limitations, projecting their anxieties into anthropomorphic deities. To Hitchens, religion offered simplistic answers to profound mysteries, stifling the pursuit of truth and intellectual progress. He saw in the sacred texts of various traditions not timeless moral guidance but the vestiges of ancient ignorance, often rife with violence, bigotry, and outdated ideas that had no place in a modern, rational world.

For Hitchens, religion was not a unifying force but a source of division, separating humanity into believers and nonbelievers, the saved and the damned. This tribalism, he argued, had fueled countless wars and conflicts throughout history, perpetuating cycles of persecution and hatred. Religious doctrines, when taken literally or wielded by those in power, became tools of oppression, stalling progress in science, education, and human rights. He pointed to clashes between creationism and evolution, the suppression of LGBTQ+ rights, and the subjugation of women as stark examples of how religion impeded humanity's ethical and intellectual evolution.

Hitchens was equally skeptical of the moral claims of religion, asserting that ethical behavior predates religious teachings and thrives without them. In his view, morality rooted in divine command was often arbitrary, and doctrines such as eternal damnation or martyrdom seemed to him not only irrational but also deeply immoral. The history of religious institutions, rife with exploitation and corruption, further cemented his belief that faith had done more harm than good. For him, secular justice, grounded in reason and evidence, offered a far more reliable and equitable foundation for morality than the canon laws of any religion.

Central to Hitchens's philosophy was the celebration of skepticism and the power of reason. He championed the Enlightenment's legacy of liberating humanity from the grip of religious orthodoxy, emphasizing that freedom and intellectual growth require a willingness to question and seek truth without preconceptions. Religion, in his view, infantilized its followers by offering comforting illusions, such as an afterlife, that undermined personal accountability and discouraged a mature grappling with life's realities. Even progressive reinterpretations of faith, he believed, failed to escape their dogmatic roots, leaving religion inherently resistant to meaningful reform.

Despite his criticisms, Hitchens acknowledged the cultural and artistic contributions inspired by religion, though he regarded these as human achievements rather than divine gifts. He also expressed a grudging respect for individuals whose religious beliefs motivated extraordinary acts of humanity, even as he challenged the theological foundations of their convictions. Ultimately, Hitchens called for a world where humanity embraced its intellectual and moral potential without reliance on the supernatural, constructing meaning and ethics through reason, evidence, and the best aspects of human nature. His critique was a rejection of religion and a call to rise above it, to seek progress and unity in a world unencumbered by the limitations of ancient dogmas.

On the other side of the coin, Dinesh D'Souza's position on religion emerges from a conviction that faith provides a foundational framework for morality, purpose, and the human quest for meaning. He argues that religion, far from being an outdated relic of superstition, continues to offer profound insights into the human condition, addressing questions that secularism struggles to answer. While acknowledging the critiques of religion, especially those advanced by Christopher Hitchens, D'Souza contends that these critiques often overlooked or underestimated the positive contributions of faith to individuals and societies.

D'Souza's beliefs are firmly rooted in theism, particularly within the Christian, or in his case, Catholic, tradition. His worldview includes a personal God who interacts with humanity, provides moral guidance, and underpins the universe with purpose and meaning. This active and relational concept of God sets him apart from deists, who believe in a more detached, nonintervening creator.

At the heart of D'Souza's argument is the idea that religion serves as a moral compass, grounding ethical behavior in a transcendent reality. He suggests that belief in a divine creator offers a coherent explanation for human dignity, moral law, and the universal yearning for justice. In contrast, he views secular approaches to morality as often lacking a stable foundation, vulnerable to relativism, and disconnected from deeper existential truths. For D'Souza, the moral structures provided by religion, though sometimes imperfectly expressed, gave humanity a sense of accountability and purpose that purely materialistic worldviews cannot replicate.

D'Souza also emphasizes religion's role in explaining the complexities of life and the universe. He introduces the "presuppositional argument," which posits that the existence of God accounts more fully for the intricacies of human consciousness, morality, and the order of the cosmos than atheistic perspectives. In his view, religion offers a comprehensive narrative that integrates science, philosophy, and human experience, providing answers to life's profound questions that secularism either avoids or fails to address adequately.

In defending religion,[3] D'Souza does not ignore its historical flaws or the violence carried out in its name. Instead, he argues that such critiques should be weighed against the immense good that faith has inspired. From humanitarian efforts to the development of art, music, and literature, he sees religion as a wellspring of human creativity and a catalyst for societal cohesion. Moreover, he points to the resilience and hope that religious belief brings to individuals facing suffering and adversity, a quality he believed secular ideologies often lack.

D'Souza's argument is also deeply pragmatic. He challenges the notion that a purely secular society could thrive, highlighting the historical and contemporary failures of ideologies that rejected religious foundations. For him, religion offers not only metaphysical insights but also practical benefits, fostering community, shared values, and a sense of belonging. He believes that these social dimensions of faith are essential for the health and longevity of civilizations.

Ultimately, D'Souza's defense of religion is both rational and passionate, rooted in the belief that faith is not merely a private matter but a cornerstone of human flourishing. He sees in religion an enduring relevance that transcends its flaws, a force capable of guiding humanity toward a deeper understanding of itself and the world. His arguments are an invitation to consider religion not as a relic of the past but as a vital, rational, and necessary aspect of the human journey.

However, in areas that intersect with Hitchens, D'Souza acknowledges the scientific theory of evolution and argues that theists should not fear Darwin's theory of natural selection. He suggests that Christians should not seek to introduce creationism or intelligent design into science curricula through legal means but should instead engage with evolutionary theory on its own terms. D'Souza has expressed opposition to same-sex marriage and has been critical of the LGBTQ+ rights movement. In debates, he has argued against the redefinition of traditional marriage to include same-sex couples. D'Souza's views on women's roles align with traditional conservative perspectives reflecting a commitment to traditional interpretations of religious and cultural norms.

Morality Dissected

On one hand, Christopher Hitchens (and his kindred spirit, Sam Harris) had a knack for cutting through apparent religious claims, and one of his boldest was the idea that morality doesn't owe its existence to religion. He believed humans were ethical long before priests and holy books showed up, and he had a straightforward way of explaining it: We're social creatures, and we've always had to get along to survive. Picture early humans huddled together in caves or around fires. To make it in such close quarters, they had to come up with some basic ground rules—don't steal food, don't hurt each other, and maybe help out if someone's struggling. These weren't handed down from on high; they were common sense born out of necessity.

Hitchens pointed out that this kind of natural morality didn't stop with humans. You can see it in animals too. Have you ever watched a group of chimpanzees share food or comfort one another? That's empathy in action, plain as day. It's not sophisticated, but it shows that fairness and care have roots deep in the animal kingdom, long before humans started building temples or carving commandments into stone tablets. To Hitchens, this was proof that morality isn't a divine invention; it's something we inherited as part of being alive and needing each other.

Religion, in Hitchens's view, came along later and did what it does best: it took these already existing moral ideas and claimed them as its own. Suddenly, "don't kill" and "don't steal" weren't just good ideas—they were sacred laws, supposedly handed down from the heavens. For Hitchens, this was less about divine insight and more about a clever way to keep people in line. Sure, religion added some bells and whistles, but it also mixed in a fair share of bad ideas, like justifications for slavery or rules that oppressed women and minorities. For him, that showed religion wasn't inventing morality; it was just dressing it up, sometimes badly.

When you get down to it, Hitchens believed humans didn't need religion to be good, and he had the modern world to back him up. Look at secular societies today, he'd say—they're often more peaceful and fairer than their more religious counterparts. They rely on reason and compassion rather than divine commandments. Hitchens opined that Enlightenment thinkers like Kant and Voltaire figured out how to build moral systems without needing a God to weigh in, and those systems have helped shape the best of what we call human rights and justice today.

For Hitchens, the real beauty of morality was that it didn't need holy books or prophets to flourish. It was there all along, growing out of our shared humanity, polished by reason, and tested through experience. The idea that we need religion to tell us right from wrong? He'd say that's just another myth. And like so many myths, it falls apart when you look at the evidence and trust in the natural goodness of people figuring out how to live together.

On the other hand, D'Souza has a very different take on where morality comes from. Whereas Hitchens sees ethics as something that naturally evolved in primates to help them get along, D'Souza argues that morality has its roots in something much bigger—God. To D'Souza, moral principles like justice, fairness, and compassion aren't just handy social tools we picked up along the way. They're reflections of God's character, and humans, made in God's image, have an innate sense of right and wrong because of this divine connection.

One of D'Souza's big points is that morality isn't just a matter of convenience or survival; to him morality is objective. He believes that if morality came from evolution alone, it would always be shifting, depending on what helps the species survive at any given time. But certain values, like the idea that murder is wrong or that all humans have intrinsic worth, seem to apply universally, regardless of culture or circumstance. For D'Souza, this consistency points to a divine source, an unchanging moral lawgiver.

D'Souza also points to the human conscience as evidence of this divine influence. People feel guilt, strive for justice, and make sacrifices for others, often at great personal cost and without any direct benefit. Why would evolution lead us to act against our own self-interest? He sees these traits as signs of a higher moral standard that's been written into our very being, something that evolution alone can't fully explain.

But D'Souza doesn't just stop at critiquing naturalistic explanations for morality. He also highlights the role religion has played in keeping moral values alive and well throughout history. Sure, people can be moral without religion, he acknowledges, but many of the moral frameworks we take for granted today, like the value of human rights, were shaped and passed down by religious traditions. In his view, religion has been the glue that holds these values together across generations, giving them depth and staying power.

Ultimately, D'Souza ties morality to the larger question of life's meaning. He argues that if we're just products of random evolution, then morality has no ultimate purpose. But if there's a God behind it all, morality becomes part of a bigger plan. For him, the existence of moral principles is evidence of a universe that isn't just random but intentional, infused with meaning and guided by a personal God. In D'Souza's view, that's what makes morality not just a practical tool for living but also a profound link to the divine.

Both positions are delimited by the lack of revelation and confined to a cul-de-sac without a revelational GPS to get them out. Hitchens's materialistic view of morality confines it to a conceptual dead end by reducing it to evolutionary and social constructs. Though practical, this perspective fails to address transcendent aspects of morality, such as the universal sense of duty, the pursuit of justice, or self-sacrificial acts that transcend survival needs. By equating human morality with animal behavior, Hitchens—that is, the secularist-atheist view—reduces the rich tapestry of human moral experience to instinctual responses, dismissing the uniquely human capacity for abstract ideals and spiritual insight. Furthermore, his framework risks moral relativism, as it lacks a transcendent foundation to provide universal and enduring moral principles. This limitation disconnects his view from the lived experiences of individuals who perceive moral duty and spiritual conviction as realities beyond mere social conditioning or biological programming.

The Urantia Book offers a profoundly different perspective on morality, rooted in its expansive cosmology and understanding of what makes humans so important in the cosmos. It asserts that morality is not a mere social construct or survival mechanism but an intrinsic part of what makes a human different from the animals—particularly primates. As a result of the sixth and seventh adjutant mind-spirits along with what it calls the Holy Spirit, humans can contact cosmic mind through the superconscious mind arena. This moral intuition, coupled with scientific curiosity and spiritual insight, distinguishes humans from animals. The most important capability humans have beyond animals, which learn primarily through trial and error, is *foresight*. Humans can evaluate not only the means to achieve their goals but also the worthiness of the goals themselves. The capacity for moral discrimination and spiritual insight enables humanity

SEAT AT THE TABLE | 303

to transcend the instinctual behaviors seen in the animal kingdom; moral and ethical decisions are deeply connected to humanity's unique endowments as **personal** beings.

In addition, the revelation discloses a unique concept called "personality."[4] It is one of the two realities that God does not delegate—the Thought Adjuster being the other one. Think of personality as the "I" that observes the "me." The personality is the unique bestowal that the Universal Father makes upon the living and associated energies of matter, mind, and spirit and that survives with the morontial soul. Personality is the reality of selfhood; it is the source of free will:

> *Only a personality can know what it is doing before it does it; only personalities possess insight in advance of experience. A personality can look before it leaps and can therefore learn from looking as well as from leaping. A nonpersonal animal ordinarily learns only by leaping. 16:7.3 (193.2)*

Now let's look at how the revelation interacts with the theistic positions. Whereas D'Souza ties morality directly to God as the moral lawgiver, *The Urantia Book* introduces a broader cosmic framework, emphasizing the interconnectedness of material, intellectual, and spiritual dimensions. It posits that morality transcends intelligence and arises from personality's ability to discern and evaluate not only the means to achieve goals but the worthiness of the goals themselves. Such moral discernment is further enriched by spiritual insight, allowing humans to align their actions with universal values and purpose. *The Urantia Book* also highlights the role of revelation as a means to compensate for humanity's inability to fully comprehend the mota, or superphilosophical wisdom, that bridges the material and spiritual realms.

While acknowledging religion's role, *The Urantia Book* suggests that morality exists independently of religious systems and is enriched by spiritual insight and cosmic revelation and responses from cosmic mind. These revelations transcend conventional religious traditions. *The Urantia Book* describes moral intuition as a direct result of human personality's unique capacity for foresight and spiritual discernment, allowing humans to evaluate both means and ends. D'Souza, in contrast, ties moral intuition to *direct divine influence* and focuses on its manifestation through religious teachings. In this belief, humans are essentially passive while revelation teaches that morality requires active participation. D'Souza's reliance on theistic traditions as the sole foundation of morality limits the universality of his argument, as it does not fully address the moral insights found outside religious frameworks or the innate aspects of morality independent of religious doctrines.

D'Souza's view of morality accentuates its theistic roots and practical benefits for society, but the *Urantia Book* expands the discussion by situating morality within a cosmic framework that integrates human personality, spiritual insight, and universal values. *The Urantia Book* challenges humanity to recognize morality not just as a divine mandate or static social construct but as a bridge to higher spiritual realities, ultimately guiding humanity toward its cosmic destiny. This expansive vision offers a richer understanding of morality, encompassing both its practical significance and its transcendent purpose. I envision this particular topic would achieve lively dialogue at the table.

Get Out of the Box

I bring up Dr. Weinstein again, as he has another profound thought, this time related to why sitting at a table is well-nigh necessary. Weinstein claims that science is "stuck."[5] He refers to his broader critique of the state of modern scientific inquiry. He suggests that for the past several decades, science has largely ceased to ask the most profound, fundamental, and difficult questions, those that once drove revolutionary discoveries and changed our understanding of the universe. Let me expand upon what Weinstein likely means by this critique and why he feels it is important to unstick science.

Weinstein has this idea, and it's a big one: science, the grand pursuit of knowledge and understanding, has somehow gotten itself stuck. He's not talking about the kind of stuck where you need a push to get out of the mud—he's talking about the kind of stuck where, for decades now, science seems to have stopped chasing the really big questions. You know, the ones about life, the universe, and everything. The kind of questions that kept folks like Einstein and Newton up at night.

Now, Weinstein's not saying science isn't doing anything. Sure, there's plenty of progress in applied fields like AI, medicine, and technology. But when it comes to the deep, profound stuff, like figuring out the fundamental laws of nature or what consciousness is all about, science has been spinning its wheels. Physics, for instance, hasn't had a big shake-up since the days of quantum mechanics and the standard model.[6] And don't get him started on string theory—it's been stuck in theoretical limbo for decades.

Eric thinks part of the problem is the way science works these days. Academia has become, in his view, a kind of machine that rewards safe, predictable research. If you're a scientist and you want to ask bold, risky questions, you might find yourself out in the cold without funding or a job. So, scientists stick to what they know will work, aiming for small, incremental progress instead of aiming for the moon.

Another problem, he says, is that science has become way too specialized. Back in the day, the great minds were often generalists who dabbled across fields, drawing connections that no one else had thought of. These days, everyone's so focused on their tiny slice of the pie that they don't see the bigger picture. In other words, one can't get the picture when in the frame. Weinstein believes this hyperspecialization has kept us from making the kind of breakthroughs that only come when you look at things from a broader perspective.

And then there's the culture of science itself. Weinstein thinks it's become more about utility and less about wonder. He misses the days when scientists asked the big, sublime questions, like "Why are we here?" or "What is reality, really?" Instead, he sees science chasing what's practical and marketable, leaving those lofty questions.

But Weinstein has ideas about how to fix things. First and foremost, he wants to rekindle that sense of wonder in science, to make it okay again to chase after those wild, profound ideas. He's all for shaking up the system so that scientists can take risks without fearing for their careers. And he thinks it's time to break down the walls between disciplines, letting folks from different fields work together and maybe spark some revolutionary new ideas.

He also thinks science needs to reconnect with the public. Right now, a lot of people see science as cold, technical, and hard to understand and maybe even a little out of touch.

Weinstein believes that if science could get back to asking the questions that inspire everyone—not just the academics—it could reignite the public's imagination and support.

Weinstein's message is clear: science is too important to stay stuck. It's the key to solving humanity's great challenges and to understanding the mysteries of existence. But to do that, it needs to get back to its roots—its curiosity, boldness, and drive to ask the hardest, most beautiful questions of all. And he thinks that if we can unstick science, there's no telling how far we might go.

The foregoing short vignettes are intended to highlight the sad condition of both science and religion in the twenty-first century. This particular statement in *The Urantia Book* by a Melchizedek of Nebadon bring this situation out clearly:

> *Your difficulty in arriving at a more harmonious co-ordination between science and religion is due to your utter ignorance of the intervening domain of the moron-tia world of things and beings. The local universe consists of three degrees, or stages, of reality manifestation: mat-ter, morontia, and spirit. The morontia angle of approach erases all divergence between the findings of the physi-cal sciences and the functioning of the spirit of religion. Reason is the understanding technique of the sciences; faith is the insight technique of religion; mota is the tech-nique of the morontia level. Mota is a supermaterial real-ity sensitivity which is beginning to compensate incom-plete growth, having for its substance knowledge-reason and for its essence faith-insight. Mota is a superphilosoph-ical reconciliation of divergent reality perception which is nonattainable by material personalities; it is predicated,*

308 | EXPLORING THE URANTIA REVELATION

in part, on the experience of having survived the mate-rial life of the flesh. But many mortals have recognized the desirability of having some method of reconciling the interplay between the widely separated domains of sci-ence and religion; and metaphysics is the result of man's unavailing attempt to span this well-recognized chasm. But human metaphysics has proved more confusing than illuminating. Metaphysics stands for man's well-meant but futile effort to compensate for the absence of the mota of morontia.

Metaphysics has proved a failure; mota, man cannot perceive. Revelation is the only technique which can com-pensate for the absence of the truth sensitivity of mota in a material world. Revelation authoritatively clarifies the muddle of reason-developed metaphysics on an evolution-ary sphere. 103:6.7–8 (1136.2–3)

This is why *The Urantia Book* deserves to be the centerpiece of the table.

The Urantia Book critiques metaphysics as humanity's well-meaning but ultimately confusing effort to bridge the gap (I call it a gulf) between science and religion. That feels par-ticularly spot-on when we look at the twentieth and twenty-first centuries, where advances in philosophy and science have both clarified and complicated our understanding of reality. A good example is the ongoing debate about the nature of reality itself. Philosophers can't seem to agree on even a basic system of thought. Some say reality is all in the mind (idealism), oth-ers insist it's all about matter and energy (materialism), and some try to straddle both camps with dualism. The problem is, these frameworks often seem more like rival camps arguing than partners working toward the same goal. Without what *The Urantia Book* calls morontia mota—a kind of higher wisdom that connects material and spiritual realities—these systems lack the glue to hold anything together.[7]

Bridging Science and Religion

Quantum mechanics throws another wrench in the works. Scientific discoveries like wave-particle duality and quantum entanglement are fascinating but also bewildering. They've inspired a lot of metaphysical speculation, some of which veers into mysticism. Have you ever heard someone say, "Consciousness collapses the wave function"? It sounds deep, but it's often just cherry-picking science to support speculative ideas. Without a deeper, unifying insight like mota, these theories often do more to mystify than clarify.

Then there's postmodernism, which shook things up with the idea that there's no such thing as absolute truth, just individual perspectives shaped by culture and experience. This might sound freeing at first, but it's left a lot of people feeling like there's no solid ground to stand on. How do you search for universal truths about science or spirituality when everything's supposedly relative? It's like trying to build a bridge between two islands that might not even exist.

The confusion runs even deeper when you look at the hard problem of consciousness, the philosophical head-scratcher about how our thoughts and feelings arise from the physical stuff in our brains. Some theories say consciousness is just an accident of biology, while others, like adherents of panpsychism, claim everything in the universe might have a bit of consciousness. Neither side has cracked the code, and both leave out the spiritual dimension that might explain why we feel so uniquely "us" (specifically, the revelatory concept of "personality").

Things don't get much easier when metaphysics tackles morality. In today's secular world, there's been a push to explain ethics as a product of evolution or social contracts. This is what Christopher Hitchens opined about. But these approaches often miss the spiritual heart of why we strive to be good in the first place. And when you try to reconcile what *is* (human behavior) with what *ought to be* (moral ideals), the gap can feel more like a canyon.

The biggest challenge, as I see it, is the ongoing struggle to unite science and religion. Some folks try to find spiritual truths in scientific discoveries—think of New Age interpretations of quantum physics—but this often feels shallow. On the flip side, when religion tries to dominate science, you end up with clashes that widen the gap instead of closing it, eventually creating a gulf like the Mariana Trench, continually spreading apart. Meanwhile, metaphysical questions about the mind and soul are getting even murkier with the rise of artificial intelligence. Are machines capable of consciousness, or is there something uniquely spiritual about human thought? Some theories wander into sci-fi territory, speculating about "machine souls" or the future singularity, leaving more questions than answers.

Getting Unstuck

While *The Urantia Book* suggests that all these confusions stem from the absence of mota, which it describes as a superphilosophical wisdom that connects the material and spiritual, mortal humans just don't have access to it. What we need, the Melchizedek writes with authority, is revelation: "Revelation is the only technique which can compensate for the absence of the truth sensitivity of mota in a material world." Revelation is the universe's methodology for atoning for this deficiency in conceptual data that man so urgently needs to construct a logical philosophy of the universe and to arrive at a satisfying understanding of his sure and settled place in that universe. Ultimately, the Melchizedek says, "The highest attainable philosophy of mortal man must be logically based on the reason of science, the faith of religion, and the truth insight afforded by revelation."[8] Under this unified conceptual triad we can compensate somewhat for our failure to develop an adequate metaphysics and for the inherent inability to fathom the mota of the morontia realm. There is no need to despair; we have great hope because we have a revelation to lean on and the Spirit of Truth to back it up!

In part 1 of this book, I made the case for three significant Urantia-based histories that as of the beginning of 2025, have varying scientific corroboration and contrasting levels of connection to the cosmology of the papers—Adam and Eve having direct linkages to the local universe ascension schema and thus a tighter relationship to the cosmology of the revelation than that of the Precambrian supercontinent and Göbekli Tepe.

In chapter 4 ("A Baker's Dozen") Dick Bain and his team provided over two dozen scientific statements in *The Urantia Book* that demonstrate its integration of science and spirituality is groundbreaking. These statements, similar to others elsewhere in part 1, emphasize how the book harmonizes scientific facts with spiritual ideas, creating a bridge between two fields often seen as conflicting. This synthesis is presented as deliberate by the superhuman authors, aiming to expand human understanding of both science and religion while showing that neither has to dominate the other. This integration demonstrates the unique purpose of *The Urantia Book*: to offer a comprehensive perspective that embraces both material and spiritual realities.

I argue that the book's inclusion of scientific statements that later discoveries have confirmed provide prescient insights unknown at the time the book was written. This argument suggests that the plethora of the scientific content of *The Urantia Book* could not simply be lucky guesses or coincidences. Instead, I argue that these seemingly foresighted statements reflect a depth of knowledge that is truly far beyond what was available to humans in the early twentieth century. This logical approach reinforces the idea that the book is more than just a product of its time.

This type of validation of the book itself is something much, much more than a Nostradamus-type twenty-first-century canard. I point to the absolute origin of the cosmic hierarchy that all the rest of the revelation falls under as our starting point. Without the well-nigh inconceivable cosmic origin the book presents, what follows—such as the spiritual disclosure of the Creative Michael Sons—would assuredly have gaps in making sense. However, with the sublime picture of the Deo-centric spiritual structure, along with the depiction of the seven Absolutes of Infinity, everything that follows makes total sense—the truth of reality seamlessly follows and is easy to visualize, understand, appreciate, and personally experience with the validation of the Spirit of Truth and our divine fragment.

The revelation delves into topics such as cosmic genesis, the interplay between time and eternity, the concept of infinity, and the organization of the universe into various levels and structures, among other next-level cosmic concepts. It examines the creation and evolution of energy, the role of the Isle of Paradise, and the gravitational relationships within the grand universe. *The Urantia Book* discloses a central universe, seven revolving superuniverses, and four outer space levels, offering a detailed analysis of the universe's architecture from both scientific and philosophical perspectives.

It describes a cosmic framework that diverges significantly from conventional scientific and philosophical understandings. Again, central to this perspective is the Isle of Paradise, which it identifies as the eternal, absolute, immovable center of all creation. Unlike the big bang model, which lacks a defined center and attributes the universe's origin to a singular, undirected event, the revelation describes Paradise as existing outside of space and time, has a universe location but no position in space, and serves as the source of all energy, matter, and spirit. The revelation integrates finite and infinite realities within a layered cosmology, proposing that the observable universe is but a part of a much larger framework of transcendent potentials. After all, the infinite, by definition, has to include the finite. This immense structure, which *The Urantia Book* calls the Master Universe, consists of a perfect and eternal Havona universe surrounding Paradise, seven evolutionary finite superuniverses, and uninhabited outer space levels poised for future developments after the Grand Universe (the finite part) is completed in what is referred to as "light and life."[9] The revelation extends the scope of cosmology far beyond the observable, offering a purpose-driven creation where spiritual growth and unity are paramount.

Cosmic Frameworks Compared

I know that Hitchens and D'Souza, if presented with this cosmology, might just scoff it off as too abstract or too far offtrack for what they are debating. But I speculate Eric Weinstein would not. His theory of geometric unity has a strange ring to it as something to be compared to *The Urantia Book*'s cosmic scaffolding.

If I have it right, Weinstein's geometric unity theory is a bold attempt to create a new framework for understanding the universe, combining mathematics and physics into a single, elegant structure. His big idea is that physics today relies on separate theories to describe the universe. General relativity explains gravity and large-scale phenomena like planets and galaxies, while Quantum mechanics explains tiny things like atoms and particles. But these two don't fit together neatly. Geometric unity aims to unify them under one mathematical framework. Weinstein suggests that the universe can be thought of as a giant geometric object—like a complex shape in many dimensions. The geometry of this shape encodes all the rules that govern physics, from gravity to the behavior of particles.

Imagine the universe as a beautifully intricate geometric puzzle. If we could understand its shape and how all the pieces fit together, we could unlock the secrets of reality, from the smallest particles to the largest galaxies. However, this theory is not yet fully developed or widely accepted in the scientific community and remains a work in progress. I say Weinstein gets a seat at the table.

Intriguing Possibilities for Progress

The potential overlaps between Eric Weinstein's geometric unity and the cosmology presented in *The Urantia Book* are intriguing, as both aim to describe a unified vision of reality, albeit through vastly different lenses. Whereas geometric unity is a scientific framework rooted in mathematics and physics, *The Urantia Book* offers a spiritual and metaphysical perspective. Both, however, share an emphasis on the universe as an interconnected and structured whole.

Weinstein proposes that the universe is best understood as a higher-dimensional geometric object, with all physical phenomena—forces, particles, and space-time—interwoven within this structure. Similarly, *The Urantia Book* describes a cosmos intricately organized into seven superuniverses, governed by a unified cosmic plan originating from the Isle of Paradise. This shared emphasis on an underlying architecture of reality suggests a conceptual resonance, even if their approaches differ significantly.

One striking similarity lies in their treatment of higher dimensions. Geometric unity relies on dimensions beyond the familiar three of space and one of time to explain physical phenomena and unify quantum mechanics with general relativity. Likewise, *The Urantia Book* describes higher-dimensional realities, such as the morontia state, which bridges material and spiritual realms. Both frameworks recognize dimensions that transcend human perception as integral to the functioning of the universe.

Another point of convergence is their pursuit of unification. Weinstein seeks to unify all fundamental forces—gravity, electromagnetism, and the strong and weak nuclear forces—within a single framework. In parallel, *The Urantia*

Book describes the universe as a system where physical energy, mind, and spirit are unified under divine governance, with the Isle of Paradise the geographic center of infinity outside of time and space. Both approaches emphasize a singular origin from which diverse phenomena arise.

Mathematics also plays a central role in both systems, albeit in different ways. Whereas geometric unity explicitly uses higher-dimensional geometry to describe the universe's structure, *The Urantia Book* implies an inherent order in the cosmos, aligning with the idea of precise, governing laws. This shared emphasis on order reflects a belief in the universe's underlying coherence, whether expressed mathematically or divinely.

Both perspectives also highlight the interconnectedness of reality. In geometric unity, the geometry of space-time ties together all physical laws, creating a seamless framework for understanding the universe. *The Urantia Book*, on the other hand, portrays a cosmos where all beings, worlds, and realities are interconnected under divine oversight. This sense of unity underpins both visions of the cosmos.

Consciousness, while not a central theme of geometric unity, is implicit in any attempt to unify physics, as it raises questions about the role of observers in the universe. *The Urantia Book*, in contrast, places consciousness at the heart of its cosmology, focusing on the role of Thought Adjusters and the spiritual growth of intelligent beings. Both perspectives, in their own ways, acknowledge the significance of consciousness within the larger framework of existence.

Finally, both geometric unity and *The Urantia Book* convey a vision of the universe as a purposeful and unified whole. Weinstein's framework, though scientific, carries

SEAT AT THE TABLE | 317

philosophical implications of an elegant and interconnected cosmos, while the *Urantia Book* explicitly describes the universe as infused with divine purpose and direction. Together, these perspectives might be seen as complementary: geometric unity addressing the how of the physical cosmos, and the *Urantia Book* exploring the why as well as the how of its spiritual significance. This synthesis highlights how science and spirituality, though different in approach, may converge in their quest to understand the ultimate nature of reality.

Expanding Horizons Together

The **absonite levels** and the **four outer space levels** from *The Urantia Book* might seem worlds apart from something like Eric Weinstein's geometric unity, but they share some interesting ideas that could make you say, "Huh, that's kind of similar!" Both are trying to describe a universe that's way bigger, more complex, and more connected than what we see with our eyes. If you were sitting at the table, you might come up with dozens of questions.

In *The Urantia Book*, the absonite (subabsolute but superfinite) is this in-between level of reality. It's not stuck in the finite world we live in, but it's also not infinite or absolute like God. It's a sort of superlevel where things like space and time don't really matter anymore. The book also describes four outer-space levels—gigantic regions of the universe beyond the known superuniverses—where crazy new kinds of creativity and cosmic action are unfolding. Think of it as the ultimate expansion pack for the universe. Similarly, Weinstein's geometric unity paints a picture of the universe as this multidimensional geometric object. It's like saying, "Hey, space and time as we know them? That's just one slice of the cosmic pie."

Both ideas share a big theme: they see the universe as layered and connected. *The Urantia Book* says that everything—matter, mind, and spirit—is tied together under a divine plan, and geometric unity suggests that all the forces and particles in physics might actually be different faces of the same higher-dimensional structure. It's like comparing a 2D blueprint to the 3D building it represents—they're connected, but one is way deeper and more complex.

What's really interesting is how they both talk about going beyond what we know. *The Urantia Book* imagines these outer-space levels as massive, cosmic labs for new creations, and Weinstein's theory hints that higher dimensions could hold entirely new laws of physics. Both suggest we're only scratching the surface of what's out there. And then there's this idea of "transcending space and time." The absonite is all about going beyond those limits, and Weinstein's math-heavy approach to higher dimensions kind of does the same thing—it looks for a way to explain stuff that seems impossible under regular physics.

That said, they're not quite the same. *The Urantia Book* is spiritual at its core, talking about divine purpose and cosmic harmony; in contrast, geometric unity is grounded in science and math. But what if these two ideas could meet in the middle? Together, they'd tell a much bigger story about the universe, like different chapters in the same epic book. At a minimum they would both gain respectability and become conscious elements of discussion of the Father's kingdom as Jesus taught.

Both approaches challenge us to think bigger, to see the universe as more than just atoms and galaxies, more than what we can measure with telescopes or math. They're both asking us to step outside what's familiar and wonder what's really out there. Who knows? Maybe science and spirituality aren't as far apart as they seem. Maybe they're just looking at the same big picture from different angles.

Final Thoughts

The seat at the table embodies more than just a dialogue; it is a transformative opportunity for science, religion, and philosophy to converge on shared questions about existence, morality, and the cosmos. I challenge and invite bold thinkers to step beyond entrenched positions and engage with the revelatory insights of *The Urantia Book*.

The table itself represents an acknowledgment that no single perspective holds all the answers. By bringing together the rigor of science, the introspection of philosophy, and the profound insights of spiritual revelation, this dialogue could illuminate pathways toward a more integrated understanding of reality. In the end, such a table is not just an invitation to discuss ideas; it's a call to shape the future of humanity by building bridges between divided realms of thought, fostering unity in diversity, and inspiring a collective pursuit of truth.

Endnotes

1. *Nonattributional* means, in contexts such as academic settings, "a policy when statements made are not attributed to specific individuals, promoting open discussion without fear of personal

320 | EXPLORING THE URANTIA REVELATION

attribution." See Marine Corps University, "Academic Freedom and Non-Attribution," September 21, 2020, https://www.usmcu.edu /Portals/218/SchoolFiles/New%20Regs%202020/Research%20 and%20Scholarship/01-Academic%20Freedom%20and%20Non -attribution.pdf.

2. Wikipedia, s.v. "Christopher Hitchens," last modified May 7, 2025, 3:22, https://en.wikipedia.org/wiki/Christopher_Hitchens.

3. D'Souza adopts a defensive posture because it aligns with his role as an apologist, his audience's needs, and his goal of rehabilitating religion's image in a secular world. While he occasionally takes the offensive, his primary focus is on countering critiques of religion, showcasing religion's intellectual credibility, and demonstrating its relevance in addressing humanity's deepest questions. By emphasizing defense, D'Souza positions himself as a rational and measured advocate for faith, contrasting with the combative style of many of his secular counterparts.

4. J. J. Johnson, "Personality Bestowal (Before and After)," Urantiapedia, 2019, https://urantiapedia.org/en/article/JJ_Johnson/Personality _Bestowal. In this article I take what I believe to be a novel position related to the bestowal of experiential human personality. I advance the idea that the Father bestows personality specifically when an individual mortal creature "[has] ascended to the universe level of moral discernment." *UB* 2:2.6

5. Eric Weinstein, "The Real Reason Physics Is Stuck," interview by Brian Keating, *The Portal Podcast*, September 22, 2021, video, 2:36, https://youtu.be/8ncDuoA6Kmo.

6. Wikipedia, s.v. "Standard Model," last modified May 9, 2025, 3:32, https://en.wikipedia.org/wiki/Standard_Model.

7. Cf. J. J. Johnson, "The Urantia Book and the COSAR Principle," video, 2:41, August 9, 2010, http://www.youtube.com/watch?v =VKeL6XNhT1k.

8. *The Urantia Book*, 103:6.15 (1137.5).

9. The revelation uses the term *settled*, which a Divine Counselor of Uversa states functions in an enlarged capacity in a status of evolutionary perfection. Cf. *The Urantia Book*, 18:6.6 (213.1).

Chapter 14
Dishes Are Done: Call to Service/Call to Action

The phrase "dishes are done" symbolizes the completion of mundane or preparatory tasks. In the context of this book's themes of coordinating science and religion, the sacred and profane, through revelation, it emphasizes that the groundwork—studying, reflecting, preparing oneself spiritually—has been laid down as a substrate. The focus now shifts from passive preparation to active engagement in the world. It is the call to move from introspection and personal growth to outward action and service.

This chapter is meant for current and future Urantia students, plus those for whom my story resonated. My initial book, *Up Close and Personal with The Urantia Book*, with its evangelical message, isn't being replaced but has evolved with the growing community of Urantia-revelation students and those who are thirsty for the Truth of Reality. I provided my personal call to service and action and invite each truth seeker to experience that. This is analogous to when Jesus announced the time had come to be about the Father's business. It is in this sense that my story has been told and now is the time to be about our Father's business:

Just before the noon rest, Jesus laid down his tools, ***removed his work apron***, *and merely announced to*

the three workmen in the *room with him, "My hour
has come." He went out to his brothers James and Jude,
repeating, "My hour has come—let us go to John." And
they started immediately for Pella, eating their lunch as
they journeyed. This was on Sunday, January 13. They
tarried for the night in the Jordan valley and arrived on
the scene of John's baptizing about noon of the next day.
(emphasis added).*[1] *135:8.3 (1504.1)*

Over five decades ago, when I first encountered that passage,
I naturally embraced it and immediately identified with the
evangelic message. As sincere students of *The Urantia Papers*,
let's not lose sight of our loyalty, obligation, privilege, and
joy of being a "positive and missionary **ambassador**" of our
religion too.[2]

When Jesus ordained the twelve apostles during the
so-called Sermon on the Mount, he referred to them as ambassadors rather than using terms like *evangelists, envoys, emissaries,* or *missionaries.* This distinction highlights the unique
role and approach he expected of them. As ambassadors, the
twelve were not merely tasked with proclaiming a message
or delivering directives; they were representatives of the kingdom of heaven, embodying its principles and values—truth,
love, mercy, justice, and humility—in every aspect of their
lives. This elevated their mission beyond mere instruction or
conversion to one of exemplification, relationship-building,
and spiritual diplomacy. This was a relational and transformative role, requiring them to model the kingdom's ideals in
their interactions with others.

Ambassadors are tasked with fostering understanding and
building relationships between different realms or cultures.

DISHES ARE DONE: CALL TO SERVICE/CALL TO ACTION | 323

Similarly, the apostles were expected to bridge the spiritual divide between humanity and God by presenting the Fatherhood of God and the brotherhood of man. This role required tact, respect, and adaptability, as they encountered individuals and cultures with varying beliefs, traditions, and levels of spiritual awareness.

Unlike an emissary who might deliver a specific message or a missionary focused on conversion, the apostles were called to empower others. They were to inspire spiritual awakening and personal transformation, helping individuals find God within themselves. Jesus's instructions emphasized that their authority came not from imposing beliefs but from encouraging faith and fostering an individual's spiritual growth.

Ambassadors serve their sovereign without imposing their will on others. Jesus emphasized this noncoercive approach, instructing the twelve to serve humbly, help those in need, and remain in the background as much as possible. They were to live the gospel rather than preach it aggressively, allowing their lives to quietly inspire inquiry and transformation in others.

According to *The Urantia Book,* Jesus envisioned the twelve functioning as a unified body, representing the spirit of cooperation and mutual respect within the kingdom of heaven. They were not independent emissaries acting in isolation but a collaborative group tasked with advancing the kingdom's mission together, demonstrating spiritual unity even while remaining philosophically diverse.

The term *ambassador* reflects the apostles' role as representatives of a divine reality. They were to approach humanity as both teachers and servants, helping individuals see and experience God's love firsthand. In this way, the apostles were to

324 | EXPLORING THE URANTIA REVELATION

bridge heaven and earth, advancing the spiritual evolution of humanity through humility, service, and personal example.

Over a decade after my expanded edition of my initial book was published in 2011, I conjecture that cosmic universe conscious citizens in the Urantia community have been growing exponentially. My call to service and action as an ambassador has now been added to the evangelic message I advanced in *Up Close and Personal*. In like manner, *"greatness and goodness simply cannot be divorced"*; and so it is with my newly combined message.[3]

Three passages in *The* Urantia Book provide the reflective ground to think through one's intentions and one's actions. A Mighty Messenger calls these *The Secret of Greatness and the Soul of Goodness.*

In *The Urantia Book* 28:6.20, greatness and goodness are addressed as complementary yet distinct qualities that together form a higher spiritual ideal. These paragraphs build upon the idea that true greatness is not about external achievements but rather self-mastery and unselfish service. They introduce the idea that goodness, at its highest level, involves loving service—demonstrating kindness, patience, and a deep commitment to the welfare of others.

In 28:6.21, the text states that the true test of greatness is the willingness to serve others with sincerity and without expectation of reward. This reinforces the idea that real greatness is measured by selfless action, especially in aiding those in need. Furthermore, it underscores that the moral and spiritual elements of greatness must align with the values of self-restraint and service.

In 28:6.22, the focus shifts more directly to goodness, describing it as the essence of divine love expressed through service. Goodness is not merely about ethical behavior but involves an active, heartfelt desire to uplift others. It suggests that the ultimate goodness is found in selfless, loving actions that reflect divine qualities.

These passages suggest that **greatness without goodness is incomplete, and goodness without greatness lacks the strength of self-mastery and moral courage.** Greatness, in this spiritual context, involves wisdom, restraint, and leadership through service. Goodness, on the other hand, is the compassionate, loving dimension of service that ensures greatness is motivated by higher spiritual values rather than ambition or self-glorification.

Together, these qualities define the highest form of planetary leadership and spiritual maturity. A truly great person is not only disciplined and self-controlled but also motivated by goodness—a genuine desire to serve, uplift, and love others unselfishly.

The relationship between greatness and goodness in *The Urantia Book* closely parallels **planning** and **doing**. If one plans to be moral and altruistic—meaning one cultivates self-discipline, wisdom, and responsibility (greatness)—then the doing aspect naturally follows as an expression of that greatness through loving service and selfless action (goodness). This means that **true greatness is not just an internal state but must manifest through acts of goodness**, making the two inseparable.

My tagline—**"Call to Service—Call to Action"**—aligns with this concept. The call to service represents the intention and moral resolve (greatness), while the call to action represents the active expression of that resolve through deeds of kindness and service (goodness). Just as planning without action is empty, and action without thoughtful intention can be misguided, greatness without goodness is incomplete, and goodness without greatness lacks moral strength and direction.

This synthesis reinforces the Urantia revelatory perspective throughout its pages that **service is the highest calling**, and true spiritual maturity integrates both the wisdom of greatness and the compassion of goodness. This is where faith and reason, religion and science, reinforce cosmic connections.

I don't take evangelism lightly. If something in your experience has resolved itself into a religion, it is self-evident that you already have become an active evangel of that religion because you deem the supreme concept of your religion as being worthy of the worship of all mankind, all universe intelligences. If you are not a positive and missionary evangel of your religion, you are self-deceived in that what you call a religion is only a traditional belief or a mere system of intellectual philosophy. If your religion is a spiritual experience, your object of worship must be the universal spirit reality and ideal of all your spiritualized concepts. All religions based on fear, emotion, tradition, and philosophy I term the intellectual religions, while those based on true spirit experience, I would term the true religions. The object of religious devotion may be material or spiritual, true or false, real or unreal, human or divine. Religions can therefore be either good or evil.

When I first encountered the above passage, I naturally embraced it and immediately identified with the evangelic message. As sincere students of the *Urantia Papers*, we should not lose sight of our loyalty, obligation, privilege, and joy of being a "positive and missionary evangel" of our religion. An ambassador manifests Fatherly love, while an evangelist delivers *brotherly* love. With brotherly love, you would love your

DISHES ARE DONE: CALL TO SERVICE/CALL TO ACTION | 327

neighbor as you love yourself, and that would be adequate fulfillment of the golden rule. But fatherly affection would require that you should love your fellow mortals as Jesus loves you.[4]

Call to Service / Call to Action

The time has arrived, once again, to draw attention to our strife torn planet and recognize that the will of our Heavenly Father can become dominant and transcendent in our hearts. As transformed and spirit-led faithful sons and daughters of God, let us join hands in spiritual unity to go forth and transform the world. Based upon our personal spiritual experiences and guided hy the truths revealed in *The Urantia Book*, with the constant help of the spirit of truth and as universe-conscious citizens, we have the opportunity, potential, and capacity to spiritually uplift our planet and make a mighty contribution to the establishment of world-wide peace.

JJ Johnson (1947–)

Urantia scholar/author

Did I just say "our religion"? I did. Let me explain.

Religion is one of the most profound and complex aspects of human experience. *The Urantia Book* offers a unique lens through which to view religion, presenting it as both a personal journey and a societal force. Let's explore the various dimensions of religion as illuminated in its pages.

Religion as Personal Experience

At its core, *The Urantia Book* portrays religion as deeply personal—a direct connection between the individual and the divine. True religion is described as a faith-trust in the goodness of God and a dynamic experience of divinity attainment, rather than a mere collection of dogmas or rituals. This personal aspect is the soul's recognition of divine values, leading to inner transformation and moral upliftment.

Religion, according to the revelation, involves spiritual insight and an unyielding faith in eternal realities. It transcends intellectual reasoning, grounding itself in the intuitive grasp of divine truth. The book suggests that true religion "is not derived from the logic of human philosophy" but arises from the inner witness of the Spirit of God. In this deeply personal realm, religion finds its highest expression as a pursuit of supreme values such as truth, beauty, and goodness.

Religion as Catalyst for Growth

The Urantia Book emphasizes that religion is not static but dynamic. It evolves alongside human culture and society. Early evolutionary religion, often born of fear and ignorance, served as a starting point for humanity's spiritual quest. Over time, it ascended from superstition to higher levels of moral and cosmic understanding. The revelation highlights how religion acts as a lever, lifting civilization from chaos and guiding individuals and societies toward spiritual enlightenment.[5]

True religion is also depicted as the "organizing principle of the soul," encouraging individuals to live purposeful lives. It inspires courage, loyalty, and devotion while offering comfort and hope. Through its teachings, individuals are equipped to face life's challenges with strength and dignity.

Religion as Unifier

One of the significant contributions of religion, according to *The Urantia Book*, is its ability to unify human experience. It harmonizes the physical, intellectual, and spiritual aspects of life, creating a cohesive framework for understanding reality. This unity fosters a sense of belonging and purpose, reinforcing the brotherhood of humanity.

Religion's unifying power extends beyond individuals to society as a whole. The revelation argues that religion has historically served as a moral stabilizer and a conservator of values. By fostering shared ideals and aspirations, it has helped societies navigate periods of change and upheaval.

Whereas *The Urantia Book* places great emphasis on the personal nature of religion, it also acknowledges its social implications. Religion's socialization often results in the formation of religious institutions, which can either nurture spiritual growth or become barriers to it. The revelation warns against the dangers of rigid dogmatism and institutional stagnation, urging religionists to remain adaptable and open to new insights.

The social fruits of religion—love, service, and justice—are presented as evidence of its authenticity. They manifest in acts of kindness, the pursuit of fairness, and the building of inclusive communities. Religion, when true to its spiritual roots, transcends cultural and national boundaries, promoting unity and cooperation among diverse peoples.

Religion in Relation to Other Fields

The Urantia Book situates religion within the broader context of human endeavor, highlighting its interplay with science, philosophy, and art. It asserts that while science deals with facts and philosophy with meanings, religion concerns itself with values. This tripartite approach to understanding reality underscores religion's unique role in addressing the moral and spiritual dimensions of life.

Moreover, the revelation posits that religion enriches human creativity and expression. It spiritualizes art, enlightens science, and elevates philosophy, integrating these domains into a coherent vision of existence. This synthesis underscores the interconnectedness of all human pursuits and their ultimate fulfillment in the search for divine reality.

Challenges and Opportunities

The Urantia Book does not shy away from addressing the challenges religion faces in the modern world. It acknowledges the tensions between religion and science, secularism, and spirituality. However, it maintains that true religion, rooted in personal experience, is resilient and adaptable. It calls for a revitalization of religion that focuses on values and spiritual truths rather than theological disputes or institutional power.

The book also envisions a future where religion evolves beyond its tribal and cultural confines to embrace universal ideals. That would include a cooperative approach among religionists, based not on doctrinal agreement but on shared goals and values.

Noble Gesture

Ultimately, *The Urantia Book* describes religion as humanity's "magnificent reach for final reality," a journey toward discovering and embodying the divine. It is a mode of living that integrates the spiritual with the material, the personal with the social, and the temporal with the eternal.

For anyone exploring the concept of religion in terms of the Truth of Reality, this perspective offers a refreshing and inclusive framework. It invites individuals from all faiths— or none—to view religion not as a relic of the past but as a dynamic force for personal and societal transformation. Religion, when true to its essence, is a celebration of life's highest values and an enduring testament to the human spirit's capacity for growth and transcendence.

Are you getting the feel for "our religion" now? Let me accentuate the universality of how religion(s) can effectuate humanity positively for progressive growth and advancement. To do that, we look at Jesus's gospel in an unadulterated fashion.

Jesus and Religion

Imagine, if you will, a teacher so extraordinary that his lessons transcended not just cultures but centuries. This teacher, Jesus of Nazareth, didn't just teach about religion; he lived it, breathed it, and redefined it. His approach was as refreshing as a spring rain and as profound as the starlit heavens.

Jesus's religion emphasized relationship—an intimate connection with God as a loving Father. He brought a message that turned the old ideas of deity on their heads. For many, religion had been about obeying a stern ruler or appeasing a cosmic judge. Jesus changed the game by declaring, "God is love," inviting us to see ourselves as children in a divine family.

This lofty idea was also deeply practical. Jesus taught that religion required an inward focus. It wasn't about clean hands

332 | EXPLORING THE URANTIA REVELATION

but clean hearts. As he famously told the apostles, "In the kingdom, you must be righteous in order to do the work." His religion focused on being—letting the fruits of the spirit grow naturally within.

Evolutionary Religions and Jesus's Encounters

The religions of Jesus's time were varied and vibrant, though often bogged down by tradition and superstition. The Greeks sought beauty, the Hebrews goodness, and the Buddhists peace. Each had its value, but Jesus saw the larger picture. He didn't dismiss these efforts but sought to elevate them, pointing out the universal truths they glimpsed.

For instance, when traveling with Ganid, a young Indian companion, Jesus highlighted the wisdom within Buddhism but lamented its lack of a personal God. Similarly, he appreciated the moral foundations of Zoroastrianism and the ethics of Confucianism. Yet, he offered something more profound: a religion of spirit that called individuals to personal growth and service.

In his ministry, Jesus demonstrated how religion should serve humanity. At the well with Nalda, he explained that true worship wasn't tied to temples or traditions but was "in spirit and in truth." He wasn't concerned with dismantling old religions but wanted them to fulfill their highest aspirations.

Teaching the Apostles

One of Jesus's most revolutionary ideas was his insistence that religion was personal. He emphasized faith over form, spirit over ceremony. To his apostles, he taught that salvation wasn't something to be earned but received through sincere faith. This was groundbreaking. Most religions of the time were heavy with rules and rituals. Jesus stripped all that away, replacing it with the simplicity of sonship with God.

However, Jesus wasn't blind to the social implications of religion. He knew that personal faith naturally spilled over into acts of service. Yet, he was cautious about institutionalizing faith. He warned the apostles not to let religion become a mere social movement or political tool. His focus remained steadfastly on individual transformation.

In one memorable instance, he told the apostles that they were to preach fellowship with God rather than repentance—a subtle but profound shift. Whereas repentance might mark the beginning of a spiritual journey, fellowship symbolized its fulfillment. He urged his followers to live as sons of God, embodying the spirit of the kingdom in daily life.

Socialization of Religion

Jesus understood the tension between the purity of personal religion and the practicalities of spreading a collective faith. He once remarked that every new revelation of truth gave rise to a cult—a socialization of religious ideals that inevitably involved compromise. He saw this process play out as his teachings mingled with those of John the Baptist and later became wrapped in the evolving Christian church.

Despite his reluctance to institutionalize his message, Jesus recognized the need for social religion to foster community and shared values. But he cautioned against letting traditions overshadow truth. As he often reminded his apostles, "Beware of the leaven of the Pharisees." More than a warning about hypocrisy, it was also an admonition against the dangers of rigid dogma stifling spiritual growth.

Gospel of the Kingdom: A Vision for Humanity

At the heart of Jesus's teachings was the gospel of the kingdom, a vision of life in harmony with God's will. This kingdom wasn't about power or politics but about the reign of God in human hearts. It was a call to live with courage, humility, and love.

Jesus saw the kingdom as both deeply personal and profoundly social. On one hand, it involved individual transformation, or becoming perfect as the Father in heaven is perfect. On the other hand, it involved building a brotherhood of believers, united by their shared sonship with God.

To his followers, Jesus imparted a gospel that was both timeless and universal. It wasn't just for Jews or Greeks but for all humanity. His message transcended culture, speaking to the deepest needs of the human spirit.

Religion of Action and Reality

Perhaps what set Jesus apart most was his emphasis on action. His religion wasn't about passive belief but active doing. He didn't just preach love; he lived it. He didn't just talk about service; he practiced it. For Jesus, faith without works was incomplete.

His approach to religion was as natural as breathing. He used simple, relatable illustrations—mustard seeds, fishing nets, lost sheep—to convey profound truths. This naturalness was the hallmark of his teaching.

Following the Master

Jesus's life and teachings offer a road map for living a truly religious life. He showed us that religion helps to build a dynamic relationship with God. He called us to see ourselves as God's children, to live with courage and integrity, and to serve one another in love.

In a world often divided by religious differences, Jesus's vision of the Fatherhood of God and the brotherhood of man remains a beacon of hope. His religion was, and is, a call to unity, transcendence, and realization of our highest potential.

So, let us take to heart the Master's invitation to enter the kingdom, not through the gates of tradition or ceremony but through the door of faith. For in doing so, we follow not just a great teacher but the way, the truth, and the life itself.

Did you notice there hasn't been a need for calling out a specific religion?

Declaration for Transformative Religious Action: A Call to Cosmic Citizenship

The time has come for a new awakening, a unified and transformative global community of kindred spirits inspired by the sublime truths revealed in *The Urantia Book*. The principles of this transformative religious call to cosmic citizenship beckons each of us to rise above the divisions of creed, culture, and tradition and embrace a universal truth, the Fatherhood of God and the spiritual brotherhood of man. My proclamation is a clarion call for action, rooted in a profound understanding of cosmic truth, universe beauty, and divine goodness that the revelation delivers with demonstrable authority

336 | EXPLORING THE URANTIA REVELATION

and clarity. It is a call to live dynamically and courageously as universe-conscious citizens, cocreators with God in the unfolding destiny of humanity and the cosmos.

Foundation of the Call

At the heart of this vision is the understanding that religion is an active force—lived out through love, service, and spiritual unity, not necessarily philosophical uniformity.

True religion, as described in *The Urantia Book*, transcends dogmas and rituals. It is the recognition of supreme values, a way of living infused with the spiritual rhythms of the soul harmonized with the eternal melody of the divine.

Transcendent progressive outreach in loving ministry challenges us to move beyond traditional boundaries, to see individuality within spiritual unity. Each individual is urged to cultivate a personal and transformative relationship with the Universal Father, guided by the Spirit of Truth and strengthened by fellowship with spiritual brothers and sisters.

Vision of Moral Courage

The vision of this new religious transformation is one of moral courage, a willingness to face the challenges of the modern world with faith and determination. The teachings of *The Urantia Book* inspire us to infuse the world with the light of truth, the beauty of divine ideals, and the goodness of righteous action. This vision calls us to embody a morality that is dynamic and evolving, one that attracts the highest aspirations of the human mind and challenges the noblest qualities of the soul.

Morality is awakened within each individual through personal reflection, prayer, and alignment with God's will. Morality finds its fullest expression in acts of kindness, justice, and service, reaching out to uplift the downtrodden and inspire the disheartened. Morality seeks not merely to reform the world but to transform it, one soul at a time.

The Act Is Ours

The call to action begins with a personal commitment to reflect through prayer in cooperation with one's indwelling spirit. Through this communion with God, individuals discover their unique calling—a divine purpose tailored to their gifts and circumstances. The Spirit of Truth, ever present and available, provides the guidance needed to navigate the complexities of life and the courage to act in alignment with divine will.

Though the call is personal, its consequences are collective. Each act of love, each effort to do the Father's will, contributes to the realization of God the Supreme—the culmination of all good, true, and beautiful endeavors in the universe. The tasks are to be undertaken in unity with spiritual brothers and sisters, united by a shared purpose and a common destiny.

Proclaiming the Vision

As we go forth, we proclaim the Fatherhood of God and the brotherhood of man not only with our words but also with our lives. We become living examples of the truths we espouse, illuminating the world with the light of spiritual unity, not through proselytizing but by inspiring—a gentle yet powerful witness to the transformative power of divine love.

The global community will challenge humanity to rise to its full potential as cosmic citizens. It calls for a collective effort to address the material, social, and spiritual needs of the world, always with the understanding that the act is ours, but the consequences belong to God the Supreme. Together, we can create a civilization that reflects the highest ideals of truth, beauty, and goodness—a world worthy of its divine origin and destined for eternal progression.

Conclusion

The time for action is now. Let us respond to this call with courage, humility, and living faith. Let us each heed our unique calling and work together in spiritual unity to transform the world. The act is ours, the consequences God's. This is our sacred duty and our divine privilege—to cocreate with God a future that shines with the light of spiritual truth, a world that glorifies the Universal Father and reflects the eternal brotherhood of humankind. Let's take off our aprons now that the dishes are done and be about the Father's business.

Endnotes

1. The day (Sunday, AD 26) is accurate *and* computers were not capable until late in the twentieth century to validate dates from Ol' Blue before 1955.

2. I am now emphasizing the ambassadorship that Jesus referred to with respect to the twelve apostles. Cf. Johnson, *Up Close and Personal* for my earlier depiction of *evangelist*.

3. *The Urantia Book*, 28:6.21 (317.1).
4. *The Urantia Book*, 140:5.1 (1573.3).
5. See chapter 3, "Göbekli Tepe."

Chapter 15
The Search for Truth: A Journey Without End

Looking back on my journey, I see a search that began long before I even knew I was searching. There was a time when I questioned everything—science, religion, the nature of reality itself. I was restless, chasing truth through every possible avenue, but each road seemed to end in contradiction, uncertainty, or more questions.

Then came *The Urantia Book*. At first, I approached it cautiously, as I had so many others before. But as I read, something happened. The words didn't just inform me; they awakened something deep inside. They spoke to the part of me that had always suspected there was more to reality than what I could see, touch, or measure. For the first time, I saw a cosmic framework where science and religion weren't enemies, but partners—where faith had reason, and reason had faith.

The book didn't just answer my questions; it reshaped the very way I ask them. I had once believed that knowledge was something you gather, like collecting stones along a path. Now, I see that truth is something you live—it's an ongoing revelation, unfolding within and around us every day.

And yet, for all the grand cosmology, the epochal revelations, the harmonization of faith and science, it is the personal aspect of this journey that remains the most profound. *The Urantia*

Book doesn't simply describe a distant, impersonal God—it introduces us to a living, loving Creator who seeks to work through us, with us, as us. This same divine force that shapes the universe whispers within our minds, urging us forward, calling us to become cocreators in our own transformation.

This realization changed everything. It changed how I see history, how I see the future, and, most important, how I see myself. It tells me that I am not adrift in an indifferent universe; I am part of a great unfolding—a plan so vast that it stretches beyond time itself, yet so personal that it touches the innermost part of my soul.

The question now is, what comes next? For me, the journey doesn't end with understanding. It continues in action, in service, in cocreation. The world is changing rapidly—technology accelerates, knowledge expands, and new frontiers emerge almost daily. But amid all this, there remains a deeper human need: the hunger for truth, for connection, for spiritual grounding in an age of uncertainty.

Each of us stands at the threshold of discovery, just as I did when I first cracked open *The Urantia Book*. The question isn't whether revelation will continue—it always has, and it always will. The question is, will we be open to it? Will we allow the divine to work through us? Will we embrace the creative partnership that has been offered to us?

I don't have all the answers. But I do know this: when I look at where I was, where I am, and where I am going, I no longer see the random trajectory of a restless seeker. My path has found a purpose, and now walks forward with faith—not just in revelation, but in the endless adventure of discovering what it means to be truly alive in a divine universe. And that journey has only just begun. Freely received, freely give.

Appendix 1
Suggested Debates, Conferences, Discussions

In recent decades, the global stage has seen a surge in public debates and conferences addressing fundamental questions about existence, morality, and the intersection of science and religion. These events bring together leading atheists, agnostics, theists, and proponents of intelligent design to explore some of humanity's most profound inquiries. *The Urantia Book*, as a transcendent literary masterpiece, has earned the respect to be included in these debates. My book has made the case for the merit of including *The Urantia Book* in these platforms.

The following list highlights key forums, debates, and platforms for such intellectual and spiritual exchanges. We can appreciate the diversity of thought and the shared pursuit of truth that unites participants, regardless of their philosophical or theological leanings. This collection offers a gateway for deeper engagement with the ideas and arguments that shape contemporary dialogues on faith, science, and reason.

Templeton Foundation Events

Explores science and spirituality topics, often featuring prominent figures like scientists and theologians.

Closer to Truth

Hosted by Robert Lawrence Kuhn, featuring global discussions on human sentience, dialogue on existence, and metaphysical debates.

The God Debate Series

Hosted at institutions like the University of Notre Dame, featuring debates such as the following:

- Christopher Hitchens versus Dinesh D'Souza
- Sam Harris versus William Lane Craig

University of Oxford Debates

Organizes notable events, like Richard Dawkins debating Rowan Williams on human origins.

Hoover Institution Events

Puts on regular lectures and debates involving thought leaders like Jordan Peterson.

Joe Rogan Experience

Features widely viewed podcasts, featuring discussions with figures like Neil deGrasse Tyson, Matthew McConaughey, and Brian Greene on topics of religion, science, and philosophy.

Unbelievable? (The Big Conversation)

Holds debates hosted by Justin Brierley, such as the following:

- Bart Ehrman versus Peter J. Williams on the historical reliability of the Gospels

- William Lane Craig versus Joshua Swamidass on the concept of Adam and Eve

Gordon College

Organizes regular debates on theology and philosophy, such as Dinesh D'Souza debating Bart Ehrman.

American Scientific Affiliation (ASA) Annual Conference

Focuses on the dialogue between science and faith, featuring speakers like Dr. Sy Garte.

92nd Street Y Events

Features notable speakers like Neil deGrasse Tyson on science, religion, and ethics.

Biola University Christian Apologetics Events

Holds annual conferences focusing on the intersection of science and theology.

Veritas Forum

Hosts forums at universities worldwide, engaging academics in dialogues about life's hardest questions, including faith and science.

Appendix 2
The Urantia Community at Your Fingertips

Resources (By No Means Exhaustive)

UrantiaStudyGroup.org
Find a study group near you or online. The urantiastudygroup
.org website is the result of many years of multiorganizational
planning and represents the most comprehensive study group
directory on the internet.

The Urantia Book Fellowship
https://www.urantiabook.org/
Download resources or read online if you like.

Urantia Foundation
https://www.urantia.org/
Resources cover the origin, history, and destiny of humanity.

Urantia Book Films
David Kantor, a fifty-year veteran of the Urantia movement,
assesses the current state of the movement and its primary
organizations on the sixtieth anniversary of the publication of
The Urantia Book. With almost one million copies of the book
now in circulation in twenty-six languages, the movement is
crossing the threshold into a completely new phase of development unlike anything experienced by any new religious

movement before it. See "Urantia: What Do We Do Now?" at https://www.youtube.com/watch?v=-k7gYk-naxg.

Watch films and short videos about your origin, our planet's history, and your eternal destiny in the spiritual civilization that permeates our universe. Realize Jesus as a transplanetary Creator as well as a personal friend. Become oriented to the spiritual cosmology and universe philosophy of *The Urantia Book*. See the other YouTube videos at https://www.youtube .com/@UrantiabookfilmsOrg8/featured.

Suggested Videos: "Re-Imagining Jesus" and "The Urantia Book and the Quest for Cosmic Citizenship." (Materials are in English, Spanish, Portuguese, and Polish.)

Research on renowned readers of The Urantia Book
The video at https://www.youtube.com/watch?v=HQ_BeQq3SsA is an intro to a book project of **Michael MacIsaac**'s that began as a master's thesis at Stockholm University in 2004. His former academic supervisor is in the video, along with others who are familiar with this research. Michael writes, "This all began with my 220-page combined bachelor's and master's thesis, which includes sections on *The Urantia Book*'s origin, contents, readership, and broader influence. Other sections show the uniqueness of the *UB* in a comparative context and show why scholars and journalists are mistaken when they categorize it as New Age or a UFO religion. Several professors who read it insisted that the 'compelling' research needs to be published."

Michael tells us he has researched and written about the lives of around 130 famous and influential people with intriguing stories of how *The Urantia Book* has been part of their lives and often influenced their work. For example, according to Albert Goldman's *The Last 24 Hours*, Elvis traveled with a portable bookcase containing more than two hundred books, including *The Urantia Book*. Today there are millions of truth seekers just like Elvis.

On Michael's GoFundMe page he says, "I had already done extensive research and writing about the amazing spread and receptivity among stars in the country music scene, and the interview with Marti added much more valuable nuance, impressions, and perspectives. One of Marti's stories adds to the other verified information about Elvis and the *UB*. In a nutshell: Marti worked as a tour guide at a famous studio where Elvis used to record. When other employees saw her *UB*, they reported that Elvis used to bring a copy of the book to the studio and had a habit of reading it before recording. These types of stories help paint a fuller picture of various celebrities' passion for the teachings."

TruthBook
https://truthbook.com/
Discover Jesus in *The Urantia Book*.

The Untold Story of Jesus: A Modern Biography from The Urantia Book
Available from Amazon

Urantia University Institute (UUI)
https://www.urantiauniversity.org/

Urantia Book Network
https://www.youtube.com/@urantiabooknetwork

348 | EXPLORING THE URANTIA REVELATION

Spirit of Truth Podcast
"Spirit of Truth #11," with JJ Johnson
https://www.youtube.com/watch?v=whj3NLIhv0I
JJ's story about the two women in South Asia who became *UB* readers but then almost the first two martyrs of the Urantia movement is pretty intense.

Up Close and Personal with the Urantia Book, expanded Kindle edition
by JJ Johnson, Dr. Meredith Justin Sprunger (foreword)

The Center for Unity
Who was Jesus before Christianity?
https://www.thecenterforunity.org/

The Urantia Book Podcast
Gabriel Rymberg
UrantiaBookPod.com
Podcast episodes here are for *all* Urantia Papers.

Cosmic Citizen Radio
The podcast is for truth seekers.
https://www.urantiabook.org/Cosmic-Citizen-Radio

How I Found the Urantia Book: 367 Inspiring True Stories
by Saskia Praamsma
https://www.amazon.com/How-Found-Urantia-Book
-Inspiring-ebook/dp/B07Q6ZH6XV

Urantia Association International
The group fosters study of *The Urantia Book* and dissemination of its teachings.
https://urantia-association.org

The Christ Experiment
https://thechristexperiment.org/

Urantia Radio
The podcast is hosted by James Watkins
https://www.urantiaradio.com/podcast
https://open.spotify.com/show/5QWtXL6CpIWwyWA La8XMm8
https://urantiaradio.blog/contact/

Pato Banton
https://officialpatobanton.com/ministry
Pato performs at major Urantia conferences. My favorite song of his is:
Life is a miracle

Appendix 3
Photo Gallery

The photographs in this appendix capture meaningful moments from my spiritual journey and international service—both as a U.S. diplomat and as a seeker of deeper truth. Though some of these older images may lack the visual clarity of modern photography, they offer a vividness of purpose. What I hope comes through most is not the lack of sharpness of the image, but the depth of the journey—those very human moments when meaning and connection revealed themselves in quiet, unexpected ways.

For more detail from my tours (including some intense moments that may not be appropriate for this book), especially the harrowing story of the Pakistani family featured below, listen to the video podcast here (1:00:00 and 1:09:54): https://www.youtube.com/watch?v=whj3NLIhv0I

Secretary of State Condoleezza Rice thanked JJ for his service and wished him well on his upcoming assignment (April 2007).

PHOTO GALLERY | 351

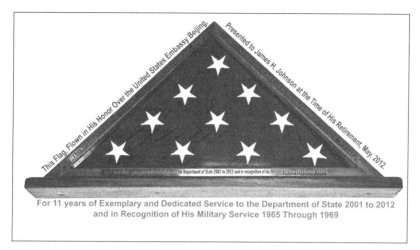

For 11 years of Exemplary and Dedicated Service to the Department of State 2001 to 2012 and in Recognition of His Military Service 1965 Through 1969

Going-away gift upon retiring from State Department. Last posting was US Embassy, Beijing. What a surprise and humbling experience September 2010–May 2012.

Twelve passports, including five for a diplomat. Since retired, I have only one current tourist passport, ready for a quick trip when I get the bug. I am still a gypsy at heart (1967–2017).

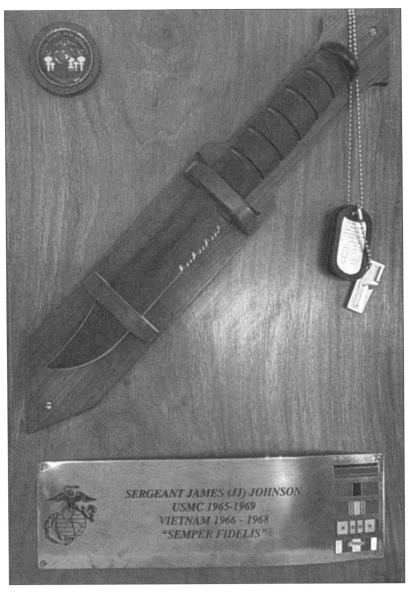

Marine Security Guard (MSG) at US Islamabad made this for me. It was my first embassy posting. Once a marine, always a marine (2002).

Most of my trips were abroad with the secretary of state. They were quite a whirlwind for me and afforded me the opportunity to place copies of *The Urantia Book* in national libraries and universities around the globe. Lots of stories are behind those flags (May 2007).

A map of my trips abroad and in the contiguous United States. It includes trips made while in foreign service (1966-2012) and before, during, and after my marriage.

JJ's intrastate cartage company in Phoenix, Arisona during the early 1990s. JJ drove these mobile billboards around Arizona with these words:

THE
URANTIA
BOOK
YOU'VE GOT TO READ IT

Ask JJ about the responses he got when you see him at a study group or conference.

Part of the Civilian Observer Unit team attached to the MFO in Sinai during my year on loan from US State Department (June 2007–June 2008). I'm lower left on bended knee. Check out MFO website for its mission.

That's me during the Sydney trip with one of the embassy support staff on my left. I was there supporting the secretary of state (March 14–March 19, 2006).

Little ones in Islamabad. I introduced *The Urantia Book* to this Pakistani family (2002).

356 | EXPLORING THE URANTIA REVELATION

It used to be five riyals to get you up, then ten riyals if you wanted to get down. Oh well. My son is on my left (2008).

Acknowledgments

First of all, thank you to the cosmic-conscious citizens in the Urantia community and those who are seekers for the Truth of Reality. During my remote assignments with the US State Department all of you have been a source of inspiration for me. Your global outreach of loving ministry was and is an unfailing inspiration that remains with me still.

Thanks to André Radatus, a Urantian scholar who added a spiritual flavor to part 1 that is deeply appreciated. André is in such demand to assist in various Urantia projects I was fortunate to snag him in becoming part of our team.

To Bob Debold, whose exceptional editing skills helped bring the draft manuscript to the point of being publisher-worthy, I give thanks. I've known Bob since my posting inside the Beltway in Washington, DC, in 2006. We met at Stevie Shaefer's house during our weekly Urantia study group. Debold's contribution as a text producer and writing partner doesn't stop there. I consider Bob a polymath. He's the type of guy who, if you ask him what time it is, not only tells you how to make a watch but also takes you to Switzerland. I cherish our friendship dearly. Bob, thank you for sharing your God-given talents with the rest of us.

To my newfound friend north of the border during the drafting of my manuscript, a proud grandpa, the scribe of Winnipeg, thank you!

I am deeply grateful to Tony Lyons and the entire Skyhorse Publishing team for believing in this book and guiding it into the world. Special thanks to senior editor Mike Campbell—not only for his exceptional skill but also for the genuine connection we built along the way. Thanks to Skyhorse and their distributor Simon & Schuster, this book has the global potential to reach those searching for the truth of reality as revealed in *The Urantia Book* that otherwise may have missed out. To everyone at Skyhorse, your dedication made this possible, and I am truly thankful.

Index

A

absonite, vii, 317-318

Adam and Eve, xiii, 16-17, 19-33, 39-41, 53, 60-63, 135-136, 139, 145-147, 149-161, 236, 239, 253, 255, 311, 344

Amadonites, 47-50

ambassadors, 226, 322

apostles, 172-176, 189, 216, 220-226, 233, 322-323, 332-333

B

bestowal, 133, 168-170, 175, 178-179, 190, 197, 219, 224, 303

Big Bang, 96-97, 106

Bob Debold, 15, 32, 61, 73, 119, 168

Brad Garner, 112

brotherhood, 173, 177, 217, 222, 229, 242-243, 249, 252, 256-258, 269-273, 323, 329, 334-338

Buddhism, xvii, 121, 332

C

call to action, xxxviii, 174, 185, 255, 325, 337

call to service, iii, 321, 324-325

Cambrian Explosion, 10-12, 15-16

Christianity, xvii, 113, 181, 204, 217, 221-222, 229-233, 255-257, 261-275, 278, 281-282, 348

civilization, xxxix, 23, 34, 36-38, 42-50, 53-55, 58-64, 121-122, 140-141, 143, 145-146, 149, 154-157, 208, 210-211, 240-241, 244, 249, 251, 253, 256-257, 262-263, 268-269, 274, 278, 280, 282-284, 297, 328, 338, 346

Condoleezza Rice, xxxii, 14, 350

COSAR Principle, xxxv, 2, 14, 15, 27, 32-33, 75, 89, 111, 117

cosmic consciousness, xii

cosmic harmony, 248, 318

Cosmic Role of Parenthood, 250

cosmology, xxxvii, 43, 62-63, 67-68, 73, 97, 101-103, 109, 125, 234, 292-293, 302, 302, 311, 313-316, 340, 346

Creator Son, 168, 178-179, 195, 212, 250

360 | EXPLORING THE URANTIA REVELATION

D
Discovery Institute, 13, 112, 118
divine purpose, xiv, 30, 32, 69, 180, 211-212, 221, 276, 317-218, 337
DNA, 24-26, 55, 72, 118-120, 124

E
Eric Weinstein, 283, 294, 314-315, 317
evangelical, 321

F
Fatherhood of God, 173, 217, 229, 242, 256-258, 323, 335-337
Fr. Martin Hilbert, 119

G
Geometric Unity, 314-318
Göbekli Tepe, xiii, 34, 38-65, 157, 311
Graham Hancock, 42-43, 65

H
Halbert Katzen, 33, 62
Herod, 190-192
Hinduism, xvii, 121
Howard Stern, 109, 114, 292

I
intelligent design, xxxvi, 13, 111-113, 118-127, 135, 298, 342
Islam, *xvii, 121*

J
Jerusalem, 78, *162, 191, 193-194, 219,* 233

Jesus,
birth, 78-79
life of, xxxvii, 132, 139, 147, 168-226
ministry, 66,
of Nazareth, 136, 147, 168-226, 255, 331
religion of, 229-246, 275, 277-280, 331-338
resurrection, 132, 264
teachings, 133, 268, 270-272, 275, 277, 279-292
Joe Rogan, 43, 343
John the Baptist, 172, 182, 185, 333
Jon Huntsman, 90
Jordan River, 172, 207
Judaism, xvii, 169, 180, 206

K
Kary Mullis, 3, 32

L
Larry Mullins, 116-117, 126-127, 313
light and life, 117, 126-127, 188
Lucifer rebellion, 41, 136, 139, 141, 143, 180, 218

M
Mark McMenamin, 7, 16
Michael Shermer, 109, 118, 124, 292
Michael Wisenbaker, 96
missing years, xxxvii, 220
Morontia, 3, 70-73, 176, 208-209, 225-226, 303, 307-311, 315

INDEX | 361

N

Neil deGrasse Tyson, 109-110, 292, 343, 344

P

Paradise, xvii, xxxii-xxxiii, 69, 101, 109, 126-127, 151, 168-169, 177-178, 238, 248, 313-316

perfection, 29, 109, 207-209, 217, 237

personal relationship, xxxvii, 216, 249, 269

personality, 3, 133-134, 169, 177-179, 209, 221, 303-304, 310

Pharisees, 190, 334

Precambrian supercontinent, xiii, 7-8, 14-16, 21-22, 63, 74, 135, 311

prescient scientific facts, xxxiv, xxxvii, 2-3, 10, 27, 43, 111, 114, 125, 261

R

revelations, xxxvii, 11, 30-34, 122-126, 133-137, 230-236, 311

bridge to, 122-126

five epochal, xxxvii, 133-137, 147

Melchizedek's, 311

revelational Delay, 230-236

Rodinia breakup, 11

scientific validation, 30-34

Urantia revelation, 116-118

Richard Dawkins, 109, 113-118, 292, 343

Rodinia, 7-13, 16

Ruthie, 112

S

Sarah Lewis, 4, 13, 115

Son of God, *19, 201, 204, 247*

Son of Man, xxxvii, 133, 212, 216, 264

Sonarington, 197

soul, xxxv, 68, 112, 132, 170-176, 184, 193, 195, 199-210, 217, 247, 264 , 270, 275-281, 293, 303, 310, 324, 328, 336-341

spiritual GPS, xxxii, 103, 134, 258

spiritual kingdom, 173, 185, 196, 200

Star of Bethlehem, 77-79, 191

Stephen Meyer, 109, 112, 118-125, 292

T

Thought Adjuster, xxxiii, 133, 141-142, 159-160, 170, 193, 207-208, 217, 244-247, 253, 286

transcendent, xv, 32, 54, 109, 120, 236, 250, 289, 292, 296, 302-304, 313, 327, 336, 342

Truth of Reality, xi-xii, xv, xxvi-xxxvii, 7-12, 20, 27, 38-44, 63, 95-99, 103, 125, 135, 147, 155-156, 160, 166-167, 183, 236, 240, 253, 258, 292-293, 312, 321, 331, 357

Tycho Brahe's *Nova*, 80